# To America

*Also by Stephen E. Ambrose*
*in Large Print:*


Citizen Soldiers
D-Day
Band of Brothers

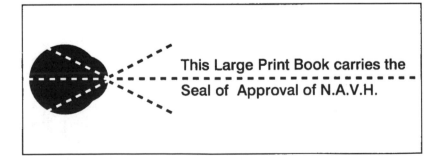

This Large Print Book carries the
Seal of Approval of N.A.V.H.

# To America

*Personal Reflections of an Historian*

## Stephen E. Ambrose

**Thorndike Press • Waterville, Maine**

Published in 2003 by arrangement with Simon & Schuster, Inc.

Thorndike Press® Large Print Core Series.

The tree indicium is a trademark of Thorndike Press.

The text of this Large Print edition is unabridged.
Other aspects of the book may vary from the original edition.

Set in 16 pt. Plantin by Warren S. Doersam.

Printed in the United States on permanent paper.

**Library of Congress Cataloging-in-Publication Data**

Ambrose, Stephen E.
  To America : personal reflections of an historian / Stephen E.
Ambrose.
    p. cm.
  Originally published: New York : Simon and Schuster, c2002.
  ISBN 0-7862-5199-9 (lg. print : hc : alk. paper)
  1. United States — History.  2. United States — Biography.
3. United States — Historiography.  4. Ambrose, Stephen E.
5. Historians — United States — Biography.  I. Title.
E178.6.A38 2003
  973—dc21                                        2002044742

For Paul Schwarzenberger, M.D.,

Alicia R. Millet, R.N.,

Suzanne Murray, R.N.,

And the Stanley S. Scott Cancer Center,
L.S.U. Health Sciences Center

# Contents

# Preface

## *Storytelling*

In 1953, when I was an eighteen-year-old sophomore at the University of Wisconsin, I took a course in American history entitled "Representative Americans." Professor William B. Hesseltine taught it. From his first lecture, I was enthralled. He spoke about presidents, generals, senators, novelists, businessmen. Who they were, what they did, what effect it had.

It was storytelling at its best, about real people whose actions had a direct impact on my life, even if they had lived a century or more ago. Some made mistakes. Some were geniuses. Some were kind, others cruel. They were far more interesting than any character in a novel or actor in a movie.

At the end of his first lecture, on George Washington, I approached the professor — short, bald, pudgy, with a big curved pipe — and told him, as he lit up, that I wanted to do what he did for a living. "How do I do that?" He laughed, then said, stick around and I will show you. That afternoon I went to the registrar's office and switched my major from premed to history.

A half-century later, I've never wavered. History is everything that has ever happened. No one can ever master everything, but your interest will never flag. When I first began teaching American history, my students would come to me before the first day of class and say, "Doc, I hate history. I'm only here because it is required."

My reply was, "You don't mean that. You don't hate history, you hate the way it was taught to you in high school. But history is about people, and there is nothing more fascinating to people than other people, living in a different time, in different circumstances."

At the beginning of the twenty-first century, our students know that they live in the richest and freest nation that ever was and they want to know how that happened. They realize that God did not decide to make the United States so supremely special. They want to know who those people were who made it so, what they did, with what consequences. One week in early 2002, I noted that four of the top six books on the *New York Times Book Review* nonfiction best-seller list were about American history.

I was taught by professors who had done their schooling in the 1930s. Most of them, like many intellectuals of their time, were scornful of, even hated, big business. They presented Andrew Carnegie, John D. Rockefeller, J. P. Morgan, and other fabulously successful businessmen

and investors as devoid of any social consciousness, men whose goal was to plunder; they
brought on the Great Depression.

My professors had praise for the anti-
Federalists of the Revolutionary era, for Jackso-
nian Democrats later on. Of course they were
four-square for Lincoln in the Civil War, but not
for his Republican Party, especially under
Ulysses Grant. In the period from the end of
Reconstruction down to the 1930s, the only parties they praised were the Populists, the Progres-
sives, and Woodrow Wilson's Democrats. After
1932, it was Franklin Roosevelt and the New
Deal Democrats, although many of the professors were Socialists who preferred Eugene Debs
and Norman Thomas to Wilson and Roosevelt.

These professors were not left-wing zealots,
but they couldn't see much good in the Republican Party. Still, they adhered to the first rule for
historians — always stick to the truth. Tell or
write only what you can prove. This they did. I
was an undergraduate less than a decade after
World War II. These men of the Second World
War were patriotic, many of them veterans, who
wished that the United States had done this or
that differently, but who loved their country nevertheless.

At twenty-four with a Ph.D. in hand, I became
a teacher of history. My subject was the Civil
War. I was a military historian, studying and
writing about the generals. Then in 1964, I went
to work on Dwight Eisenhower's biography. For

the next decade I was writing about him. That was my scholarly life. My country was at war in Vietnam, which I thought a dreadful mistake. I was a dove, not very active in the antiwar movement but very much an outspoken critic.

I spent about half of my time with World War II veterans and historians, who were mainly hawks, and the other half with students, who were doves. The first group was generally positive about the whole of American history, the second group critical. I agreed with the first on some matters, with the second on others.

In this short volume, I tell stories about Americans from the past, what they did, how they did it, with what results. I am a storyteller by training and inclination. I tell war stories, political stories, academic stories, business stories. I tell stories about some of my admired Americans — George Washington, Thomas Jefferson, Lewis and Clark, Andrew Jackson, Ulysses Grant, Crazy Horse, Custer, Theodore Roosevelt, Franklin Roosevelt, Dwight Eisenhower, Jackie Robinson, Betty Friedan. And some stories about Americans who are far from being my favorites — Andrew Johnson, Lyndon Johnson, Richard Nixon.

Whether I'm writing a story, or telling it to family or friends gathered around a campfire, or giving a lecture to students, I hope that my listener is concentrating on what is happening and wants to know how it turns out.

One of the wonderful things about a story is that it can be anything — heroic, sad, funny, triumphant, tragic, good, evil. To tell a story well, you need to help the listener identify with the main character, whether he is struggling in a small boat against a rampaging sea, or risking his or her life to secure civil rights, promoting the status of women. What happened? Who made it happen? What are the results today? Where do we need to go? It is through history that we learn who we are and how we got that way, why and how we changed, why the good sometimes prevailed and sometimes did not.

# Chapter One

# *The Founding Fathers*

Americans in great numbers are rediscovering their Founding Fathers in such best-selling books as Joseph Ellis's *Founding Brothers*, David McCullough's *John Adams*, and my own *Undaunted Courage*, about Lewis and Clark. There are others who believe that some of these men are unworthy of our attention because they owned slaves — Washington, Jefferson, Clark among them, but not Adams. They failed to rise above their time and place, though Washington, but not Jefferson, freed his slaves upon his death. But history abounds with ironies. These men, the Founding Fathers and Brothers, established a system of government that, after much struggle, and the terrible violence of the Civil War, and the civil rights movement led by black Americans, did lead to legal freedom for all Americans and movement toward equality.

Let's begin with Thomas Jefferson, because it is he who wrote the words that inspired subsequent generations to make the heroic sacrifices that transformed the words "All men are created equal" into reality.

In the fall of 1996 I was a visiting professor at the University of Wisconsin. The History Club there asked me to participate in a panel discussion called "Political Correctness and the University." The professor seated next to me taught American political thought in the Political Science Department. I remarked to her that when I began teaching I had required students to read five or six books each semester, but I had cut that back to three or four or else the students would drop my course. She said she had the same problem. She had dropped Thomas Jefferson's writings from the required reading list. She did, she said, have Vine Deloria's *God Is Red* on it. She said she wanted her students to get the Native American point of view.

"You are in Madison, being paid by the citizens of Wisconsin to teach their children American political thought, and you leave out Tom Jefferson?"

"Yes," she replied. "He was a slaveholder." More than half the large audience applauded.

Jefferson owned slaves. He did not believe that all were created equal. He was a racist, incapable of rising above the thought of his time and place, and willing to profit from slave labor.

Few of us entirely escape our times and places. Thomas Jefferson did not achieve greatness in his personal life. He had a slave as mistress. He lied about it. He once tried to bribe a hostile reporter. His war record was not good. He spent much of his life in intellectual pursuits in which

15

he excelled, and not enough in leading his fellow Americans toward great goals by example. Theodore Roosevelt called him our worst President. Jefferson surely knew slavery was wrong, but he didn't have the courage to lead the way to emancipation. If you hate slavery and the terrible things it did to human beings, it is difficult to regard Jefferson as a great man, or a good man. He was a spendthrift, always deeply in debt. He never freed his slaves. Thus the sting in Dr. Samuel Johnson's mortifying question, "How is it that we hear the loudest yelps for liberty from the drivers of Negroes?"

In his only book, *Notes on the State of Virginia*, Jefferson's chapter on slavery includes this passage: "The whole commerce between master and slave is a perpetual exercise of the most boisterous passions, the most unremitting despotism on the one part, and degrading submissions on the other. Our children see this, and learn to imitate it. If a parent could find no motive either in his philanthropy or his self-love, for restraining the intemperance of passion towards his slave, it should always be a sufficient one that his children are present. But generally it is not sufficient. The parent storms, the child looks on, catches the lineaments of wrath, puts on the same airs in the circle of smaller slaves, gives loose to his worst of passions, and thus nursed, educated, and daily exercised in tyranny, cannot but be stamped by it with odious peculiarities. The man must be a prodigy who can retain his manners and morals undepraved by such circumstances."

He knew slavery was wrong and that he was wrong in profiting from the institution, but apparently could see no way to relinquish it in his lifetime. He thought abolition of slavery might be accomplished by the young men of the next generation. They were qualified to bring the American Revolution to its idealistic conclusion because, he said, these young Virginians had "sucked in the principles of liberty as if it were their mother's milk." This despite what he had written about the effect of slavery on the slave owner's children.

Of all the contradictions in Jefferson's contradictory life, none is greater. Of all the contradictions in America's history, none surpasses its toleration first of slavery and then of segregation. Jefferson hoped and expected that Virginians of Meriwether Lewis's and William Clark's generation would abolish slavery, yet he said not a word to them about his dream. His writing showed that he had a great mind and a limited character.

William Clark owned a slave called York. They were the same age. York went with him on the Great Expedition, which crossed the hitherto unexplored continent. He paddled, pushed, hauled, made and broke camp, hunted, stood ready to fight Indians, went hungry and was often exhausted, carried his rifle, and was prepared to protect Captain Clark's life at the risk of his own. When the Corps of Discovery got back to St. Louis, and every man who had gone on the expedition got double pay and a land grant, York received nothing.

York asked Clark, How about my freedom? His owner said that that was out of the question. He asked Clark to sell him to an owner in Louisville so he could live with his wife and family. Not possible, Clark replied, and he complained, "York is but of very little Service to me, insolent and Sulky. I gave him a Severe trouncing the other Day and he has much mended Sence." In 1816, more than a decade after the expedition, Clark finally freed York, and gave him a wagon and a mule so he could move goods between Nashville and Louisville and make a living. Clark, like Jefferson, like all slaveholders and many other white members of American society, regarded Negroes as inferior, childlike, untrustworthy — and of course as property. Clark and his fellows got such ideas not from observation, not from York's actions — or the actions of many, probably most, slaves — but from a prejudice so deeply rooted that nothing, it seemed, could pull that plant from the ground.

Jefferson, the genius of politics, could see no way for African Americans to live in society as free people. He embraced the worst forms of racism to justify slavery, to himself and those he instructed. The limitations he displayed in refusing both to acknowledge the truth of his own observations on the institution, and his unwillingness to do something, anything, to weaken and finally destroy it, brand him as an intellectual coward.

In *Notes on the State of Virginia*, Jefferson describes the institution of slavery as forcing tyranny and depravity on master and slave alike. He also wrote about the character and morals of blacks in words that drip with the most vulgar assertions: Negroes have produced no scholars or poets (without mentioning that it was illegal in the South to teach a slave how to read or write); they smell different and bad; they engage in sex constantly but always without love. He said things about these fellow human beings that would make members of a nineteenth- or twentieth-century lynch mob feel comfortable. He knew — how could a man with his agile mind not know — that these were all lies. He left America's first and greatest moral problem to his successors. He could not rise above convenience. To be a slaveholder meant one had to regard the African American as inferior in every way. One had to believe that the worst white man was better than the best black man. If you did not believe these things you could not justify yourself to yourself. So Jefferson could condemn slavery in words, but not in deeds.

Jefferson had slaves at his magnificent estate, Monticello, who were superb artisans, shoemakers, masons, carpenters, cooks. But like every bigot, he never said, after seeing a skilled African craftsman at work or enjoying the fruits of his labor, "Maybe I'm wrong." He already knew that. He ignored the words of his fellow revolutionary John Adams, who said that the Revolution would never be complete until the slaves were free.

Jefferson left another racial and moral problem for his successors, the treatment of the Native Americans. He had no positive idea of what to do with or about the Indians. He handed that problem over to his grandchildren, and theirs.

The author of the Declaration of Independence threw up his hands at the questions of women's rights. It is not as if the subject of votes for women and other rights never came up. Abigail Adams, at one time a close friend of Jefferson, raised it. But Jefferson's attitude toward women was at one with that of the white men of his age. He wrote about almost everything, but almost never about women, not his wife or his mother and certainly not Sally Hemmings. He contrasted American and Parisian women he observed when he was ambassador to France. In America, Jefferson noted with approval, women knew their place, which was in the home and, more specifically, in the nursery. Instead of gadding frivolously about town as Frenchwomen did, chasing fashion or meddling in politics, American women were content with "the tender and tranquil amusement of domestic life" and never troubled their pretty heads about politics.

★ ★ ★

So it is of particular irony to admit that Jefferson was as remarkable a man as America has produced. "Spent the evening with Mr. Jefferson," John Quincy Adams wrote in his diary in 1785, "whom I love to be with. . . . You can never be an hour in the man's company without something of the marvelous." And even Abigail Adams wrote of him, "He is one of the choice ones of the earth."

Jefferson was born rich and became well educated. He was a man of principle (except with regard to slaves, Indians, and women). His civic duty was paramount to him. He read, deeply and widely — more than any other President of the United States except, possibly, Theodore Roosevelt. He wrote well and with more productivity and skill than any other President, except, perhaps, Theodore Roosevelt. He was not a great public speaker, but in small groups he shone. Wherever Jefferson sat was the head of the table. Those few who got to dine with him around a small table always recalled his charm, wit, insights, queries, explanations, gossip, curiosity, and above all else his laughter.

Jefferson's range of knowledge was astonishing. Science in general. Flora and fauna specifically. Geography. Fossils. The classics and modern literature. Languages. Politicians of all types. Politics, state by state, county by county. International affairs. He was an intense partisan. He loved music and playing the violin. He wrote countless letters about his philosophy, observations of people and places. He composed powerful essays, not always about politics — his head and heart essay is perhaps the best known. In his official correspondence, Jefferson maintained a level of eloquence not since equaled. I've spent much of my professional life studying Presidents and generals, reading their letters, examining their orders to their subordinates, making an attempt to judge them. None match Jefferson.

In spite of these rare abilities, Jefferson was not a hero. His great achievements were words. Except for the Louisiana Purchase, his actions as President fall short. But those words! He was the author of the Declaration of Independence. The second paragraph begins with a perfect sentence — "We hold these truths to be self-evident, that all men are created equal" (an affirmation he did not live out). Eventually, with Lincoln, who articulated these truths and lived them, and slowly afterward, the idea made its progress.

Abraham Lincoln, who grew up in a free state, struggled for more than a half-century with his own feelings about slavery. At one point he wanted to ship all slaves back to Africa. But in 1865, in his Second Inaugural, shortly before his death, he clarified his conclusion unequivocally. He said the whole country was guilty of the fact of slavery, not just the South. All of us.

Jefferson's declaration that all men are created

equal is quoted all over the world. Everyone, everywhere, knows these words. Those words, as the great historian Samuel Eliot Morison has said, "are more revolutionary than anything written by Robespierre, Marx, or Lenin, a continual challenge to ourselves, as well as an inspiration to the oppressed of all the world."

Jefferson was the author of the Virginia Statute of Religious Freedom, a doctrine that spread throughout the United States. He is the father of our religious freedom. It is, next to the words of our independence, his greatest gift, save only perhaps our commitment to universal education, which also comes to us via Jefferson.

In 1779, when Jefferson introduced "A Bill for Establishing Religious Freedom" in the Virginia legislature, he wrote: "no man shall be compelled to frequent or support any religious worship . . . whatsoever . . . nor shall otherwise suffer, on account of his religious opinions or belief; but that all men shall be free to profess, and by argument to maintain, their opinions in matters of religion. . . ." In *Notes on the State of Virginia* he wrote, "The legitimate powers of government extend to such acts only as are injurious to others. But it does me no injury for my neighbor to say there are twenty gods, or no God. It neither picks my pocket nor breaks my leg." In his most famous utterance on religion, Jefferson said, "I have sworn upon the altar of God, eternal hostility against every form of tyranny over the mind of man."

A pity that he did not introduce "A Bill for Emancipation" in the Virginia legislature and swear "eternal hostility against every form of tyranny over the mind and work of man, including slaves."

Religious liberty did not happen throughout the United States all at once, of course, but as Jefferson's great biographer Dumas Malone wrote: "Jefferson's vision extended farther and comprehended more than that of anybody else in public life, and, thinking of himself as working for posterity, he was more concerned that things should be well started than that they be quickly finished."

More than anyone else, even Benjamin Franklin, it is Jefferson who implanted in the United States the notion that everyone is entitled to universal education. He put no limit on the amount of time or money he would invest in education. When he was eighty years old he made the architectural plans for the University of Virginia — what he liked to call his "academical village." (In 1976 the American Institute of Architects voted his design "the proudest achievement of American architecture in the past 200 years.") When the school opened, March 7, 1825, it had five faculty members and forty students. Jefferson was startled to learn that most of the students were found by the faculty to be "wretchedly prepared." He immediately began to work on improving the elementary and secondary education in Virginia.

The Northwest Ordinance of 1787 was based on Jefferson's "Report of a Plan of Government for the Western Territory" written three years earlier. In it, he made certain that when the populations of Ohio, Indiana, Illinois, Wisconsin, and Michigan were large enough, these and other territories would come into the Union as fully equal states. They would have the same number of senators and representatives as the original thirteen. They would elect their own governors, and so on. He was the first who had the thought that colonies should be equal to the thirteen original members of the Union. No one before him had proposed such a thing. Empires were run by the "mother country," with the king appointing the governors. It was Jefferson who decided that we wouldn't do it that way in the United States. The territories shall be states. He applied the principles of the Northwest Ordinance to the Louisiana Purchase territories, and by later extension to the West Coast. It was Jefferson who envisioned an empire of liberty that stretched from sea to shining sea.

For Jefferson, the matters he was eager to address, the ones he seized on most, start with the assertion of American independence, exclude the grip of established religion on the minds of men, and provide education for the citizens. These are the accomplishments he chose to put on his tombstone, the ones by which "I wish most to be remembered."

HERE WAS BURIED
THOMAS JEFFERSON
AUTHOR OF THE DECLARATION
OF
AMERICAN INDEPENDENCE
OF THE
STATUTE OF VIRGINIA
FOR
RELIGIOUS FREEDOM
AND FATHER OF THE
UNIVERSITY OF VIRGINIA.

Washington and Jefferson were both rich Virginia planters, but they were never friends. Washington did not have Jefferson's IQ. He was not anywhere near as good a writer. He was not as worldly. He had less formal education than any subsequent President, except Abraham Lincoln. He towered over his contemporaries, literally so. He was a six-foot-three general; his soldiers averaged five-foot-eight. He was not a good general, or so his critics say. His army lost more battles than it won.

But Washington held the Continental Army together, "in being" as the military expression puts it, and he had a masterly judgment of when and where and how to strike the British in order to raise morale among his soldiers and throughout his country — perhaps most symbolic was his crossing the Delaware River at Christmastime in 1776, when in a lightning week of campaigning he picked off the British garrisons at

Trenton and Princeton, taking many prisoners and valuable supplies. The next winter he spent with his soldiers in a freezing Valley Forge. From there, he directed the strategy of the war, turned the Continental Army from a ragtag collection into a solid regular army, forced the politicians in Congress to support him, and emerged as the one who would lead the nation through the Revolutionary War.

Washington's character was rock solid. He was constant. At the center of events for twenty-four years, he never lied, fudged, or cheated. He shared his army's privations, though never pretended to be "one of the men," and was careful to keep a distance between himself and his subordinates and his enlisted men. They respected him, even loved him. Washington came to stand for the new nation and its republican virtues, which was why he became our first President by unanimous choice and, in the eyes of many, including this author, our greatest.

Washington personifies the word "great." In his looks, in his regular habits, in his dress and bearing, in his generalship and his political leadership, in his ability to persuade, in his sure grip on what the new nation needed (above all else, not a king), and in his optimism no matter how bad the American cause looked, he rose above all others. He established the thought, "We can do it," as an integral part of the American spirit. He was indispensable, in war and in peace, "first in war, first in peace, first in the hearts of his countrymen." Abigail Adams, again, so insightful in her descriptions of this or that Founding Father, quoted John Dryden to describe Washington: "Mark his majestic fabric. He's a temple sacred from his birth and built by hands divine." Congress wanted Washington's body to rest in a room beneath the Capitol rotunda, somewhat like Napoleon's tomb in Les Invalides. He is buried at his home, Mount Vernon.*

Of the nine Presidents[†] who owned slaves, only Washington freed his. (One of their descendants is a guide at Mount Vernon.) He resisted efforts to make him into a king and established the precedent that no one should serve more than two terms as President. He voluntarily yielded power. His enemy, George III, remarked in 1796, as Washington's second term was coming to an end, "If George Washington goes back to his farm he will be the greatest character of his age." Napoleon, then in exile, was as stunned as the rest of the world by Washington's leaving office. He complained that his enemies "wanted me to be another Washington." As George Will wrote, "the final component of Washington's indispensability was the imperish-

---

* When Lieutenant Dwight Eisenhower first saw Napoleon's tomb in 1927, he told his wife, Mamie, "That's disgusting." He is buried in Abilene, Kansas, his home.

[†] George Washington, Thomas Jefferson, James Madison, James Monroe, Andrew Jackson, William Henry Harrison, John Tyler, James Polk, and Franklin Pierce.

28

able example he gave by proclaiming himself dispensable."

Washington was a slaveholder. In New Orleans, in the late 1990s, George Washington Elementary School was renamed Charles Richard Drew Elementary School, after the developer of hemoglobin. Although I advocate naming schools after Martin Luther King, Jr., or George Washington Carver, and others, I don't see how we can take down the name of the man whose leadership brought this nation through the Revolutionary War and who turned down a real chance to be the first king of the nation.

"But he was a slaveholder," students sometimes say to me.

"Listen, he was our leader in the Revolution, to which he pledged his life, his fortune, and his sacred honor. Those were not idle pledges. What do you think would have happened to him had he been captured by the British Army?

"I'll tell you. He would have been brought to London, tried, found guilty of treason, ordered executed, and then drawn and quartered. Do you know what that means? He would have had one arm tied to one horse, the other arm to another horse, one leg to yet another, and the other leg to a fourth. Then the four horses would have been simultaneously whipped and started off at a gallop, one going north, another south, another east and the fourth to the west.

"That is what Washington was risking to

29

establish your freedom and mine."

Our nation's capital abounds with statues to our president heroes, including the Lincoln Memorial, the Jefferson Memorial, and the FDR Memorial. The one that stands out is the Washington Monument, the tallest, grandest, the most superbly designated, and most immediately recognized. It is our tribute to the man who led our nation to victory in the Revolutionary War and who, as our first President, did more than anyone else to create the Republic. Jefferson extended it from the Mississippi River to the Rocky Mountains. Lincoln preserved it. Franklin Roosevelt led it to triumph in the greatest war ever fought. But it was George Washington who set the republican standard. So long as this Republic lasts he will stand first.

Washington's monument was unfinished at the time of the Civil War, which was fitting, as Washington came from Virginia, a state that in 1861 had seceded from the Union, and he was a slaveholder. In his Republic only white men of west European descent could vote. But in his person he was Father of a Union that was expansive not only in its territorial possessions but in its being. In his Republic the blacks would be freed — albeit after a horrible struggle. He certainly never thought of white women as those who could be full citizens. But the Constitution which he swore to defend would eventually have room in it for freed slaves, for women, for minorities.

The Mall that stretches out from Washington's monument has been the scene of controversy, protest, and persuasion, which is as it should be in a democracy. There more than anywhere, our national discord has been on display, and our national step-by-step progress demonstrated for. There the women's suffrage movement was advocated. There Martin Luther King, Jr., spoke the words that characterized and led the way to civil rights for African Americans and all other Americans, "I have a dream." There citizens gathered in huge numbers to protest the Vietnam War, including my wife and me.

In the shadow of the Washington Monument, we come together to protest, to grieve, to affirm. It is there, above any other place, that we have the monument that stands for our greatest national strength, our democracy, and that symbolizes our greatest national pride, our unity.

The Washington Monument and the Jefferson and Lincoln memorials remind us that greatness comes in different forms and at a price. Jefferson, by his words, gave us aspirations. Washington, through his actions, showed us what was possible. Lincoln's courage turned both into reality.

Slavery and discrimination darken our hearts and cloud our minds in the most extraordinary ways, including a blanket judgment today against Americans who were slave owners in the eighteenth and nineteenth centuries. That the

31

masters should be judged as lacking in the scope of their minds and hearts is fair, *indeed must be insisted upon,* but that doesn't mean we should judge the whole of them only by this part.

In his last message to America, on June 24, 1826, ten days before he died on July 4, the same day that John Adams died, Jefferson declined an invitation to be in Washington, D.C., for the fiftieth anniversary of the adoption of the Declaration of Independence. He wrote, "All eyes are opened, or opening to the rights of man. The general spread of the light of science has already laid open to every view the palpable truth that the mass of mankind has not been born, with saddles on their backs, nor a favored few booted and spurred, ready to ride them."

He died with hope, that the future would bring to fruition the promise of equality. For Jefferson, that was the logic of his words, the essence of the American spirit. He may not have been a great man in his actions, or in his leadership, where he did little or nothing to bring about his hope. But in his political thought, he justified that hope.

# Chapter Two

# The Battle of New Orleans

In 1815, New Orleans was a city with a diverse population of clannish eccentrics, which is pretty much the way it is today. For that reason, and others, it has been my hometown for most of my adult life. In its ethnic diversity — French, English, Irish, German, African, Mexican, Central American, Vietnamese, Chinese, others; in its food, from around the world; in its music, from the blues and jazz and marches and dirges; in its everyday phrases, such as "I'm going to make groceries" or "where ya at?"; in its fear of a hurricane and not much else; in its love affair with itself, it is singular. It is America's favorite party city. At times it seems that the party is continuous, but two especially stand out — Mardi Gras and the Jazz and Heritage Festival. It is the city that care forgot. It is sometimes also called the city that forgot to care, but in 1815 all of New Orleans's residents knew its importance.

It was the port at the mouth of the great Mississippi River, therefore one of the most valuable pieces of real estate in the world. The river drained a vast territory of rich farmland; an abundance of metal; almost unlimited fur pelts, deer, bear, elk, and many other animals; scores of rivers all headed toward the Mississippi — a richer drainage than existed anywhere else in the world.

In 1815, New Orleans city was growing. Americans were settling west of the river, in Missouri, Iowa, Arkansas, Minnesota, and sending their corn and other products to a world market through New Orleans. The site had belonged to the Indians, the French, the Spanish, the French again, then to the Americans. In 1803, when Jefferson purchased Louisiana, he did not ask the French citizens of New Orleans if they wanted to be Americans. He just did it. Despite their new American citizenship, the French in New Orleans felt removed from American life.

In January 1815, the British were coming to take control of the port and make it their own. Britain was entrenched in Canada, at the northernmost end of the Mississippi River. Britain had an alliance with some of the Native American tribes in U.S. territory on the west bank of the river, stretching far inland. It had the seafaring skills to sweep its men-of-war up the river, perhaps to St. Louis, even beyond. And after the June 1815 battle at Waterloo, in which Napoleon was defeated, Britain had experienced troops available to challenge the Americans west of and along the river. For the French residents

34

of New Orleans, no matter what they thought of the Americans, a conquest by the British was an even worse prospect.

General Edward Pakenham — a veteran of the Napoleonic Wars and the Duke of Wellington's brother-in-law — had 9,000 veterans serving under him in the United States. Theodore Roosevelt described them in his *The Naval War of 1812* as "fierce and hardy veterans of the Peninsular War." These were perhaps the finest troops in the world. They were headed toward New Orleans.

Pakenham's goal was to take New Orleans, then establish British forts along the Mississippi River, wrest the Louisiana Purchase from the Americans, and extend Canada's boundaries south to the Gulf of Mexico. The Battle of New Orleans was of supreme significance, as American independence was at stake. In that sense it might be called the last battle of the Revolutionary War. The British committed their best regiments under one of their best commanders.

To stop them, the United States had Andrew Jackson and his men. Jackson was the youngest of three sons of Scotch-Irish immigrants. His father died in 1767, shortly before Jackson's birth, and his older brothers and mother died during the Revolutionary War. As a fourteen-year-old captured American soldier, Jackson refused to polish a British officer's boots. The officer slashed the boy with a saber across his hand and forehead. Of all the blood drawn by

British sabers over the centuries, that was the blood they had most cause to regret.

Jackson was a lawyer, a slaveholder from Tennessee who despised the British and had contempt for almost anyone who was not a white American. He had served in the U.S. House of Representatives and in the Senate. In 1798 he became a judge on the Tennessee Supreme Court. In 1802 he was elected major general of the Tennessee militia, more an honorific job than a demanding one. But he took his military duties seriously enough to study a translation of French Army regulations and he tried to instill French methods to his militia.

When war with England came in June 1812, Jackson offered the Tennessee militia's services. President James Madison accepted, but did not call Jackson to active duty because of his intense dislike of the man. Disgusted, Jackson returned to Tennessee, where he became involved in an act of violence that was typical of the American frontier: a duel, with Thomas Hart Benton's brother, who was a colonel of the militia under Jackson's command. Benton shot Jackson in the shoulder and gravely wounded him. Despite his wound, in November 1813 Jackson fought two successful battles against the Creek Nation. By March 1814, with 5,000 men in his force, Jackson attacked the Indians at one of their fortified camps at the Horseshoe Bend of the Tallapoosa River, routing the Creek Nation and breaking its power forever.

To show its gratitude, the United States on May 28, 1814, appointed Jackson major general in the U.S. Army and put him in command of the Seventh Military District, in the South. He was, in effect, that unique American creation, a citizen soldier serving as a general officer. In September, he defended Mobile, Alabama, from a small British force, and went on to Pensacola, Florida, which he captured. In late November, he hurried west to New Orleans, correctly surmising that the British intended to use the Mississippi River to launch an amphibious attack on the city.

Jackson had a couple of thousand frontiersmen and militia to stop the British. He was sick with dysentery and recovering from a bullet wound he had received in the battle with the Creeks, but his will kept him going. He once said Napoleon should have burned Paris to the ground rather than let it fall to the enemy. He appeared ready to do that to New Orleans.

Jackson put together an army of citizen soldiers. He marched Kentucky militia and Tennessee volunteers from Mobile to New Orleans, where he prepared defenses south of the town, on the east bank of the Mississippi River, at the Plains of Chalmette. He enlisted anyone who would fight to reinforce the militia, eventually forming an army of roughly 4,000. In addition to the men from Tennessee and Kentucky, he had the pirate Jean Lafitte and his men, black men from New Orleans, some of them "free men of color," some slaves (even though he himself was a slaveholder), along with Germans, Irishmen, Spaniards, Cajuns, Italians, and Portuguese and Norwegian seamen. His drummer boy, Jordon B. Noble, was a fourteen-year-old former slave from Georgia who volunteered for the duty. Jackson said the British were "the common enemy of mankind." As disparate as his soldiers were, nothing drew them together more than their hatred of the British Empire, made intense by the fear that Pakenham intended to turn New Orleans into a southern version of Montreal.

Just as the Mississippi was the great river that drew the nation together rather than dividing it into separate parts, so was the mixture of races come together to fight the British — something even Napoleon had never been able to do. Jackson put together the first multi-racial army, one that stands as a model to today's American armed forces, except that it had no women. It was a ragtag force, barely trained, ill-equipped, led by a brawling frontiersman who had no formal training for his command, and who had been a general for less than half a year. That was the army that prepared to stand up to Britain's proud veterans.

Theodore Roosevelt, in his book on the War of 1812, took special notice of the African-American soldiers. "One band had in its formation something that was curiously pathetic. It was composed of free men of color, who had gathered to defend the land which kept the men

38

of their race in slavery." Some of them were seamen from the various ships in the harbor; at the time, one sailor in six serving on the U.S. frigates was a free black. In Roosevelt's words, they "were to shed their blood for the Flag that symbolized to their kind not freedom but bondage; who were to die bravely as freemen, only that their brethren might live on ignobly as slaves. Surely there was never a stranger instance than this of the irony of fate."

Jackson's troops called him "Old Hickory," which signified his unbending nature and his strength. On December 2, 1814, Jackson marched his militia and a few regulars (two regiments, about 800 men) into the city. There he proclaimed martial law, seized all available artillery and every ounce of war matériel that the city contained, suspended all general business, and put all the residents to work to build earthworks and other defenses.

Theodore Roosevelt, himself a citizen soldier, wrote of those troops who marched with Jackson and of those he recruited within New Orleans: "They loved and feared him as few generals have ever been loved or feared; they obeyed him unhesitatingly; they followed his lead without flinching or murmuring, and they ever made good on the field of battle the promise of their courage held out to his judgment."

On the afternoon of December 23 the British advance guard of 2,000 was camped on the east bank of the Mississippi, downriver from New Orleans. Jackson determined to attack at once. In the city alarm guns were fired, drummer boy Noble beat on his drums, shouts were heard calling the troops to their duty. About 2,000 men were assembled. As the gray of winter twilight settled, Old Hickory took his place at the head of the force and marched down the riverbank toward the enemy camp. At nine P.M., well past full dark, the Americans came up on the British and immediately attacked. For three hours the sides exchanged fire. Around midnight, smoke from the guns and a fog that had come up obscured everything. With a loss of some 200 men, Jackson turned about and marched upriver. The British, with about 300 killed, returned to their camp.

Jackson fell back about three miles, where he took up a position in the Plains of Chalmette along the Rodriguez Canal. The line was around a mile long, running from the low levee along the river to a cypress swamp. The ground in front of it was a stubbled sugarcane field that gave the American artillerymen a clear field of fire. Jackson had his men dig the canal wider and deeper, filled it with water, and placed cotton bales to the front, along with log defenses to form breastworks. He also placed a battery of smoothbore cannon on the west bank of the river, protected by breastworks, with a few hundred troops to defend the guns.

The British command figured that Jackson

had retreated back into the city. On December 26, Pakenham put his whole army in motion, nearly 10,000 men. He rode at the head, and after three miles, to his great surprise, he stumbled on the American army. Jackson had his breastworks defended by 3,000 men, plus half a dozen guns, plus the corvette *Louisiana* anchored in the river. As Pakenham's columns appeared the Americans opened mortar, cannon, and muskets on them. The *Louisiana* joined in. Pakenham pulled his army back out of cannon range and pitched his camp, facing the Americans.

After dark on New Year's Eve, Pakenham sent forward some workmen to within 300 yards of Jackson's line. Shielded by darkness, the men threw up stout earthworks. In them Pakenham placed fourteen cannon, to face Jackson's thirteen. At dawn on New Year's Day, he opened fire, confident his veteran artillerymen would blast the Americans out of the way. But the American artillerymen proved their skill in handling their guns. Some guns were served by New England seamen, taken off one of the American gunboats for that purpose. Others were handled by the privateersmen of Lafitte, who knew their guns as well as anyone. Others were serviced by the trained artillerymen of the regular army.

The British gunners fired as fast as they could and managed to set some cotton bales used in the American embrasures on fire and blow up two powder caissons. The American cannon-

41

balls began hitting the sugar hogsheads that protected part of the British batteries. They were shattered. As Theodore Roosevelt notes, although the British were vastly more experienced in artillery fire, they failed to adjust their aim and most of their cannonballs went sailing over the Americans' heads. The American fire was slower but much surer. Through the fight they coolly corrected their faults and hit their targets. By noon, the Americans had two of their guns disabled and thirty-four casualties. The British, by then, had all their cannon silenced or dismounted, and had lost seventy-eight men.

Pakenham's attempt to breach Jackson's breastworks had failed. This came as a great surprise to him. British artillery had never before been bested, not even by Napoleon. Pakenham and the Duke of Wellington had defeated the greatest of Napoleon's armies and marshals, time and again, driving them in headlong flight over the Pyrenees. For the British to be beaten by a ragtag army from a former colony was humiliating. Pakenham pulled back.

Jackson kept after him. He did not attack over the open ground, which would have been madness, but he kept his cannon firing at intervals, to prevent the British from getting more guns up to the line. And at night, he did not allow the wearied British to sleep undisturbed; throughout the hours of darkness Jackson's backwoodsmen engaged the British sentries, drove in their pickets, and allowed none of those on guard a moment's safety or freedom from alarm.

Pakenham was being outthought, his men out-fought. His own pride was high, so also that of his men. In a dozen battles, these men had conquered the armies and captured the forts of the mighty French Emperor. Could they possibly be stopped by a ragged army of militia, pirates, African Americans, who had only a mud wall to protect them? Men who could not even do a close-order drill? Whose commander was a grizzled old Indian fighter who had not been heard of outside the South, and whose only claim to a victory was over the Creek Indians? It was time to close on them, drive them away, march into New Orleans and run up the Union Jack.

Unlike Pakenham, who hardly bothered with reconnaissance, Jackson kept a constant watch on the British and had surmised that the enemy would make the main assault on the east bank of the river. He therefore kept 4,000 or so of his army along the Rodriguez Canal. He had a small, still unfinished redoubt in front of the breastworks on the riverbank. His thirteen pieces of artillery were in place, scattered along the line. On his right he had the Seventh regular infantry, 430 strong; then came 740 Louisiana militia, French Creoles and men of color, Germans, Irishmen, Spaniards, and others; to their left were 500 Kentucky military and then 1,600 Tennessee militia. On the extreme left he placed 250 Louisiana militia. In the rear he had 230 dragoons, chiefly from Mississippi, along with some other troops in reserve.

Through the night of January 7–8, 1815, the Americans could hear hustle and bustle in the British ranks, only a quarter of a mile away. When the sun came up it glinted on the sharp steel bayonets of the English — every man had his bayonet fixed, while in the American line only about half were so armed. The British were about 400 yards from the Americans, out of range of their muskets. They were in their battle array, in scarlet uniforms. They, and Pakenham and the other generals, were fully confident that after marching in perfect rank and file into the American lines and taking a few casualties, they would drive away the Americans with their bayonets and then — on to New Orleans!

Pakenham pulled his sword, pointed it forward, and the British moved ahead in silence. The bulk headed toward the American left, where the Tennessee militia was in place, standing motionless. The British crossed 100 yards, then 200, then 300. So close to the American lines, the troops gave a cheer and broke into a run, holding their muskets, bayonets pointed.

Drummer Noble began beating on his drum, calling for commencing fire. Theodore Roosevelt described what happened next: "Then a hell of a fire smote the British column. Rank after rank of the wild marksmen of the backwoods rose and fired, aiming low and sure. Aghast at the slaughter, the reeling files staggered and gave back. Pakenham rode to the front, and the

44

troops, rallying round him, sprang forward with ringing cheers. But once again the pealing rifle blast beat in their faces; the life of their dauntless leader went out before its scorching and fiery breath. With him fell the other general who was with the column." Reinforcements rushed forward, a third general was killed, the remaining British troops driven back.

On Jackson's right, near the river, the British managed to capture the redoubt, killing the defenders to a man. Then they attacked the breastworks behind. But this time they and their leader were "riddled through and through by the balls of the riflemen," according to Roosevelt.

Within a half-hour, all along the line, it was over. The British had suffered almost 2,000 casualties, the Tennessee militia six killed and seven wounded, the defenders of the American redoubt about forty casualties.

One hundred and seventy years later I took Major John Howard to the battlefield. He had been the commander of the company of British glider troops who had been the first to invade France on June 6, 1944 — D-Day — at 0016 hours. His company was a part of the Oxfordshire and Buckinghamshire Light Infantry — the "Ox and Bucks." John and I walked across the ground over which the British had launched their charge, then along the length of the Rodriguez Canal. We went to the Beauregard House, an antebellum home overlooking the river that today serves as a small museum. There was a display of the regimental patches of the British units involved in the battle. John and I looked, and he began to cry. What? I asked him. He pointed. There was the patch of the Ox and Bucks. It was one of Britain's oldest, and best, regiments.

The next year I took British military historian and World War II gunner Ronald Lewin to the battlefield. In front of the same display, he too began crying. His comment was, "They sent the cream over here."

Pakenham's body was put into a rum barrel and taken by the retreating British to a ship for transportation home. He had suffered a bloody and disastrous defeat and its cause was British contempt for the Americans. Up to this time, the British had won almost every land engagement in the War of 1812 and were certain they would again. Pakenham neglected reconnaissance, he made no use of surprise or maneuver. He simply sent his men forward, marching in step, shoulder to shoulder in their scarlet uniforms, anticipating that the Americans would run as the columns came close. That did not happen. As Roosevelt wrote, "No troops, however steady, could advance over open ground against such a fire as came from Jackson's lines." The Battle of New Orleans was, for the British, about as badly conceived and as ineptly carried out as any battle could have been. America's citizen soldiers had decimated the British regulars.

It was the great event of the war. It saved

American self-respect at home and gave the United States prestige abroad. The highest praise for the victory goes properly to Jackson, for his concept of a flexible defense until the British revealed their intentions, his daring night attack once they had done so, his ability to get his men to work together effectively at the preparation of defensive works at the Rodriguez Canal, his insistence that they stand shoulder to shoulder behind the breastworks and fire only aimed shots, and those as quickly as they could reload. His men were superb. So was he. He became the most famous and successful general of his generation. Theodore Roosevelt described him as "the ablest general the United States produced, from the outbreak of the Revolution down to the beginning of the Great Rebellion."

Drummer boy Noble, a free black, became a celebrity. He served in various military units in the Indian skirmishes, and in 1847 he joined the New Orleans Washington Artillery to participate in the Mexican War. At age sixty, he served in the Union Army under General Benjamin F. Butler. When he was in New Orleans and not involved in fighting, he played his drum at funerals (a slow, dirgelike "Streets of Laredo") and weddings (an upbeat version of "Amazing Grace").

The battle transformed Andrew Jackson overnight into a national hero. His fame helped propel him to the presidency in 1828. Yet there is much to criticize Jackson for, his slaveholding to begin with, and his treatment of the Cherokee and Creek tribes, and more. As a young teacher I went after him in my lectures, especially on his Indian policy before and while he was President, but I now realize that despite his shortcomings and failures, he was a great man, not only but above all else because of his victory in the Battle of New Orleans. Had he not brought the disparate elements of the city together, had he not led frontiersmen from Kentucky and Tennessee and Mississippi and Alabama to the battle, the British would have won. We can only speculate on what would have happened next, but we do know that the general belief that the battle made no difference because the peace treaty between Britain and the United States had already been signed (the Treaty of Ghent on December 24, 1814) is not true — even though I used to teach it that way.

The British did not become a world power or gain a vast empire by retreating from victories. Indeed, after the Battle of New Orleans, the British army turned east and attacked Mobile, where on February 12 they captured Fort Boyer and were in position to take Mobile. Had that happened, could the Americans have ejected them? We cannot know. But immediately afterward the news of peace arrived and all hostilities terminated.

As Jackson was leaving the White House in 1837, at the end of his second term, a congressman asked him if there was any point to the Battle of New Orleans. Jackson's eyes flashed. He stared up and down at the congressman. He said, "If General Pakenham and his ten thousand matchless veterans could have annihilated my little army . . . he would have captured New Orleans and sentried all the contiguous territory, though technically the war was over. Great Britain would have immediately abrogated the Treaty of Ghent and would have ignored Jefferson's transaction with Napoleon."

On the twenty-fifth anniversary of the battle, Jackson visited the site, where the Chalmette Monument had just been erected, to speak about his men. He praised his troops for their "undaunted courage, patriotism, and patience under hardships and fatigues." He alluded to their many differences and how they came together to defend their country. "Natives of different states, acting together, for the first time, in this camp, differing in habits and in language have reaped the fruits of an honourable union." The combination of Creoles and Tennesseans, Cajuns and Kentuckians, blacks and whites, slaves and freedmen, Germans and Irishmen, Italians and Norwegians, made them realize for the first time they were all Americans. Together with Jackson they had won a battle of the most fundamental importance.

# Chapter Three

# *The Indian Country*

Free land, or very cheap land, and the promise of political freedom and education for their children drew nineteenth-century immigrants from Europe to the United States in one of the greatest mass migrations in history, and in many ways the most consequential. It certainly was as unstoppable as the tide, or the melting of the snow in the spring. Even before the Louisiana Purchase in 1803, or the Lewis and Clark expedition of 1803–1806, American settlers, led by Daniel Boone, had crossed the Mississippi River and started their farms in Missouri. Well before 1836 Americans had moved into and begun farming in Texas. Long before the Mexican War began in 1846, Americans had settled in California, already a land of milk and honey even before the discovery of gold and annexation by the United States. There were great disputes between the various frontiersmen from Texas out to California, over slavery most of all, but as well over land titles, mineral rights, boundaries, and more. But the Americans agreed on the even more important principle, that they wanted their land to be democratic with freedom of worship and universal education. And they could not be stopped.

It was called "Manifest Destiny," or "The American Way." It meant rounding up the Indians who had occupied the land for centuries and segregating them in reservations. It meant extending the borders of freedom for the white man. As to the Indians, the guiding principle was, promise them anything just so long as they get out of the way.

Who is to say the Americans were wrong? Who today is willing to say that Texas and California and the remainder of the Southwest would be better off if they were governed by Mexico? Who would be willing to tell the European immigrant or the American frontiersman that he can't go to the Texas grasslands or the Kansas prairie because the Mexicans already own the land or the Indians need it, so he had best go back to Prague or Dublin or Chicago or New York? Who is willing to tell a hungry world that the United States cannot export wheat or beef because the Cheyenne hold half of Kansas, the Sioux hold the Dakotas, the Mexicans have Texas and California?

Before I began a study of George Armstrong Custer and Crazy Horse in 1970, I took for granted — and taught — what I had been taught. That America ought to be ashamed of what it did to the Indians of the Great Plains. I did not know then what I do now, that it is totally irresponsible to state — as so many have done — that the

51

United States pursued a policy of genocide toward the Sioux, Cheyenne, and other Indian tribes. Some tribes were wiped out, many others decimated, not by a policy of genocide but because of the introduction of European diseases, most of all smallpox. In its own inept way the United States government did try to find a solution to the Indian problem. The consistent idea was to civilize the Indians, incorporate them into the community, make them part of the melting pot. That it did not work, that it was foolish, conceited, even criminal, is true. But it was not a policy of genocide, certainly not genocide as we have come to understand it in the twentieth century.

My first experience with Indians came in the summer of 1971. My wife, Moira, and I had sold our house in Kansas and had to be out by June, and bought a house in New Orleans but could not occupy it until September, when I took up my job at the University of New Orleans. We had no money to amount to anything, no home, nothing in our possession other than a Volkswagen bus. We decided to go camping in the Black Hills of South Dakota, then in August to go to Dad's cabin in northern Wisconsin. We spent June in the Hills, a delightful place. We hiked, fished, climbed mountains. I always read about the history of the area where we were camping, and this time it was the history of the Black Hills and the Indians and whites who once lived there. I would read aloud to our children around the campfire, then talk about what had happened here.

In early July we decided it was time to go to Wisconsin. We loaded up the VW bus — all our camping gear; our Labrador dog; our five children, Stephenie, Barry, Andrew, Grace, and Hugh — and headed east. A VW bus (which cost in those days, as I recall, $2,100; for $1,800 you could get a VW Bug) could hold immense amounts of stuff and on a flat stretch, with no head wind, could get up to sixty miles per hour. Going downhill, seventy miles per hour. But headed uphill, fully loaded, you were lucky to keep it at thirty miles per hour, and near the top at twenty.

We were headed east from the Black Hills. We got to the top of a hill, and before us was a long, gentle slope down, then the next hill rising up. Our technique was to get that VW going as fast as possible on the downhill, keep the pedal to the floor when we started up, and hope for the best.

Moira was driving. Ahead, at the bottom of the hill, there was a sign with an arrow pointing left: "Wounded Knee, 12 miles." I had told the family about the massacre in 1890 of Big Foot and his band of Sioux at Wounded Knee by the U.S. Seventh Cavalry. The children wanted to see it. Moira wanted to see it. I wanted to keep going, not lose the momentum, get up that next hill. But she put on the brakes and over my protest turned left. It was a turn that changed our lives.

We got to the Wounded Knee site. I had a book on the massacre with a map. We went into the trading post. I saw a buckskin dress, beaded, and had to have it for Moira. She and the children all found items they could not live without. We were entranced by the setting. A nearby ranch had a small campground. We went, set up our tent, and stayed through July and August.

I read. Mari Sandoz's *Crazy Horse*, Jay Monaghan's *Custer*, George Hyde's *Red Cloud's Folk*, George Custer's *My Life on the Plains*, other books that were available in paperback. I decided I wanted to write a book about Custer, but there were too many already. Besides, I was a great fan of Plutarch's Lives. So I decided to do a dual biography, Custer and Crazy Horse. They were born at the same time and died within a year of each other. They were war lovers, men of supreme courage, natural-born leaders. They were always first to charge the enemy and the last to retreat. Neither man drank liquor. Both were avid hunters. Each man loved horses and riding at full gallop across the unfenced Great Plains of North America. Had they been born in the same society they would have been great friends. As it was, they were great enemies. They met only twice, each time on the battlefield, first on the banks of the Yellowstone River in 1873, second on the banks of the Little Bighorn in 1876.

I was able to persuade my editor at Doubleday that there was a book in this subject and got an advance sufficient to support us through three summers of camping and researching. From 1971 to 1974, we camped for extended periods of time with the Oglala Sioux at Pine Ridge Reservation in South Dakota; at the Crow Reservation at Crow Agency, next to the Little Bighorn battlefield; at the North Cheyenne Reservation at Lame Deer in eastern Montana; with the Shoshoni and Arapahoe at Wind River, Wyoming; and at Fort Robinson in northwestern Nebraska and Custer National Forest in the Black Hills of South Dakota. At Crow Agency, our children pleaded with the organizers and got themselves into a staged re-creation of the Battle of the Little Bighorn — not as Sioux warriors riding bareback or soldiers dressed in uniform, but as immigrants crossing the Plains in covered wagons, attacked by the Indians. They still talk about it three decades later.

During our time on reservations, and throughout our more than twenty years of camping out in the West, I observed, learned, explored, thought, absorbed. The vast spaces, the snow-covered mountains, the swift-running rivers, the Native Americans, the cattle and the deer and other game, the buttes, the horses, the mountain trails, the attitude that all this public domain belongs to you and me, seized my imagination. I had gone to graduate school in a department once headed by Frederick Jackson Turner, whose frontier thesis grabbed and held most American historians living west of the Appalachian Mountains. I had been taught about the frontier, why it was important and what it meant to America. Most of all, the frontier brought democracy. That view, widely accepted at the beginning of the twentieth century, was widely rejected by the 1950s. Either way the Turner thesis was regarded, it dealt with the history of the West from the white man's point of view. The Indian was peripheral. He was the "other," the one who had to be gotten out of the way.

Beginning in 1971, camping in the West, my views began to broaden. The Indians were not in the way; they were an integral part of the scene. There were not enough of them to stop the coming of the white man. They could not unify their politics to stand together — one of the few times they did was at the Little Bighorn, where Cheyenne and Sioux joined and defeated George Armstrong Custer. But had there been fewer Indians in the Great Plains, or none at all, it would have been far more expensive to explore. Without the native tribes, Lewis and Clark would have gotten lost, or starved. Indians showed the white man the way. Without them, fur trappers and traders would have had a much different and more difficult task. Yet in the history of the West, as written in the white man's textbook, the Indian is as forgotten or neglected as are the black slaves who built and maintained the plantations.

But the Indians were there. They still are. In our travels throughout the West, I got to know some about my age, went horseback riding with them, swimming, driving into town, just sitting around and talking. I learned something about a way of life.

Sometimes I learned through jokes. Once, sitting with a Sioux man of my age on his porch, I looked at my watch. It was twelve noon. "Time for lunch," I said and started to get up. He laughed and said, "White man only man I know who looks at his watch to see if he is hungry or not."

I learned through stories. Many modern Indians join the U.S. armed forces and compile outstanding records. I got to know one, a veteran of the Korean War living at the Pine Ridge Reservation, who told me about his experiences in Korea. I've spent much of my life hearing veterans tell their war stories. When he came to his discharge, I asked him what happened to him when he came home from Korea.

"Well," he said, "it was like this." He had become a sergeant, earned some decorations, had an honorable discharge, money in his pocket after two years of combat pay and no place to spend it. So he went to a bank to borrow some more money to build a gasoline station in Pine Ridge. With his war record as his collateral he got the loan, built the place, and opened for business.

His first customer was his mother. She helped herself to two new tires on the rack, filled her tank with gasoline, said thanks, and drove off.

Then came his younger brother, who filled up, changed his oil, said thanks, and drove off. Then a friend, same thing. By the end of the day he had taken in no money but dispensed gallons of gasoline, a few tires, quarts of oil, and more. The Sioux would never charge their relatives or friends for anything, much less something as essential as gasoline.

"So," he said, "after the first day, I knew that I either had to be a capitalist or an Indian. I could not be both." He sold the station to a white man, paid the loan back to the bank, and got what work he could as a cowboy.

In August 1971 we attended a Sun Dance at Wounded Knee. In a Sun Dance warriors pierce their chests with grizzly bear claws, which are attached to long leather thongs that are tied to the top of a twenty-foot pole in the middle of a circle. For hours, the warriors dance, sing, lean back to get the claws to tear open their flesh and free them from the thongs.

One of the dancers was Russell Means. He later was active in the American Indian Movement, which for some weeks took over the trading post at Wounded Knee and was besieged by the FBI. There were some shootings, some jail sentences — not involving Means. He had the most extraordinary good looks. He was tall, with no excess weight, bulging muscles. He was a model for Hollywood, and indeed became in the 1990s a well-known Hollywood actor. In 1971 he managed to tear open his skin and release himself from the claws and thongs.

In 1972 we were at a powwow run by the Northern Cheyenne at Lame Deer in Montana. We camped with them for four days of dancing, singing, and talking. Our children joined the dancers and became fairly proficient. Moira and I would join the dance circle, close our eyes, and sway and dream. Mr. Red Bird had the loud-speaker and he would signal to the drummers when it was time to begin playing, then call out, "All you singers, all you dancers. Intertribal! Everybody powwow!" As we danced he kept up a constant stream of jokes, gossip, news, and instructions — "Now you big kids. You leave those little kids alone!" We would rise to his voice in the morning, go to sleep when he told us to do so at night. In the mornings, the tribe dis-tributed rations — bread, peanut butter, canned vegetables, chunks of frozen beef or buffalo, Cokes, more. At first we protested that although we were camped in the circle, we didn't need the distribution and could afford our own food. That was ignored and we gave up protesting.

Mr. Red Bird called all of us together for a cer-emony. A young Cheyenne, perhaps fifteen years old, named Harry Has Many Horses, was joined in the center of the circle by a married couple from the Sioux Reservation at Standing Rock, South Dakota. The couple, Red Bird explained, had lost their son in action in Viet-nam. They had come to the powwow hoping it would help them shake off their grief. They watched Harry Has Many Horses dance. He danced just like their son. So they asked him if he would let them adopt him, thus taking the place of their lost boy. It is an old Indian custom, for parents who are bereaved to adopt someone else who reminds them of the lost one. Harry said yes. So did his parents. The adoption took place then and there, and Red Bird announced that after the powwow Harry was going to his new parents' home at Standing Rock for a visit.

During the powwow the Cheyenne had a give-away. One family would give whatever it had, clothes, pipes, implements, furniture, even a car and more to another family, who in turn would give away their possessions. It promoted the feeling, common among the nineteenth-century Plains Indians, that whatever I have is yours, and vice versa.

After I finished my book on Crazy Horse and Custer, I thought I might do one on Geronimo and the Apaches, so I drove out to Ruidoso, New Mexico, to meet with Eve Ball, who was the white authority on the tribe and one of the very best of all historical writers. Eve and I talked for a week and I ended up deciding that I wasn't capable of doing Geronimo and his people, because I didn't know the Apache language and despaired of learning it, and I didn't know enough about the Apache customs and practices, and there was not much written about the tribe in English.

In the process of discovering that I wasn't up

to the task, I still learned a lot. Eve lived on the edge of the Apache reservation and had been a friend of the tribe for decades. She knew the men and the women, the leaders and the led, and had stories about each of them. She was especially close to a man named Ice, who was a medicine man.

One day Ice had come to her house to announce that the Apache had just made her into a tribal member. With her great modesty and realization of the honor that had just been done her, Eve said thank you. Ice then said, "This means you can go to the Happy Hunting Ground with us and we can always be together."

"Oh, Ice," Eve replied. "I'd love to. But I know there are no books in your Happy Hunting Ground, and you know how much I love books and must have them around me, so I've got to say no."

Ice frowned, thought, then asked, "Are there books in the white man's heaven?"

"Of course there are," Eve answered. "Thousands of them. Entire libraries."

Ice brightened. Then he declared, "We'll make a raid!"

I like to think that today, Eve is with Ice, reading about her beloved Southwest from one of the books Ice brought back from his raid on heaven.

Getting to know something about the Indians, even in my own modest and incomplete way, got me to looking backward as well as forward, to studying not just what the white man or the U.S. Army soldiers did to the Indians, but what the Indians did to each other. That is, the Indians of the Great Plains before Lewis and Clark came. The Sioux, Cheyenne, the Crow, and others tried in the nineteenth century to convince the U.S. Army and government that the lands they lived on were their ancestral lands, but they were not. They had become Plains Indians because they were pushed westward by tribes moving into Wisconsin. When they acquired the horse, they became warriors and hunters without equal, and spread out, taking more land from previous inhabitants.

Thus I learned that the Indians lived by the same rules or system as all the human beings that went before or came after them — the right of conquest. The land, or a portion of it, belongs to those who can seize it and hold it. In pushing the Great Plains tribes out of the way and taking their land, the whites were doing to the Sioux and the others what they had done to the tribes that preceded them. At the Fort Laramie treaty conference of 1851, where the Americans attempted to confine the Sioux to lands north of the Platte River, a Sioux spokesman named Black Hawk protested that the Sioux held lands south of the Platte by the same right the Americans claimed the lands they took from Mexico; the right of conquest. "These lands once belonged to the Kiowas and the Crows," Black

Hawk said, "but we shipped those nations out of them and in this we did what the white men do when they want the lands of Indians."

The "turnabout is fair play" argument can't be taken too far, however, because much of what the whites did in their dealings with the Plains tribes was shameful. All Americans need to hang their heads — and this includes African Americans, who made up the 24th and 25th regiments, the so-called Buffalo Soldiers. They, along with the white regiments in the horse cavalry, fought, rounded up, put the Indians into camps.

But what hurt the most, for the Indians, was the forked tongue with which the white men spoke. Lies and more lies and then more lies were told by government negotiators to get the Indians out of the way. The Sioux were told that the Black Hills would be theirs so long as the grass grew and there were buffalo to graze. That promise was made in the early 1870s and broken as soon as gold was discovered in the Black Hills. The people of the frontier wanted to dig it out. The U.S. Army made only a feeble attempt to protect the rights guaranteed the Sioux. Some 130 years later, the U.S. government has done nothing to rectify the situation or to pay for the theft — even though the grass is still growing in the Black Hills, and one of the largest buffalo herds in North America roams through Custer National Forest.

The lies continue. Sometimes they are designed to glorify the Indians. In the last third of the twentieth century, it became common-place for environmental groups to tout the Indians as the first conservationists. It was said that they killed only what they needed for food. This is hardly true. It was said the slaughter of the buffalo herd for hides, done in the 1870s, could only have been done by white men. This was correct because only the white man had the rifles and the trains to move the hides. But it is not correct to assert that the Indians never left rotting carcasses. In fact even before the horse arrived, the Plains Indians learned how to use a pishkin, where they would drive a herd of buffalo off a ledge. The animals would break a leg; the Indians would slaughter the helpless ones. Then they would cut out the tongues and leave the rest for the wolves. Hundreds of buffalo.

The Indians were presented, in advertise-ments, in classrooms, in movies, in books as the most generous and helpful of people. They would never hurt anyone. In fact Indian warriors were guilty of great gruesomeness. They tor-tured their captives in bloodcurdling ways. So did the white soldiers commit atrocities of a gruesome nature on captured Indians. One called the other savages. It is politically incorrect to say so, but they both were.

That there have been a multitude of injustices done by the whites to the Indians is apparent to everyone. But it is also true that things can be improved and are beginning to be so. Indians are a part of our national life, a part of our culture, which is good for them but even better for us. To some small extent, which badly needs to be extended, we are more willing than before to allow Indians to be Indians — hunting, fishing, going to powwows, speaking their own language, herding cattle on horseback.

But we have made so many promises to the Indians that were so soon broken as to make it impossible for the Indians to trust or for the white man to hold up his head. Sometimes it appears that the white man's only "gift" to the Indians has been alcohol, which turns out to be the bane of the Native Americans, as they have had only two or three hundred years to become accustomed to it, as opposed to those of European descent who have two millennia of boozing behind them.

Young Indian males join the Army and Marines in large numbers. In the wars of the twentieth century they have made a splendid reputation for themselves, have received many medals, taught their comrades and learned from them. One of the most famous groups of the Second World War is the Navajo Code Talkers. As children they were forced to go to school in English-only classes, chained when they insisted on speaking Navajo, but welcomed into the Army and Marines when they enlisted right after December 7, 1941. The United States, after trying to beat their language out of them, realized that the Navajo language would be ideal for combat communications, because on the battlefield it didn't matter if they spoke over the radio in their own language, as the Japanese and the Germans could listen all they wanted. They would never crack the code. The Navajo are much celebrated, and rightly so, for this and other accomplishments.

The migration that hit the Great Plains after the Civil War is generally described as a "tide," and that is an apt description. Nothing could stop it — not drought, not fire, not flood, not famine. As much as anything can be with human beings, it was inevitable. And so were the changes it wrought. With it came fences and plows and railroads.

Whether it is called progress, or civilization, or a land grab, or theft, or conquest, it happened. In 1868 the commander of the U.S. Army, General William T. Sherman, was appointed by President Andrew Johnson to a Peace Commission to parley with the chiefs and sign treaties that would contain an Indian promise to let the Union Pacific Railroad go through their territory without molestation. At North Platte, Nebraska, Sherman made a speech. In it, he told the Indians, "This railroad will be built, and if you are damaged by it we must pay you in full [a promise that was broken] and if your young men will interfere the Great Father, who, out of love for you, withheld his soldiers, will let loose his young men, and you will be swept away."

That was blunt enough. So was what followed:

"We will build iron roads, and you cannot stop the locomotive any more than you can stop the sun or the moon, and you must submit, and do the best you can."

Cheyenne chief Pawnee Killer, who had already stopped two locomotives, stomped out of the council in a rage. He swore to end the railroad building. Sherman was as determined as he. "Whether right or wrong," he wrote, "those roads will be built, and everybody knows that Congress, after granting the charters, and fixing the Routes, cannot now back out and surrender the country to a few bands of roving Indians."

The transcontinental railroad was going to be built. The Indians were not going to stop it, although they could make it more costly. Almost everyone in the United States wanted it built, even if it was going to divide the buffalo herd, bring farmers and ranchers to Nebraska, Wyoming, Utah, and across the West, thus disrupting the Indians' pattern of life. That the federal government should have done something to compensate the Indians for what the whites were stealing is true. It is a sad, even a pitiful, thing that it did not. That it should have stopped the building of the railroad is absurd.

On the Plains, as in the Eastern woodlands, as on the Pacific Coast, there were irreconcilable differences between the Indians' way of life and the life the white immigrants wanted to build. One had to give way. The white man had the numbers and the technology. It is easy today to sit back and criticize the United States for its treatment of the Indians, or the individual settlers and frontiersmen for what they did to the Native Americans, but for them the choices were to go back to where they came from or to go forward and seize what they wanted or needed. Few today are willing to say they should not have done what they did, although many of us are prepared to say they should have paid for what they took, especially by giving more consideration to preserving the Indian way of life.

The trouble is, the only payment the Indians wanted was to retain possession of their lands. That they could not have. Instead, the Indians got reservations, run by reformers, who called themselves "Friends of the Indian." They came mainly from the churches, and in 1869 President Ulysses S. Grant, in his "Peace Policy" toward Indians, gave the reformers control over the reservations. They did not believe the Indians were inferior to whites, but rather that like children they were still advancing up "the ladder of civilization" and the reservations were the way to help them do so.

As historian Richard White puts it, the reformers were "all the greater enemies of Indian cultures, for they believed that for Indians to survive they had to shed all that made them obviously Indian. If Indians would not do so willingly, then the reformers would have to force them to do so for the Indians' own good. This determination to destroy Indian cultures in order to save Indian peoples gave the peace policy of the reformers a ferocious edge."

On the reservations, the goal was to get the Indians to drop their native language and speak English, to become farmers and Christians, and thus be more like the whites. To a very large extent, little of this has worked.

Moira and I were at Cut Bank, Montana, in the 1990s. We were researching Lewis and Clark and the Blackfoot tribe. Wilbur Werner, a lawyer in Cut Bank, was an expert on both and he spent the day with us, traveling in our four-wheel-drive truck, sometimes walking, showing us the site on the Two Medicine River where Lewis fought the Blackfeet, killing two of them, and Lewis's "Camp Disappointment" on Cut Bank Creek.

Then Wilbur took us to a brick schoolhouse, two stories high, in the middle of the Plains, some twenty-five miles from the Rocky Mountain Front and the eastern edge of Glacier National Park. It had been abandoned since the Depression, chairs and tables and other furniture gone. Wilbur explained that it had been the schoolhouse for young Blackfoot males, run by the Catholic Church. His brother had been a monsignor of the Church and in charge at the school. Upstairs was a large, airy room with lots of windows and great views. But at one place there was a prison, large enough for one or at the most two boys, with one window and bars across the opening. Wilbur said this is where the boys got punished, not for theft or other crimes (unusual within the Blackfeet tribe), but for refusing to speak, read, or learn in the English language.

The view was of Glacier Park, always snow-covered, beyond the prairie. It contained much of what the Blackfeet loved and is why they have lived there for more than two centuries, resisting all efforts by other Indians and then by whites to force them out. Thinking of Blackfeet boys and their love of freedom, of their own language and of their culture, being in a tiny prison on their own land where they could see but not touch what they loved, punished for refusing to abandon those attributes that made them Black-feet, Moira began to cry, then to sob.

Wilbur put his arm around her. He said he understood and in many ways could sympathize. But, he went on, consider that some of those boys who were educated in this building, who learned English and how to read while there, went on to high school, college, and in a few cases to law school. "Today," he said, "they are the only ones the tribe can turn to for a defense against an arbitrary government action. The only ones."

Later, Moira and I were talking about what Wilbur had said, and what the Church had done. I was pretty much persuaded by his explanation and argument. The modern tribe can retain much of its culture — fishing, hunting deer and elk, living in tipis, riding horses — but like it or

70

not, though they were living on an Indian reservation, it was in a white man's world and under the control of the white man's government. At least some of the Blackfeet had to know how to deal with that situation.

Moira could not see any force in my argument. She was ashamed of what white people in general, and in this case her Church, had done to the Blackfeet. Rather than trying to destroy their culture, we should have done all we could to make sure it flourished.

Back then, I could not see her point of view. Today, much has changed. I've watched immigrants come to the United States from all over the world. In many cases they have established their own living space where they continue to maintain their culture. It is a pity, and worse, that we cannot make that possible for the tribes.

Indian policy is one of the places where the United States has failed and continues to do so. Thomas Jefferson thought that someday "we shall all be Americans," that is that the Indians would live as individuals side by side with the whites, sharing the same culture. That yielded to Andrew Jackson's assertion that Indians had "neither the intelligence, the industry, the moral habits, nor the desire of improvement" to do so. So he removed the Cherokees from Georgia to Oklahoma. His successors, after the Little Bighorn battle of 1876, forced the Indians onto reservations and there tried to drive the Indian out of them. That didn't work either. Today we are stuck with a problem to which we have no solution. Like their predecessors, the Presidents of today just throw up their hands.

One proposal has almost no adherents or following, and it by no means covers all the tribes and reservations in the country, but it might work. It is this: In the eastern third of Montana and the western third of the Dakotas, the great cattle and wheat ranches of the past are giving way and are abandoned or about to be. This is because of the feed lots and irrigation problems. It might be possible to buy up those ranches and turn parts of the entire area into a grasslands peopled by Indians and covered with buffalo.

In his greed, the white man wanted everything. He took from the Indians the grasslands, slaughtered the buffalo, built fences, brought in cattle. In today's world, none of that needs to be. This is not to advocate turning the whole of the western half of North and South Dakota, or of eastern Montana, to the various tribes, but it is a way to try to emulate the Canadians, who have managed to live peacefully with their Indians. It is a disgrace that the United States, with all its money and its people from around the world and land that goes far beyond what is needed for agricultural purposes, has not done the same.

# Chapter Four

# The Transcontinental Railroad

By 1866–67 nothing was going to stop the transcontinental railroad. But until 1862, the unanswered questions were who would build it, when, how, and what it would cost. It was a stupendous project, the biggest engineering challenge ever undertaken. To invest money and time in the railroad would be risky beyond anything ever before attempted, but when and if it were completed it would link the continent, changing forever the nation's politics and economics and bringing great profits to the men who built and owned it.

Even by 1850 the transcontinental railroad was something everyone in America wanted built, and the technology was ready to do it. But the cost would be heart-stopping and only the federal government had the resources — including all the land it owned — to finance the project. The Southerners in Congress wanted it to run from New Orleans through Texas to southern California, thus increasing the slave states' economy and political clout. The Northerners wanted it to run from Chicago to Sacramento and San Francisco, or from Minneapolis to Portland, increasing the free states' economy. The two sides blocked each other throughout the decade of the 1850s.

In the 1860 campaign, Abraham Lincoln and the Republican Party pledged to get the construction going immediately. When Lincoln won the election, the South did the most stupid of all the stupid things it had done until then — it seceded from the Union, and its senators and representatives walked out of the Congress. That opened the way for the railroad, over the northern route, through the Great Plains, over the Rocky Mountains, through the Great Basin, over and through the Sierra Nevada.

With the nation at war from 1861 to 1865, it seemed impossible. Nevertheless, one of the first things Lincoln and the Republican Party did after secession was to propose a bill authorizing and providing loans and land grants for the construction of a line from Omaha to Sacramento. There are many reasons why the South lagged so far behind the North in the century after the Civil War, and losing the war was certainly at the top of the list, but right behind came walking out of Congress and allowing the North to have the transcontinental railroad.

After the bill was passed in 1862, the road was completed in seven years. On May 10, 1869, the golden spike was driven at Promontory Summit in Utah and the United States had a continuous track running from the East Coast to the West Coast.

The men who prepared the roadbed, laid the rails, drove in the spikes were the heroes of the enterprise. Their names are unknown today, and were even at the time, but their accomplishment has been celebrated in stories, songs, books, movies, and documentaries. They were mainly Chinese on the Central Pacific, building east from Sacramento. Irish immigrants predominated on the Union Pacific, headed west from Omaha to Promontory Summit, with Union Army and Confederate Army veterans mixed in, along with former slaves, Jews, Germans, many others.

On each road, the men pounded the spikes with sledgehammers, carried forward the rails to lay them precisely, shoved the gravel or dirt, dug through the cuts, used powder to blast tunnels through the mountains, built bridges over creeks, rivers, and gullies, constructed culverts where needed, worked from sunrise to sunset and sometimes longer, at a pace that seemed to exceed the toil that any man can be asked to do in a day. They did it six days a week. In the summer, in Nebraska or Wyoming or Utah or Nevada, they worked in a boiling hot sun, with the wind blowing like fury. In the winter they were sometimes buried in snow. They froze their ears, their toes, fingers, hands, noses. On the Union Pacific in Nebraska and Wyoming they fought off Indian war parties. There is no way to measure or accurately compare, but it can be asserted that no men ever worked harder under more dangerous conditions than those who built the UP and the CP.

What they had going for them was their youth, their lithe bodies, their back and arm and leg muscles, their determination and their pride in what they were accomplishing. In this they were not much different from the heroes who went before and came after them — George Washington's troops at Valley Forge, Andrew Jackson's mixed bag of citizen soldiers in the Battle of New Orleans, Ulysses Grant's men at Vicksburg, Theodore Roosevelt's Rough Riders at San Juan Hill, Black Jack Pershing's doughboys in World War I, Eisenhower's GIs at Omaha Beach in 1944, the men of Korea, Vietnam, and Desert Storm. They were ordinary men called on to do extraordinary things. Slave labor could never have built that road in six years — and that is not a guess, it is a fact, as the Russians tried to build their railroad across Siberia with slave labor (200,000 Chinese forced labor, along with hundreds of thousands of convicts) and they did not complete it until thirty-two years after the Americans built theirs.

Of course those who worked on the railroad had leaders — surveyors, foremen, construction bosses, engineers, those in charge of equipment, rails, spikes, and the rest — all of whom made invaluable contributions. And the big bosses, the directors, whether on the UP or the Big Four of the CP, took great financial risks to bring it off. But it was the workers who did the job who capture our imagination.

Even that bare outline would lead any observer to suppose that those who built the Union Pacific and those who built the Central Pacific would have their names trumpeted, statues erected to them, their birthdays celebrated across the land. Nothing remotely like that happened. What the builders thought should be regarded as a splendid achievement was widely and correctly viewed as full of serious abuse. The directors of both lines told lies, cheated, outright stole money. Three abuses stood out above all others: the Crédit Mobilier, the construction company under contract to the Union Pacific; the government bonds handed over to the railroads as each twenty-mile section was completed; the land grants given by the government to the railroads.

The Crédit Mobilier, trumpeted in bold headlines on September 4, 1872, in the *New York Sun,* was the biggest scandal of the nineteenth century. It had everything investigative reporters lust after — big money, stolen money, congressmen, a Vice President, and a future President among the guilty, along with high-ranking corporate officials. There was a congressional hearing that lasted for six months and produced daily headlines. A chief target was Congressman Oakes Ames ("Hoax Ames" one newspaper called him) because he had distributed Crédit Mobilier stock to some of his colleagues in Congress. They included Representatives James G. Blaine, James Garfield, and James Brooks, and Vice President Schuyler Colfax. Ames had written, in a private letter discovered by a reporter and published by his newspaper, that he was placing the stock "where it would do the most good."

The Crédit Mobilier was supposed to oversee and pay for construction on the Union Pacific, but all it really did was distribute money, in large amounts, to its stockholders, who were either UP stockholders or congressmen. And the distributions were on levels never before seen, or dreamed of. In 1868 the UP directors made distributions of UP first-mortgage bonds, stock, and cash to the Crédit Mobilier. Thus in 1868 alone a man holding a hundred shares of Crédit Mobilier stock, which if he were a congressman was given to him and if not had cost him $10,000, received a dividend of $18,000 in cash, $7,500 in UP bonds then selling at par, and forty shares of UP stock worth about $1,600 in cash. All together, he received in distributions $27,100 for his $10,000 investment.

The money came, mainly, from government bonds. The railroads received $20,000 in bonds for each mile of road built over flat land, $32,000 for each mile in the foothills, and $48,000 for each mile in the mountains. With the money generated by selling the bonds, the railroads were supposed to pay the men who laid the track, but in fact the UP paid the lowest possible wages to the men who built the lines, and delayed or actually ignored payments of bills to the subcontractors and the workmen. Instead of using the money from the bonds to pay its legitimate debts, the UP directors distributed it to the Crédit Mobilier, which in turn used it to pay dividends to the UP directors. Most Americans found it difficult, even impossible, to believe that the directors had actually earned those profits. There were cries of outrage. The general sentiment was, We have been bilked!

In one way or another, many of those involved in Crédit Mobilier suffered from it. Thomas "Doc" Durant, who had been a key figure in setting up the Union Pacific and then the man who created the Crédit Mobilier, died less than ten years after the scandal, broke and forgotten. The Ames brothers, Oakes and Oliver (once the UP president), were men who had a sixty-five-foot monument built by the UP at the highest point on the entire line, Sherman Summit, in Wyoming. The monument, with the Ames brothers' faces in bold relief, has been defaced. Men and boys with rifles have shot off their noses and obliterated their eyes. It is but a mile from Interstate 80 coming out of Cheyenne and headed toward Ogden, Utah, and has its own exit on the highway. But only a handful of hard-core railroad buffs go there, and most of them once only. In the words of the historian of the UP, Maury

79

Klein, the Ames brothers "risked their fortunes and their reputations on the grandest enterprise yet undertaken by Americans. In return they received not praise but censure as participants in the major scandal of an age busy with scandals."

At the Central Pacific the same method as the Crédit Mobilier was used. The CP's company was called the Contract and Finance Company. Fortunately for the Big Four who were the CP directors (Collis Huntington, Mark Hopkins, Charles Crocker, and Leland Stanford), all its books had been burned — whether deliberately or by accident was and is in dispute — so the Congress was able to pin nothing on the Big Four, even though they were as vulnerable as the men of the UP. The Big Four became extraordinarily rich thanks to the way the CP was financed. They spent their fortunes lavishly, to the point that they became the very models of conspicuous consumption.

It was the land grants and the bonds the government passed out that caused the greatest outrage, at the time and later. The federal lands belonged to the government, to be handed out or sold by Congress, all in the name of and for the benefit of the people. The lands given to the CP and the UP amounted to 6,400 acres per mile of track (five alternate sections per mile on each side of the road, with the government retaining and then selling to settlers the remainder). The bonds, to be sold by the railroads, usually at par because the government stood behind them, brought in $64,623,512. Even in the corporate world, that is big money. But it was the lands that got the most notice.

My professors in the 1950s, like the reporters before them and the public at the time and later, denounced, lambasted, derided this giveaway. In one of the most influential textbooks ever published, *The Growth of the American Republic*, Samuel Eliot Morison and Henry Steele Commager wrote: "The lands granted to both the Union Pacific and the Central Pacific yielded enough to have covered all legitimate costs of building these roads." A colleague of theirs, also distinguished, Fred Shannon, wrote, "The half billion dollars in land alone to the railroads was worth more than the railroads were when they were built."

Professor William B. Hesseltine, my mentor, was one of the leading critics. Among other things, in his lectures he pointed out that the railroads enjoyed a monopoly that allowed them to charge what most users came to regard as inflated rates for freight and passenger traffic. And there was a great deal of shoddy construction that had to be replaced. Collis Huntington of the Big Four had lied and probably used bribes and certainly had drawn a fictitious map to get revisions on the original Pacific Railroad Bill highly favorable to the CP. He and his partners and their opposite numbers at the UP also lied to the various government commissions set up to examine the track. The CP lied about where the foothills east of Sacramento began (right outside the city line, according to the Big Four) and about the width of the Sierra Nevada, in order to get extra bond money from the government. In these and other matters, the directors of the UP and the Big Four justified the concern and attention of the investigative reporters and the politicians. And they ran the UP and the CP and later its addition the Southern Pacific like medieval kings. In California, their word was law. According to Hesseltine, there was almost nothing good to say about these robber barons.

The professors of American history nearly all insisted that the robber barons were exactly what the two-word description means. The directors who constructed the Union Pacific and the Central Pacific were thieves who worked directly in collusion with the Republican Party and politicians in Congress. They made obscene profits in building the roads and by overcharging the farmer shipping his grain or the passenger going from Chicago to San Francisco. They used those profits to dominate state and national politics to a degree unprecedented before or since. John Robinson's book *The Octopus: A History of the Construction, Conspiracies, Extortions, Robberies and Villainous Acts of Subsidized Railroads* expressed what the professors thought, felt, and said.

The professors said that political opposition to the UP and the CP was based on how the corporations misused the monopoly granted them by the government, overcharging so heavily and brazenly for their services as to break the financial back of farmers from Nebraska to California. This had led to the formation of the Populist Party and then the Progressive Party. Like my teachers, I regarded those parties as the saviors of late-nineteenth- and early-twentieth-century America. Like them, I wanted nothing to do with those railroad thieves.

Then in 1997, my editor asked me to write my next book on the building of the first transcontinental railroad. I told her I didn't want to do it. She insisted that I at least think about it, that what she wanted was not an exposé or a defense of the Big Four or the directors of the UP but a book that would answer the question, How did they build that railroad? Not, How did some profit from it? Or, How did they use their power for political goals? But, How did they do it?

I needed six months to read the major items in the literature so I could see if there was a reason for another book on the subject. In the process I discovered what a fascinating subject the building of the line was and is. I discovered that there was an alternative proposed to having the railroad built by private corporations. The government built wagon roads, dug and maintained harbors and canals, constructed bridges. Why not have the government build and own the railroad?

Grenville Dodge, the chief engineer of the UP,

proposed just that. In a meeting with Lincoln in 1863, even as Robert E. Lee's army was moving into Pennsylvania, Dodge told the President that a provision of the act of 1862 made it difficult for a corporation to raise capital. Lincoln agreed and said he would see what could be done, as he was very eager that the road should be built and wanted to do his part. Dodge said he wanted the government to step in and take over, to build and maintain it. Lincoln interjected that the government would give the project all possible aid and support, but could not build the road. As Dodge remembered his words, Lincoln said that the government "had all it could possibly handle in the conflict now going on, but it would make any change in the law or give any reasonable aid to insure the building of the road by private enterprise."

As in writing about a battle, I knew I couldn't write about building the railroad without first seeing the ground. So my son Hugh and I drove from Omaha to Sacramento and back, mainly on Interstate 80, which parallels the track. We stopped in the small towns, nearly all of them built by the railroads. We walked along the tracks. We picked up discarded spikes. We marveled at the bridges, tunnels, fills, and roadbeds built by the workers. Chairman Richard Davidson of the UP, and Philip Anschutz of the Anschutz Corporation, gave us permission to ride in a locomotive the entire length of the road.

I wanted to see the track from up front, not through windows on the sides of the cars. We rode in a UP diesel locomotive from Sacramento to Reno, going around California's Cape Horn, climbing and descending the Sierra Nevada, having experiences of sight, sound, and touch that will never be forgotten. How the surveyors did their job, how the workers did theirs, could be seen best from up front.

At one point Mike Furtney of UP, who was with us, said to me, "You know, Steve, there are thousands of men in this country who would pay us anything we might choose to ask to be up here on this ride." I said I knew that. He said, "You take the controls for a while."

I said I wouldn't dare. He said the engineers, Larry Mireles and Mike Metzger, would be right behind me and he insisted. So I got to drive the train up the Sierra Nevada, tooting on the whistle before every crossing of a road. Now, everyone knows that there is no human experience that can match an orgasm — but I'm bound to say that pulling on that cord, tooting the whistle of a locomotive three, four, or five times at each crossing, comes awfully close. I don't know if the Big Four or Durant or Dodge ever got to toot the whistle on their locomotives, but they sure missed a good one if they didn't.

On the westbound trip, we rode in locomotive No. 844, with Stephen Lee as engineer. We got out and walked through the tunnels in the Sierra Nevada. It was extraordinary to watch Lee at work, adjusting the more than thirty-seven handles and knobs on the cab's panel as we sped along. He worked them without looking at them. Riding with Lee, I learned that the locomotive is sacred for many reasons. It is in the cab that a mere man can control all that power, it is from there and there only that a man riding on the train can see ahead. It is the eyes, ears, brains, motor power, and central nervous system for the long string of cars it is pulling along.

Seeing the mountains, the desert, the rivers and creeks, the buttes, the grasslands, and all the terrain that the railroad had to cross strengthened my determination to learn how the railroad was built. By 1998, after I had spent more than a year riding the trains and reading and doing research in the archives about building the road, I began to write. My first lesson was clear and simple: my teachers were wrong when they called the first generation of American big businessmen "robbers." It took courage and a willingness to take on huge risks to build the railroad, something the government was unwilling or incapable of doing.

The Central Pacific could not raise money in San Francisco, not when the Civil War was on and investors with money to lend could make 2 percent or more per month on their loans. The railroad offered nothing but hopes. Charles Crocker, one of the Big Four who built the Central Pacific Railroad, later said of this time, "We could not borrow a dollar of money. We had to give our personal obligations for the money necessary to carry us from month to month. There was not a bank that would lend the company a cent. I would have been glad to have got a clean shirt and absolution from my debts. I would have been willing to give up everything I had in the world in order to cancel my debts."

In 1873, four years after the last spike was driven in and the railroad was complete, Collis Huntington tried to sell the whole Central Pacific to a California financier for a total price of $20 million. He was rebuffed. Six years later the railroad was worth $160 million. As the Big Four were the ones who were willing to take a risk when no one else would, for sure they felt they had earned their profits. They completed the railroad in six years, a momentous accomplishment. The cost was staggering. Of course there was corruption, theft, corner cutting, profiteering. But the road was built, the first to cross a continent, done in much less time than the Canadian Pacific Railway or the Russian Trans-Siberian, not to mention the time it would have taken the U.S. government to build it.

The road was built in a democracy. Congress voted the land grants and the government bonds, granted the exclusive right of way, made it possible for the nation's first corporations to get a charter and go to work. And made it possible for the crews to dig through the mountains or bridge the streams and rivers as fast as was humanly feasible. The government "inspections" of the roadbed, of the tunnels and bridges, were perfunctory, which was just what the Congress wanted. And the government seemed, if anything, too eager to hand out the land grants and pass around the government bonds to the railroad magnates.

The reason for all this haste was that haste was exactly what the people wanted. Had there been a national poll in 1866 or '67 or '68 over the question, Do you want the road built well, or built fast? — to build it fast would have won an overwhelming victory. Thus, although most, maybe even all, the charges brought against the Crédit Mobilier were true, the accused sitting in the box should not have been a few congressmen or the directors of the railroads or the government inspectors, but the people themselves. It was their insistence on getting it done as soon as possible that led to the corruption.

I was further surprised to discover that the land grants given to the railroads by the government, about which so much was made by the railroads' critics, were not worth much, or anything. Despite what historians Morison and Commager or Shannon wrote, those grants never brought in enough money to pay the bills, or even came close. If the railroads had managed to sell all the land they received, there might have been enough to pay the cost, but that never happened. And they absolutely wanted to sell the land to bona fide settlers as soon as possible, because those farmers would quickly become the shippers the railroads knew they would depend on.

The total value of the lands distributed to the railroads was estimated by the Interior Department as of November 1, 1880, at $391,800,000 — but that figure assumed that all the land granted to the railroads would be sold at a minimum of $2.50 per acre. Nothing like that happened. In most of Wyoming, Utah, and Nevada, the railroads never could sell the land. Unless it had minerals on it, it was virtually worthless, even to cattlemen, who needed far more acres for a workable ranch. The government too has been unable to sell the alternative strips it held on to, for the same reason, which is why the federal government is the biggest landholder in the American West, by far. The railroads come next.

In Nebraska and in California, the government was able to sell the alternate sections it held for big sums, often much more than $2.50 per acre. Those were lands that grew wonderful crops or fed fat cattle, but they would have been worth nearly nothing, or in some cases absolutely nothing, if not for the railroads.

Another surprise: the government bonds, so denounced, were in fact loans, not gifts. The railroads paid back the loans — by 1899, the government had collected $63 million of principal plus $105 million in interest on the bonds, making a total repayment of $168 million for an initial loan of $65 million. That is not a bad investment.

I have come to respect the Big Four of the CP and some of the directors of the UP, but those I admire are Abraham Lincoln, without whose prodding and urging and persuasive powers there would have been no railroad; Theodore Judah, the engineer who got the CP organized and did the surveying and provided the imagination on how to get through the Sierra Nevada (and then died just as his dreams began to come true); and Grenville Dodge, a Civil War hero who became the driving force behind the UP.

But even more, I admire the Chinese who built the CP and the Irish, and others, who built the UP. I admire them for how hard and in what danger they worked, how they stuck to it, how proud they were of what they had done. They wanted to be a part of something big, and they were. They had that American quality of seeking change, of living in new places, of conquering territory, of belonging to this new nation and contributing to it. They also wanted to be paid and, in the case of the Irish, to blow some money on beer, whiskey, dance, and women — and they did.

So were the engineers ambitious as only Americans can be. They demonstrated how far ahead American engineers were compared to the European engineers. It was American engineers who developed switchbacks. They built the locomotives with enough power to get a train up the hill. They could survey better than anyone else. The lantern, cowcatcher, the snow plow, snow sheds in the Sierra Nevada (copied today by railroads in the Alps and other European mountains), T-rails, brakes, wheels that could turn to follow a curve in the track, were all American developments or inventions. As one observer noted, "the key to the evolution of the American railway is the contempt for authority displayed by our engineers." European engineers were taught that this or that can't be done. American engineers said to hell with that, we can do it. And they did, including drilling tunnels through the Sierra Nevada and the Wasatch Mountains, making snow sheds for the tracks over the mountains, developing snow blowers, more.

Before the transcontinental railroad was built, it took as much as six months to go from New York to San Francisco, either by land through the desert or over the isthmus at Panama or around South America and back up the Pacific Coast of South and North America, at a cost of $1,000 or more, and you had to risk your life. With the railroad, the time had been cut to seven days — "so fast," they used to say, "you don't even have time to take a bath" — at a cost of $100. It linked California to New York.

Ulysses Grant had just been inaugurated as President when the golden spike was put in and the line completed. He had been its supporter from the first. He made critical decisions when he was a candidate for President that got the Central Pacific built. At a meeting of the big shots of the UP at Fort Sanders, Wyoming, on

July 26, 1868, attended by Generals Grant, William T. Sherman, and Philip Sheridan, Doc Durant took the floor. He denounced the UP's chief engineer, General Grenville Dodge, charging that Dodge had selected extravagant routes, wasted time and money on useless surveys, ignored sound judgment, intended to bypass Salt Lake City, and more.

Grant turned to Dodge: "What will you do about it?" he asked.

"Just this," Dodge answered. "If Durant, or anybody connected with the Union Pacific, or anybody connected with the government, changes my lines, I'll quit the road."

There was a tense hush. Then Grant spoke. "The government expects this railroad to be finished," he declared, speaking as if his election — he was only a candidate for President — was assured. Then he turned to Dodge, "The government expects you to remain with the road as its chief engineer until it is completed."

Dodge had been one of Grant's favorites during the Civil War, and still was. He was and remained the engineer most responsible for the UP. The Army officer most responsible for protecting the workers on the line from hostile Indians was General Sherman, Grant's close friend. And General Sheridan was there to put in his support. That was quite a group.

Grant and the other generals had put the full weight of the Army behind the building of the road. Grant had added the full support of his soon-to-be administration. Congress had given its backing. All the big-city newspapers had reporters out with the working crews, reporting to avid readers the progress — proof, if any were needed, of the public's absorbing interest. That interest was strong enough to make the railroads by far the number one story from 1866 to 1869.

The people, as they almost always are, were right. Next to winning the Civil War and abolishing slavery, building the first transcontinental railroad was the greatest achievement of the American people in the nineteenth century. Not until the completion of the Panama Canal in the early twentieth century was it surpassed as an engineering feat. The railroad took brains, muscle, and sweat in quantities and scope never before put into a single project.

It might not have happened if different choices had been made, by the politicians, by the engineers, by the Irish and Chinese and all the other laborers coming from around the world, by capitalists willing to take high risks for great profit, by men willing to challenge all in order to win all. It would not have happened without teamwork.

But a choice was made, and it cannot be changed. Things happened as they happened. It is possible to imagine all kinds of different routes across the continent, or a better way for the government to have helped private industry, or maybe to have had the government build and own the railroad. But those things didn't happen, and what did take place is grand. So we admire those who did it — even if they were far from perfect — for what they were and what they accomplished and how much each of us owes them. Most of all, we praise the workers who built it, and the line bosses who directed them. Between them, they developed a camaraderie so binding as to be unsurpassed anywhere, even in an army, and seldom equaled.

# Chapter Five

## Grant and Reconstruction

Ulysses S. Grant was the most popular American of the nineteenth century, both at home and abroad. According to historian Geoffrey Perret he was even more popular than Abraham Lincoln. As no one held a plebiscite during the century, it cannot be proved. And what about Jefferson? Jackson? Or, my wife insists, Mark Twain?

To the people of the nineteenth century, Grant was the only Union general who beat Robert E. Lee, so he was the Man Who Won the War. But after being at or near the top to his contemporaries, Grant in the twentieth century fell precipitously. He became "Butcher Grant." To the nineteenth-century mind, he was the President who tried to bring about reconciliation with the South, but by the twentieth century his presidency was so disgraced by scandal that Americans ranked him at the absolute bottom of all the Presidents, behind even Andrew Johnson.

The cause of such extraordinary shifts in opinion was certainly not anything Grant did, or did not do. His record is his record. No investigative reporter or historian uncovered documents showing that President Grant had conspired to do this or that, or that he secretly used his positions to enrich himself, or to commit any other criminal or immoral act. Historians teaching the American history survey courses in the twentieth century denounced General Grant for his drinking, his recklessness, his wanton disregard for the lives of his troops, his appalling waste of the tools of war, his bullheaded insistence on attack, and more. They taught that President Grant ran a corrupt administration that was guilty of widespread financial scandal, that abandoned the newly freed African Americans to the mercies of their former owners, that turned the care of Native Americans over to do-gooder religious types, who knew nothing and learned even less, and otherwise was a disgrace. Worst of all, Grant turned the party of Lincoln from one of hope for the common man and for the newly freed slave into the party of big business. Those of us sitting at the professors' feet absorbed what they said and went out to teach it ourselves.

The historians were enunciating and sharpening the public's changed perception of what Grant had done, and why. Before World War I, people regarded Grant's losses in battle as regrettable but necessary. But after the losses incurred between 1914 and 1918, Grant came to be regarded as a general who was no different from Field Marshal Douglas Haig, or Joffre, or

Ludendorff, or any of the other generals who want only to sacrifice their men's lives for their own glory. No longer were Grant's losses inevitable, yet suffered in a good, indeed a supreme cause — they were after 1918 regarded as inexcusable. Instead of praise, they brought on Grant's head calumny.

Actually Grant was a great general, as good as any America ever produced, far better than most. In his first campaign in the Civil War, in Missouri, he learned a lesson that he adopted as his constant guide: the enemy general is more afraid of me than I am of him. He was determined to win, whatever the cost. He personified an axiom used by Dwight Eisenhower in World War II, that in war, everything is expendable, even generals' lives, so long as you win. He won at Fort Donelson, at Shiloh, at Vicksburg, at Chattanooga. The essential elements in his victories were his willingness to make decisions and the will to carry them out. After the Chattanooga campaign, his chief of staff, General John Rawlins, said of him, "It is decisiveness and energy in action that always accomplishes grand results, and strikes terror to the hearts of the foe. It is this and not the conception of great schemes that makes military genius."

Grant displayed his tenacity and force of will most effectively in the Wilderness Campaign of 1864. After a drawn battle, the kind that his predecessors in command of the Army of the Potomac used as a reason to withdraw from

Lee's front and retreat to the North, he told Lincoln, "I intend to fight it out on this line if it takes all summer." He marched south, not north, until he finally forced Lee to surrender at Appomattox.

His success came about not because he was stubborn, but because he was smart. He knew much more than to simply tell his troops to charge. He knew how to handle his subordinates, what to tell them and what to order them to do. More, he understood the nature of the war. Despite the terrible losses the Army of the Potomac suffered, or those it inflicted on the Army of Northern Virginia, Grant knew his purpose was not to annihilate the Rebels but to force them to lay down their arms and rejoin the Union.

Thus at Appomattox, Grant knew full well Lincoln's wish for leniency toward the enemy. Agreeing with it wholeheartedly himself, he was determined not to humiliate Robert E. Lee or the Southern army. This was partly because he had learned to respect his opponent, even more because he wanted to restore the Union. So he made the surrender terms as generous as possible, indeed the most generous ever given to a defeated army after a long and bloody war. Lee and his army were released on parole, not sent into a prisoner-of-war camp. There would be no reprisals, Grant promised, nor any trials for treason. Grant had the Union quartermasters distribute rations to the near-starving Rebels.

The Confederates were allowed to keep their horses "for the spring plowing."

Grant carried no grudge against his former classmates at West Point who had fought against the government. At Appomattox, he talked to Lee about their experiences together in the Mexican War. Later that day, inspecting the Confederate lines, Grant met James "Pete" Longstreet, who had been his best man at his 1848 wedding. "Come on, Pete, let's play another game of brag [a card game]," he said.

These extraordinary terms were granted to an army that had inflicted a half-million casualties on the Northern forces, fighting for one of the worst causes people ever fought for, and with the least excuse. But what Grant wanted, above everything else, was to sheathe his sword. There had been enough bloodshed and there was no need for reprisals.

The total casualties in the war were more than one million; for the Confederacy 94,000 battle deaths, 164,000 killed by disease, and 194,000 wounded; for the Union, 110,000 battle deaths, another 225,000 deaths by disease, and 275,000 wounded. Such losses could never be forgotten and could not soon be forgiven, yet it was essential that a reconciliation take place.

Sadly, the President for the next four years was Andrew Johnson. Abraham Lincoln had chosen him for the number two spot on the 1864 Republican ticket because he was a Democratic senator from Tennessee who had stayed with the

Union, the only senator from the South to do so. Lincoln needed the votes of the Democrats and the support of the border states. Johnson brought some of them into line for the Republicans, but he was a Southerner generally who proclaimed that his native state of Tennessee was "a country for white men."

On April 15, 1865, he succeeded the assassinated Lincoln as President. He indicated he wished to follow the politics of moderation that had been outlined by Lincoln, and in his first half-year in office he oversaw the reestablishment of civil government in the South. Ordinances of secession were formally repealed, and the Thirteenth Amendment (that neither slavery nor involuntary servitude can exist in the United States) was ratified in all but one of the former Confederate states. But the most important issue, that of suffrage for the former slaves, he left to state determination — with the Southern states under the control of former Confederates.

In December 1865, Congress met and the radical Republicans took control, dismantling Johnson's program and substituting its own ideas of Negro suffrage and disenfranchisement of former Confederate soldiers. In 1866 the Radicals won enough seats in Congress to override Johnson's vetoes of their bills, and in 1867 Radical Reconstruction began.

Meanwhile, in 1866 the Ku Klux Klan was founded in Tennessee. The KKK was a continuation of the war, an attempt on the part of white

Southern planters to maintain at least a part of what they had enjoyed before the war. Slavery was based on terror. Every African American in the slave states had been subjected to random terror — beatings of all kinds, mutilation, sale to another master, having marriages broken up, the children sold down the river. By law, slaves could not be taught to read or write. They could not organize, or communicate with slaves on another plantation. All this was done by private individuals, reinforced by sheriffs and the law.

By 1867 the KKK's primary goal was to oust the Republican parties from the state capitols in the South. The KKK wanted to replace the former slaves with former Confederates. It was a terrorist organization that usually operated at night, resorting to lynching, murder, arson, rape, whipping, mutilation, and economic coercion to achieve its goals. The aim of the KKK was to terrorize any African American who tried to be a leader of his people, who learned to read and write, or who otherwise displeased his former master.

By the time of the election of 1868 the KKK had about taken over the South, helped in some measure by President Johnson, who had pardoned former Rebels and restored their full rights as citizens at a breathtaking, many thought reckless, pace. Johnson refused to punish the white South, or promote the fortunes of the black South. He was impeached by the House and survived in office by only one vote in the Senate.

Had Lincoln lived, no one knows what he might have done. We do know that Grant stood with him on Reconstruction. For some time, Grant attempted to support Johnson, but soon gave it up, turned against him, and, in 1868, won election.

So it fell to Grant to bring about a reconciliation. The only other men who took over as President when the country was so badly divided were Gerald Ford and Jimmy Carter, and even in their cases the nation was not as deeply split as it had been in 1868. Both men were honorable, intelligent, hardworking, but neither could win reelection because of their failure to heal the wounds left by Vietnam. The wounds of 1868 were far more widespread, and deeper.

To denounce Grant as a venal politician, stupid, ignorant, corrupt, is to miss entirely what his administration tried to do, and in some ways succeeded in doing. Most of all, for a time at least, the Grant administration disproved the Democratic assertion in the 1868 election that "This is a white man's country."

When Grant took over, some of the South was still occupied by Federal troops. Southern whites were furious, of course, as were many Northern Democrats, who figured their chances at taking control of the White House were thwarted by the occupation. Like Dwight Eisenhower, the only other West Point graduate to become President, Grant never wanted the job and had tried to avoid it. William T. Sherman said of him early in the election year, "Grant don't want it — will only take it if he feels it is necessary to save the country."

Grant saw his task, as any decent man would have, as being to bring about peace and reconciliation between the North and South and to enforce the rights of citizens for blacks. He soon learned that he could not do both. In effect, by the end of his two terms he had abandoned the African Americans to white supremacy and conceded the political leadership of the South to former Confederates, in return for keeping a Republican in the White House.

As President, Grant wanted peace and reconciliation and to be President of all the people. There were hundreds of thousands of ex-Confederate soldiers living in the Southern states. They hated the Yankees and everything the Yankees stood for, including most of all peace and reconciliation. And there were millions of former slaves, now citizens. They wanted their rights — first of all the right to vote. How could Grant be an effective President of both the ex-Rebels and the ex-slaves? Bringing the white South back into the Union could be accomplished only by excluding the former slaves from the body politic, or so it was thought. But denying the rights of citizens, especially the right to vote, to African Americans would be to betray them and the cause for which the Union had fought, and to which Abraham Lincoln had committed the nation and the Republican Party.

What to do with the freed slaves was the number one concern for the North (which had fought to free the slaves and now had the responsibility for them) and the South (which had fought to keep them in slavery and now had to live with them). Difficult enough by itself, the problem was compounded because many people had mixed feelings or, even more commonly, hardly knew what they thought and had no clue as to what to do. That included Grant. Although born in Ohio, with his father, Jesse Grant, an abolitionist, he had many Southern friends while at West Point. His best friend was Simon Buckner, later the Confederate commander at Fort Donelson, captured by Grant in 1862 for the first victory for the Union in the war. Grant had borrowed money from him in 1855. James Longstreet of Georgia, as noted, was Grant's best man. Jesse Grant had refused to attend the wedding because Julia Dent's family were Missouri slaveholders.

Neither Ulysses nor Julia Grant were slaveholders, but they were not abolitionists either. During the war Grant welcomed escaped slaves into his lines and put them to work digging ditches, erecting living quarters, repairing railroads, and other jobs. When he was fighting Lee in Virginia, in 1864 to 1865, Grant organized the Negro troops into regiments and divisions and used them extensively. In the ill-fated Petersburg Mine Assault, July 30, 1864, the 4th

Division, the first Negro unit to serve with Grant in Virginia, was badly mauled. The Rebel infantry fought with a special hatred against armed African Americans. And the Southern leaders from West Point gave their best to their cause.

In the first stages of Reconstruction, Andrew Johnson had refused to grant the demand of the Radical Republicans that African-American males be given the vote. The Radicals had passed the Fourteenth Amendment: "All persons born or naturalized in the United States, and subject to the jurisdiction thereof, are citizens of the United States and of the State wherein they reside. . . . Nor shall any State deprive any person of life, liberty, or property, without due process of law; nor deny to any person within its jurisdiction the equal protection of the laws." That amendment also barred many former Confederates from holding Federal office. But with Johnson's approval, the Southern states, then being run, mostly, by former Confederates, had rejected the amendment.

In January 1867, a delegation from Arkansas — all white, mainly ex-Confederates — called upon General Grant. To them, he gave his advice: go home, ratify the Fourteenth Amendment, and grant Negro suffrage. Not committing himself, he told the delegation that the North was heartily in favor of the amendment and if it were not adopted by the South, Congress would impose more stringent terms. Still, the amendment was not adopted until July 1868 — when Grant was already the Republican nominee for President and a certain winner.

My mentor, William B. Hesseltine, wrote in 1935 *Ulysses S. Grant: Politician*, the only full-scale study of President Grant. It was sixty-six years after Grant was elected President before anyone assessed his two terms, and in the sixty-seven years after Hesseltine's book there have been no other books written only about his presidency. In the 1950s Hesseltine liked to say in his seminars that in his view his book would last forever. One attendee said, jokingly, that he thought every book over thirty years old should be pulled from the library's shelves and burned, thus making room for new books written by younger scholars. We all laughed, including Hesseltine, but none of us expected then that fifty years later there would still be no competition for *Ulysses S. Grant: Politician*.

Hesseltine opens his book with this sentence: "Over Grant's tomb in New York's Riverside Park is inscribed the phrase — 'Let Us Have Peace' — which marked the Civil War General's formal entrance into politics." Grant wrote these words at the end of a letter accepting the Republican nomination for the presidency in 1868. Hesseltine goes on to say that the phrase "might well have been the prayer which accompanied his exit from the White House nine years later. In his two presidential terms, fierce political warfare supplanted and almost surpassed in bitterness the military conflict of the four preceding years." Grant was "unprepared by experience and unendowed with the native gifts necessary for a successful political career. Historians and biographers . . . have written him down as the least worthy of the Presidents."

Hesseltine came down heavy on Grant. He was, Hesseltine charges, "peculiarly ignorant of the Constitution and inept in handling men. His mental endowment was not great and he filled his state papers with platitudes rather than thoughts. . . . His militant qualities of decisiveness and obstinacy which brought success on the battlefield only insured defeat in politics." He set out in 1869 to be the President of all the people, only to end up in 1877 as a partisan hack who was "the 'safe' representative of the more reactionary economic interests of his day."

As the nation's leader, Grant felt he had inherited Lincoln's responsibility to mend the nation, but also Lincoln's self-imposed charge to protect the rights of the freed slaves. In 1870 his administration had seen the ratification of the Fifteenth Amendment, which guaranteed the right of citizens (except women) to vote. When in 1871 white groups in South Carolina led by the Ku Klux Klan were attacking the State's Republican government, Grant's Attorney General told him that "There was no question of the existence of these disorders and crimes and as the elections approached they would be increased." Grant moved to prevent it. In a message to Congress, he said "the proof is there" that the state officers were incapable of suppressing disorder. "Therefore I urgently recommend such legislation as shall effectually secure life, liberty, and property and the enforcement of law in all parts of the United States." In the final sentence of his message, Grant said, "There is no other subject upon which I would recommend legislation during the present session." This was called the Ku Klux Act, and was the first Civil Rights Act.

Before it passed, the South Carolina Republican government asked Grant for troops to suppress disorders. He complied by sending twelve companies of infantry and four of cavalry. When more outrages were committed anyway, Grand declared there was more disorder in South Carolina than in any other state and he would use all his power to put down the disturbers. If two regiments would not suffice, he would send ten and keep them there. He issued a proclamation describing conditions in the state and threatening the "use of military force" unless the "insurgents" dispersed within twenty days. They did and the Ku Klux Act was passed.

The white South was not pacified. The determination to keep the votes and the right to hold power from the former slaves ran deep and wide throughout the South. In the summer of 1874, riots broke out in New Orleans. White opposition to Republican Governor William P. Kellogg, who was supported by Grant, tried to wrest control from him and take over the government. Barricades appeared overnight in the streets. Kellogg found refuge in the custom house and wired Grant for troops. Instead, Grant issued a proclamation ordering the rebels to disperse, which in September, under the threat of military action, they did.

Congressional elections were approaching. The national Democratic Party press went after Grant with vigor and delight. You cannot fight a war for the Constitution, the Democrats argued, and then ignore it. Louisiana was entitled to her senators and representatives — who, if only white men voted, would all be Democrats. "General Grant has vanquished the people of Louisiana," proclaimed the *New York Tribune*. "He has telegraphed to his generals and his admirals; he has set the army and navy in motion; and the lawful government of Louisiana surrenders." Grant's proclamation was an "outrage" which stood out "in all its naked deformity." It was an unpardonable crime against popular suffrage and the sovereignty of a state. This approach helped in November, when the Democrats took control of Congress.

In his annual message to Congress in December 1874, Grant defended himself. He reminded Congress that he had already called attention to the "fraud and irregularity" in the

1872 election in the state — this was hardly new nor unique — before imploring Congress to make sure "there be fairness in the discussion of Southern questions." He said honest, truthful reports from the area, reports that "condemned the wrong and upheld the right," would soon insure that "all will be well." A Negro voter, he added, voted Republican "because he knows his friends are of that party." Many "good citizens" voted Democratic, not because they agreed with the national policy of the party but because they are "opposed to Negro rule."

For those of us who lived in the American South from World War II to the 1980s, we can only say how right Grant was. Since then the rise of the Republican Party in the former Confederacy has brought about major changes in politics. But we still have not achieved what Grant spoke for in his last two sentences: "Treat the Negro as a citizen and a voter, as he is and must remain, and soon parties will be divided not on the color line but on principle. Then we shall have no complaint of sectional interference."

Troubles never ceased in Louisiana. In December, when the newly elected legislature came to New Orleans to organize for the session, Democrats and Republicans alike claimed a majority. Anticipating trouble, Grant sent General Philip Sheridan at the head of a body of troops to the Crescent City. Upon arrival, Sheridan informed Grant that it was obvious that the disorders were the result of the organized and armed White Leagues of the state (Louisiana's version of the Ku Klux Klan). "I think that the terrorism now existing in Louisiana could be entirely removed and confidence and fair dealing established by the arrest and trial of the ringleaders of the armed White Leagues." Sheridan wanted Congress to declare the Leaguers "banditti" and allow him to try them by military courts.

The Democrats set up a howl at this. There were countless condemnatory editorials about Sheridan's use of the word "banditti." Congressional Democrats demanded an investigation. When Grant nevertheless approved Sheridan's course, there was talk of impeachment — quite a bit of talk, actually. The Senate demanded that Grant provide information on Sheridan's actions.

Grant complied. "Lawlessness, turbulence, and bloodshed have characterized the political affairs of that State," he began. Few residents, before or after the 1870s, would disagree. He spoke of the many instances of mob violence and even political murder in Louisiana. He concluded that Sheridan's words were thoroughly justified. "Honestly convinced by what he has seen and heard there, he has characterized the leaders of the White Leagues in severe terms, and has suggested summary modes of procedure against them, which, though they cannot be adopted, would, if legal, soon put an end to the troubles and disorders in that State."

What he could do, Grant said, he would. The Ku Klux Act gave him the power to prevent White Leagues or any such organization "using arms and violence" from governing any part of the country. He would use the act to protect "Union men or Republicans from being ostracized, persecuted, and murdered on account of their opinions."

Those were brave words, sincerely uttered. But whatever the facts or the law, Grant realized that he could not have both peace and reconciliation and suffrage and other full rights for Negroes. It had to be one or the other. Even the Radical Republicans were deserting him as the 1876 presidential election drew nearer. One of them, the American consul at Nuremberg, Germany, asked the consul at Liverpool, "Is it not too dammed bad that our party should be ruined. I believe Genl. Sheridan told the simple truth — but the truth is our people are tired out with this worn out cry of 'Southern outrages'!!! Hard times & heavy taxes make them wish the 'nigger,' 'everlasting nigger,' were in hell or Africa."

Grant had never surrendered in his life. He had never given in to the Confederates. But this time he succumbed to the deep rage of the white Southerners, whose fury at the "impudence of those niggers" was so monumental. This was politics, not a shooting war. Grant gave up. He sent no more Federal troops into the South.

The presidential election of 1876, to pick a successor to Grant, was disputed. It pitted Samuel Tilden, Democrat, against Rutherford Hayes, Republican. It was so close that the Congress had to set up a fifteen-member Electoral Commission to decide who won. The commission had eight Republicans, seven Democrats, and as expected each member voted his party's choice. Not until March 2, two days before Grant's term expired, was the count completed. Hayes won with 185 electoral votes, to 184 for Tilden. What had happened was a deal between the Southern Democrats and the Northern Republicans.

The deal was concluded on February 26, 1877, at the Wormley Hotel in Washington. The Southerners said that if the Republicans promised to withdraw all Federal troops from the South, thus insuring "good" government in South Carolina and Louisiana (which otherwise would remain Republican), the South would forgo any proposals to use force to inaugurate Tilden. The promise was made. The South also promised to treat the former slaves humanely.

Of February 26, Hesseltine wrote, "Reconstruction ended, for the Hayes men promised that the troops would be withdrawn from the South. In other words, the Republicans surrendered the Negro to the Southern ruling class, and abandoned the idealism of Reconstruction, in return for the peaceable inauguration of their President [Hayes]."

Grant had sent in the troops that Hayes withdrew. Grant did not complain, but accepted what had been done. He had earlier set a precedent no other President until Eisenhower dared to emulate. He did so to enforce civil rights for African Americans. So did Eisenhower, in 1957, when he sent troops into Little Rock, Arkansas, to enforce a court order desegregating Central High. Until then, for eighty years, and more, Southern blacks lived in a system that banned private slavery but kept alive a public segregation that was the disgrace of the nation.

Over the half-century since I first sat in on an American history survey course, I've always been ready to praise Grant as a general, damn him as a politician. I was especially furious at the way he gave in to, or sold out to, the white supremacists. Today I know that he tried to do more for the African Americans than any President until Lyndon Baines Johnson. I realize now that when Grant threw up his hands, he had a reason. It is hard to put anything ahead of "Let Us Have Peace" as a motto, but sometimes I almost wish Grant had done so. Had he been able to garner any support from prominent white Americans, he might have. But with Lincoln gone, there was no chance.

The criticism of Grant the President did not come about so much because of his efforts to help the African American enjoy his rights as a citizen — something that most white Americans just ignored from the election of 1876 to 1964. Rather, Grantism as a term of opprobrium referred to the scandals of his administration. They were supposedly wide and deep and did irreparable harm to the nation. There was Orville Babcock, Grant's secretary, who pocketed money from the Whiskey Ring for sale of tax revenue stamps. The ring also distributed money to the Republican Party. There was corruption in the War Department and the Indian reservations, where trading post operators paid a kickback to higher officials. There was more, but the scandal of the age was the Crédit Mobilier — which although Grant gets most of the popular blame for, had taken place before he became President. Grant was never charged with dishonesty himself but he became the target of reformers and critics of all kinds — including American history professors.

It was the Gilded Age, after all. The Civil War was over, the boom times had arrived. Fortunes were being made, and lost. In its own way, the United States during Grant's administration was somewhat like the United States in the 1990s.

In foreign affairs, Grant's record, thanks in large part to his Secretary of State Hamilton Fish, was solid. Most notably, he managed to support Fish in negotiation of the Treaty of Washington (1871), which lay the foundation for the amicable arbitration of U.S.-British disputes left over from the Civil War, including the

*Alabama* claims by Northern shippers against the British for building the commerce raider and selling it to the Confederates.

Grant sent his Farewell Address to Congress in December 1876. He began with a personal note: "It was my fortune, or misfortune, to be called to the office of Chief Executive without any previous political training. Under such circumstances it is but reasonable to suppose that errors of judgment must have occurred." He continued, "Mistakes have been made, as all can see and I admit." He defended himself: "I have acted in every instance from a conscientious desire to do what was right, constitutional, within the law, and for the very best interests of the whole people. Failures have been errors of judgment, not of intent."

As to the white South and Reconstruction, he characterized the struggle as having been over "whether the control of the government should be thrown immediately into the hands of those who had so recently and persistently tried to destroy it, or whether the victors should continue to have an equal voice with them in this control." It had been expected that the enfranchisement of the Negroes would mean an "addition to the Union-loving and Union-supporting votes."

With the swearing in of Hayes, Grant was gone. He and Julia and their son went on a two-and-a-half-year round-the-world tour, on which he was greeted everywhere by huge, enthusiastic crowds. At the Republican convention of 1880, no delegate wanted Hayes again, and a number of replacements were nominated — led by General Grant for a third term! When New York Senator Roscoe Conkling presented Grant, he opened:

> When asked what State he hails from
> Our sole reply shall be —
> "He hails from Appomattox
> With its famous apple tree."

To the Grant delegates it seemed like sublime poetry. On the first ballot, James G. Blaine of Maine got 284 votes, Senator John Sherman of Ohio got 93, two others got 34 and 30 respectively, and Grant led the way with 304 votes (370 were necessary to nominate). Grant held in there for a while, but finally he and Conkling and his supporters gave it up. Dark horse James A. Garfield won on the thirty-sixth ballot, with Chester A. Arthur as Vice President.

Grant moved to New York, where he invested all his money — it wasn't very much — in a banking firm that soon was bringing in big profits. The trouble was that his partner, Ferdinand Ward, was a swindler. On the night of May 5, 1884, Grant learned that the bank had failed and all his money was gone. He and Julia went over their assets. He had $80 in cash in his pocket. Julia had $130 in the house. There was a house in Washington, and a small trust fund. The Grants were almost destitute.

Grant recuperated by, of all things, writing. The Century Company asked him to prepare some articles for their projected series, "Battles and Leaders of the Civil War." He agreed to write four articles at $500 each. The articles were an immediate success. Grant raised his fee to $1,000 per article. Pleased with the results, he announced he would write his memoirs. Publishers swarmed to sign him up, but his friend Mark Twain of the Webster Company knew the American public's reading taste better than anyone else and his company offered by far the most liberal contract.

Grant was diagnosed with throat cancer, but managed to keep writing. A few days after finishing, he died on July 23, 1885. The book was an immense success, in sales and for his reputation. It proved what a splendid intellect Grant had, what a superb storyteller he was. Whatever my professors thought of him, whatever I told my students about him, he was a great American who did far more good for our country than most generals or Presidents can even approach.

# Chapter Six

# Theodore Roosevelt and the Beginning of the American Century

In my days as a student, Theodore Roosevelt was denounced in the history books and in lectures by my professors as America's leading imperialist. Together with his intimate friends Elihu Root, John Hay, and Henry Cabot Lodge, Roosevelt took up the cause of Alfred Thayer Mahan to champion the historic, geopolitical, military, and economic necessity of American commercial, ecclesiastical, and territorial expansions abroad, especially in the Caribbean, at the isthmus of Panama, and in the Pacific in Hawaii and the Philippines. Roosevelt and his friends conspired, I was taught, to turn America into an imperialistic nation.

Almost no historians approved of what Roosevelt had done. In his seminal work *Theodore Roosevelt and the Rise of America to World Power* (1962) Howard Beale concluded: "One comes away with a sense of tragedy that his [Roosevelt's]

119

abilities were turned toward imperialism and an urge for power, which were to have consequences so serious for the future." Roosevelt, as President William McKinley's assistant secretary of the navy, played a major role in 1898 in sending U.S. troops to take Puerto Rico from the Spanish, and in ordering Admiral George Dewey and the American Pacific fleet into Manila Bay to destroy the Spanish fleet and seize the Philippines as an American colony. As President, Roosevelt took the Panama Canal Zone from the Colombian government and had the United States create and hold a lease on the canal. Explaining his actions, T.R. boasted, "I took Panama." He made Cuba — which he had helped free from the Spanish — into an unofficial protectorate of the United States and gave the United States the right to intervene on the island whenever it disapproved of the Cuban government.

Roosevelt's imperial reach extended in every direction. He supported John Hay's "Open Door" policy in China. When in December 1904 he learned that European powers were threatening to intervene in the Caribbean to collect debts owed by the Dominican Republic, he asserted the right of the United States to exercise international police powers in the Western Hemisphere. In a statement later called the Roosevelt Corollary to the Monroe Doctrine, he changed the Doctrine from prohibition of intervention by European powers in the New World to the right of intervention by the United States. In January 1905, the Dominican Republic signed an agreement with the United States giving the Americans full control of its finances, to be exercised by a comptroller appointed by Roosevelt. The agreement was rejected by the U.S. Senate, but Roosevelt carried it out anyway.

Fifty years later, when I was in college, Roosevelt's jingoistic nationalism did not sit well with most students, including me. Imperialism meant Japanese aggression, Nazi aggression, the post–World War II aggression of the Soviet Union. The acquisition of the Philippines at the turn of the century didn't look all that good to us after America had just fought a bloody war in the Pacific that she was drawn into in large part because of her colony in the Philippines. Further, the tactics the American army used in suppressing the Philippine "Insurrection" of 1898 to 1901 were almost Nazi-like, and were widely reported in the nation's press. So far as we students were concerned, Teddy Roosevelt and his Rough Rider mentality were discredited by his own actions.

Roosevelt had catapulted into the national spotlight during the war with Spain. He had resigned his post with the McKinley administration to become the colonel of the Rough Riders of the 1st U.S. Volunteer Cavalry. He led the charge up San Juan Hill that broke the Spanish army. Shortly after the battle he set sail for New

York, where in 1899 he published a book entitled *The Rough Riders* in which he claimed the victory was his doing. One humorist, Mr. Dooley, said the book should have been called "Alone in Cuba."

His heroism in Cuba, according to my mentor, Professor Hesseltine, was contrived. Roosevelt did not lead the Rough Riders up San Juan Hill but up the nearby Kettle Hill, and he was not in the front, but together with his men was following Captain Jack Pershing, who commanded a Negro Regular Army regiment — thus his nickname "Black Jack."

In describing the action at Kettle Hill, Hesseltine said that when Roosevelt was ordered by his superior Colonel Leonard Wood to charge Kettle Hill, he pointed to the Negro regiment to his right and said, "See those Negroes over there. They are regulars. It's their job. Send them." It was done at a heavy loss to the regiment, while the Rough Riders followed, suffering almost no casualties.

But San Juan Hill made Roosevelt into a hero and propelled him into the presidency. So he got to live in the White House because of his incessant bragging, his wild claims about what he had done. His posturing as President was worse. Mark Twain, who so often spoke for his contemporaries, said, "Mr. Roosevelt is the Tom Sawyer of the political world of the twentieth century; always showing off; always hunting for a chance to show off; in his frenzied imagination the Great Republic is a vast Barnum circus with him for a clown and the whole world for audience." Henry Adams wrote of Roosevelt as "pure act" but even more pure ego. In a 1904 letter, he said, "Never have I had an hour of worse social *malaise*. We were overwhelmed in a torrent of oratory, and at last I heard only the repetition of I-I-I attached to indiscretions greater one than another. . . . The wild talk about everything belonged not to the bar-room but to the asylum."

But there was much more to Theodore Roosevelt than showmanship and false claims. He did exaggerate, and sometimes stretched the truth, especially when it was about one of his exploits. But his greatness lay in preparing America to become a world power, strengthening the nation's defenses, improving its diplomacy, and in his contribution to the power of the presidency in domestic affairs, in his trust busting, and most of all in conservation.

Regarding his incessant bragging about his actions in Cuba, recall how the charge up Kettle Hill was closer to the Civil War, fought thirty-five years before, than it was to World War II, fought forty-six years later. Roosevelt's Rough Riders assaulted a prepared position — without benefit of naval gun support, with insignificant artillery support, poor reconnaissance, with no handheld automatic weapons, no rocket launchers, no air cover, no hand grenades, no communication system other than runners, no tanks, trucks, or bulldozers, no hygiene and only the most primitive first aid. Many of the men were wearing Civil War uniforms. The charge up Kettle Hill, in short, was like Grant's men going up Lookout Mountain, not at all like Eisenhower's men going up the bluff at Omaha Beach. Indeed some of the men in the American force were Civil War veterans.

Still there were similarities between 1898 and 1944. The bluff above Omaha was not much different than San Juan Hill. Men hesitated to go forward and up against well-aimed enemy fire (much, much heavier at Omaha). It was their officers who got them going. Among those, T.R. stood out. He rode ahead of the entire line of dismounted cavalrymen and the Negro regiment, which in fact charged beside the Rough Riders, not in front. He was the only man on horseback. Some forty yards from the top of Kettle Hill, he got to a fence, dismounted, and led the rest of the charge on foot. He attracted Spanish rifle fire. No one who saw him ever forgot it; the correspondents and artists implanted the image in the American mind and it became the symbol of the war. Later it was charged by historians that it was a false symbol. It was not.

To add to an already stirring story, Roosevelt's son, General Theodore Roosevelt, Jr., was at Normandy. He went in shortly after dawn at Utah Beach, the oldest American to go into the battle. General Omar Bradley had ordered him not to go — he had suffered a heart attack — but Teddy Jr. insisted. He landed with General Joe Collins. They jumped into a shell hole, pulled out their maps, looked and cursed. They were one mile east of where they should have been. One of them (it is not certain which one) folded up his map and said, "Well, we will start the war from right here," and they began moving the troops inland. Two weeks later Teddy Jr. died of a heart attack.

Theodore Jr.'s son Quentin Roosevelt II was at Omaha Beach on D-Day. Quentin and Ted Jr. were the only father and son combination in the invasion. Quentin II was later killed in China when he was with the CIA. Theodore Roosevelt and his son Ted Jr. were the only father-son recipients of the Congressional Medal of Honor (for 1898 and 1944).

The biggest problem Roosevelt faced when he became President in 1901 was war. It had become more destructive, widespread, and consequential, to a degree undreamed of less than a generation earlier. It had come to the point that war could threaten the nation itself. On this problem, Roosevelt was magnificent. He led America into the new century, knowing that there were as many threats out there as there were opportunities. He did more to prepare the country for world conflict than any other American who went before him or who came after — until Franklin D. Roosevelt. He wanted his legacy to be a strong, independent America prepared to defend itself and its allies, no matter what.

T.R. was certain that the best way to avoid war was to be armed and prepared. To make this happen, he built the Great White Fleet. First he had to build up the power of the presidency, which he did. Then he transformed the fleet from one small in size to one second only to the British fleet, and dispatched it on an unprecedented voyage around the globe, boasting, "I determined on the move without consulting the Cabinet, precisely as I took Panama without consulting the Cabinet." He put through reforms in the War Department that began the process of modernization of the armed services for the complexities of modern war.

As a diplomat he knew that avoiding war was the best policy whenever possible, so in 1905 he mediated an end to the Russo-Japanese War (for which he was awarded the Nobel Peace Prize). In 1906 he prevented another outbreak of war by resolving the First Moroccan Crisis between Germany and France.

Roosevelt realized that in the new century America would have to assume more responsibility, expand its reach and interests, reject its nineteenth-century role of isolationism, and take up its twentieth-century burden of leadership. He knew it was his lot to lead the nation toward its destiny. His advocacy was always for a greater military preparedness and an insistence on national honor. By no means did the nation always follow his advice; between 1914 and 1916 his call for increasing the size and equipment of the armed forces went mainly unheeded by President Woodrow Wilson.

Here is a "what if?" In 1912 Roosevelt ran on the Progressive Party ticket, against incumbent President William Howard Taft, a Republican and Roosevelt's chosen but disappointing successor, and New Jersey Governor Woodrow Wilson, a Democrat. Suppose Teddy Roosevelt had won the election. (He came in second with 4.1 million votes to Wilson's 6.3 million and Taft's 3.5 million.) He would have taken office in March 1913. He would have been the commander-in-chief in the summer of 1914 as the great world war blazed in Europe. Once the shooting started, he might have taken a pro-British and pro-French stand as he meanwhile built up the American Army and Navy. He might have seized the sinking of the Lusitania as a compelling cause for entering the war. He might have gotten the United States into the war sooner and in a better position to fight it than Woodrow Wilson did. Then what? A quicker, less bloody defeat of Germany?

According to author Bruce Miroff, in the period of 1914 to 1916 Roosevelt came to loathe President Woodrow Wilson "as he had no other political foe before." He was Wilson's "most vocal critic," calling the President "a physically timid man" who failed to prepare for his great challenge. Roosevelt tried to convince the American public of the need for military preparedness and the duty to punish Germany for its aggression against the weak. But Wilson had won the 1916 election on the slogan "He kept us out of war," which T.R. saw as pandering to the German-American, pacifist, and Socialist vote.

As a result, when Wilson did lead the nation into the war in April 1917, the armed forces were woefully unready. Rather than entering the large-scale combat that characterized World War I on the Western Front, in 1917 the hastily raised American Army spent the year in training. Only the U.S. Navy, thanks to Roosevelt's Great White Fleet, was ready for war. When the American Army did become fully involved, in the spring of 1918, its pilots flew mainly British and French aircraft, its artillerymen fired mainly French 75mm cannon, its trucks and what few tanks it had were British-made for the most part, and altogether it was a sad performance, except for the men themselves. They were entering combat for the first time and were hale and hearty, in good health, eager to crush the Germans.

The shortcomings and mistakes of the Wilson administration before World War I were studied and generally corrected in the buildup for World War II. Teddy Roosevelt's cousin, Franklin, started drafting and training the troops a couple of years before they were called on to fight. He improved their equipment — fighter and bomber aircraft, rifles and machine guns, jeeps, trucks, and tanks, and technology across the board, including a start on the atomic bomb — and picked the right men to lead the armed forces, starting with Army Chief of Staff George C. Marshall.

Nineteen forty was the darkest year for democracy ever, a time when it looked all but certain that the Nazis were going to control the whole of Western Europe and perhaps the British Isles as well, when it appeared that Hitler and Stalin had entered into a partnership that would guarantee Soviet domination from Eastern Europe all the way to the Pacific, and that the Japanese Empire would engulf China, Manchuria, Vietnam, Burma, plus most if not all the offshore Asian islands, a time when the American people were divided over the question of how to respond to the totalitarians. The evil ones were on the march everywhere, bringing a new Dark Ages with them.

President Franklin Roosevelt, however, was preparing to stand up to them, taking some of his cues and programs from Theodore Roosevelt. It was at this time, 1940, that Henry Luce dared to proclaim that this was to be the American Century. He based that prediction in part on what the two Roosevelts had done to get the country ready to do its duty.

Luce had made as accurate a prediction as has ever been made on so grand a scale. And it began to come true a year later, even as things got

129

worse. At Pearl Harbor, the U.S. Navy suffered a stunning defeat. Hitler, who six months earlier had broken his pact with the Soviet Union, had his armies almost at the gates of Moscow. France had fallen, along with Norway and Denmark. Only Great Britain, supported by Australia, New Zealand, and Canada, was still in the fight.

But America was much better prepared to do her part in December 1941 than she had been in April 1917. Franklin Roosevelt and his successors have adhered to Theodore Roosevelt's admonition to "speak softly but carry a big stick." The result has been victory in World War II and in the Cold War and the spreading of democracy to many parts of the world. It has come about because our navigators have hewed closely to a line laid down by the first President of the century.

Theodore Roosevelt the imperialist, often rightly criticized for his seizing of Panama and high-handed methods in building the canal, and for much else, was in fact America's leader in getting the nation prepared for the American Century. The canal made it possible for the American fleet to operate in both the Atlantic and the Pacific oceans. As one example, the battleship USS *Nevada*, which began construction in Theodore Roosevelt's second term and was completed just before America entered World War I, was at Pearl Harbor. *Nevada* was the only battleship to get underway on the morning of

December 7. She was seriously damaged, but repaired and in 1944 sent to Europe, where she participated in the invasion of Normandy. Then she was back in the Pacific, supporting the landings on Iwo Jima and Okinawa. None of these movements would have been possible without the Panama Canal.

Roosevelt was way ahead of his time in the domestic arena as well. He advocated the vote for women and civil rights for African Americans. Roosevelt put himself in the front, at the cutting edge, on facing and conquering the problems brought by the great industries, with their thousands of employees and a monopoly market. It was clear to him that only the federal government had the power to regulate the corporations. When the anthracite miners' strike of 1902 began to cause massive coal shortages, he forced the recalcitrant owners to negotiate with the miners' union by threatening to use the Army to work the mines. In his trust busting, T.R. got started by revitalizing the Sherman Antitrust Act of 1890 and hauled more than thirty corporations into court on antitrust charges. The most notable of these were the Northern Securities Company and the Standard Oil Company of New Jersey. The Supreme Court ordered them both dissolved, although both later revived under somewhat changed names.

In legislation, Roosevelt got started with the

Elkins Act of 1903 and the Hepburn Act of 1906 to regulate the railroads. He pushed into legislation the Meat Inspection Act and the Pure Food and Drug Act, which marked the beginning of consumer protection by the federal government. From his administration on through the twentieth century, the federal government has been increasingly involved in the regulation of the marketplace and working conditions.

In traveling in his car through London and the countryside during World War II, Winston Churchill would note things that needed fixing. Back at the office, he would send letters demanding the change to the head of the department whose jurisdiction covered the matter. He would end those letters with these words: "Action this day."

On January 21, 1902, in a letter to the Board of Commissioners for the District of Columbia, Roosevelt wrote: "Some four months have passed since I first communicated with you about the smoke nuisance in this city. I would like to know in writing what has been done. . . . This black smoke is thoroughly deleterious and a nuisance which can be readily abated. From the windows of the White House I can see two chimneys disfiguring the entire landscape. One I think is a Government building. It is not excusable to permit these nuisances longer to go on. If you have power you should stop them out of hand. If you have not power then you should go to Congress, and indeed should have done so six weeks ago, demanding a bill giving you power. Please report in writing at your earliest convenience."

Roosevelt recognized that the continued expansion of the American economy would bring problems — the relationship of capital to labor, to start with — and threats to the environment of great magnitude. So strongly did he feel about the second subject that he declared, "There can be no greater issue than that of conservation in this country." In 2001 I told Vice President Dick Cheney that Theodore Roosevelt committed the Republican Party to the cause of conservation, and that of all the things he is remembered for — San Juan Hill, the Panama Canal, the Great White Fleet, federal regulation, and more — the one that stands above all others is conservation.

In saying that there was no greater issue than conservation, Roosevelt was going against the sentiment of his time, which was to drill for oil and natural gas, burn the prairies, cut the forests, dam the rivers, dig canals, build ever greater cities with even taller buildings. For T.R., preserving what was precious was his self-ordained task. He expanded the forest reserves of the nation from 43,000 acres to 194 million acres, an increase of over 400 percent. In 1907 lumber interests secured an amendment to an agricultural bill that forbade the President from setting aside any additional forest lands. Before it took effect, Roosevelt put out an executive proclamation creating thirty-two new forest reserves. In triumph, he explained: "When the friends of the special interests in the senate got their amendment through and woke up, they discovered that sixteen million acres of timberland had been saved for the people by putting them in the National Forest before the land grabbers could get at them."

Roosevelt worked for and then signed the Antiquities Act of 1906, which gave the President authority to set aside natural wonders, historic sites, and prehistoric structures as "national monuments." He proclaimed eighteen national monuments, a record no President until Bill Clinton matched. Monuments created by Roosevelt include Devils Tower in Wyoming, the Petrified Forest of Arizona, California's Muir Woods, the Gila Cliff Dwellings in New Mexico, Utah's Natural Bridges, Mount Olympus in Washington, and the Grand Canyon. I was visiting the sites designated by Roosevelt when I thought again about the man. His willingness to act for the common good, his ability to see into the future, his ability to conserve the priceless sites for all Americans to come — including me and my family and grandchildren — made me realize what a great man he was in preservation.

When coal deposits were discovered at the bottom of the Grand Canyon and entrepreneurs wanted to dig it out, Roosevelt created the Grand Canyon National Monument (later to become the National Park). He said of the canyon, "Leave it as it is. You cannot improve upon it, not a bit. What you can do is keep it for your children, your children's children, for all who come after you."

Roosevelt established the first federal bird reservations, fifty-one in number. His interest in the subject went back to the days in 1898 to 1900 when he was Governor of New York. He had then insisted that the state forbid factories to make bird skins into articles of apparel because birds in the trees and on the beaches were much more beautiful than on women's hats. In the period of 1900 to 1903, ornithologists had been trying to get protection for the birds on Pelican Island, a pinpoint of land in Florida's Indian River, where plume hunters had been making such inroads on the egrets and other species that it was feared they would soon be exterminated. When all their efforts failed, they appealed directly to Roosevelt. The President asked, "Is there any law that will prevent me from declaring Pelican Island a Federal Bird Reservation?" None, was the reply, the island being federal property.

"Very well," Roosevelt responded, "then I so declare it."

That was the first federal wildlife refuge. Roosevelt also created the first four national game preserves, including the Wichita Forest in Oklahoma and the National Bison Range in Montana. In all, he placed under the protection of the federal government some 230 million acres of America's natural heritage, a legacy, he said, for "the unborn generations."

In his *Autobiography*, Roosevelt expressed his view that the President "was a steward of the people bound actively and affirmatively to do all he could for the people. . . . I declined to adopt the view that what was imperatively necessary for the Nation could not be done by the President unless he could find some specific authorization to do it. My belief was that it was not only his right but his duty to do anything that the needs of the Nation demanded unless such action was forbidden by the Constitution or by the laws."

In his promotion of the power of the President, Roosevelt was following the lead of the first President of the nineteenth century, Thomas Jefferson. When the Federalists complained about the Louisiana Purchase and pointed out that nowhere in the Constitution is the President given the power to buy land, Jefferson's response was that nothing in the Constitution says he cannot.

Even as America's Industrial Revolution expanded, Roosevelt was warning against and struggling against the waste of irreplaceable natural resources. In 1907 he declared, "We are prone to speak of the resources of this country as inexhaustible; this is not so." He was pleased that he had been able to save so many forest lands, but he warned "it is only a beginning."

Public lands generally had been subject to "great fraud" by corporations with no objective save the largest profit in the shortest time. In contrast, Roosevelt declared the conservation of natural resources to be "the fundamental problem which underlies almost every other problem of our national life."

In Buffalo, speaking informally at a breakfast with some business and professional men, he talked as earnestly as only he could on the subject of the purification of Lake Erie's waters. "We must keep the water supply unpolluted," he said, "and to do that you must see that it is not polluted at its source." That was not a subject that got discussed very often in Buffalo at the beginning of the twentieth century.

Roosevelt led the way for the conservation movement. It was so critical to him because he was the first President, and one of the very first Americans, to recognize — in Walter Lippmann's words, written in 1935 — "that justice, opportunity, prosperity were not assigned to Americans as the free gift of Providence. He saw that once the period of settlement and easy expansion had come to an end, the promise of American life could only be realized by a national effort."

Lippmann went on: "The mentality against which his whole career was a protest, the mentality of weak and complacent and selfish unpreparedness for responsibility, has been the radical cause of our greatest difficulties. Theodore Roosevelt began the work of turning the American mind in the direction which it had to go in the Twentieth Century. His immortality resides in this change of direction. Though he did not see all that was in the world or its whole future, he was the first President to see that even for Americans the world is round and that even for them the future is not to be a repetition of the past."

The genius of this man was his remarkable vision. He was President just three years after the closing of the American frontier. Buffalo still roamed the Great Plains. Progress was king, but Roosevelt almost single-handedly committed the GOP to conservation.

Lippmann gave Roosevelt his highest marks for his "unremitting sense that American unity is plural, that it can be preserved, therefore, only by a continuing equilibrium among its many regions, classes, interests, and faiths."

Roosevelt's interests were also plural. His curiosity was immense: How does this work? What is this for? His eagerness to try out whatever was new was legendary. He was the first President to travel outside the United States while in office; he went to Panama to oversee the construction of the canal (which was one of the great engineering feats of all time, anywhere, and where perhaps the most famous photograph of him was taken, at the controls of a huge earth-moving steam shovel; the canal was begun in 1904, completed in 1914). He was, probably, the first President to ride in an automobile. He was the first to go down in a submarine, in 1905, and until Jimmy Carter, the last. Roosevelt bought the government's first airplanes, from the Wright brothers, and assigned them to the Army. He sent the first transglobal message; twelve minutes after he dispatched it from the Oval Office, it returned.

Roosevelt always amazes. As President, he camped out in Yellowstone Park. At Yosemite he camped out for three days with John Muir. On Long Island, President Roosevelt and his sons and their boy cousins rode all night one summer, leaving Sagamore at sunset and arriving at dawn in Sayville to visit cousins. So the President and some boys were all alone all night on a journey in the open. Musician Duke Ellington enjoyed telling of his experience with Roosevelt. Duke was a boy, playing basketball on the court in his Washington, D.C., neighborhood. When he looked up, there was Roosevelt on his horse. The President was out for a ride by himself. He said hello. Ellington said hello. Duke did notice that the President had a big, shiny pistol stuck into his belt.

Just imagine the President out on his own, in wilderness and in city streets. He had become President because his predecessor had been shot while speaking at the Pan-American Exposition at Buffalo, and he himself would be shot during the 1912 campaign. One would have thought something would be done to protect William McKinley's successor. But whatever might have been done, Roosevelt was himself. When he was President, he issued a directive that required officers stationed in Washington to ride ninety miles in three days. The officers grumbled. Roosevelt thereupon got up before dawn and, employing a relay of four horses, rode nearly fifty miles to Warrenton, Virginia, then remounted and rode back to the White House. It was great fun. He told his son Kermit, "The last fifteen miles were done in pitch darkness and with a blizzard of sleet blowing in our faces."

He looked to the future. Speaking in 1903, T.R. said, "To each generation comes its allotted task; and no generation is to be excused for failure to perform that task. No generation can claim as an excuse for such failure the fact that it is not guilty of the sins of the preceding generation." In May 1901, when he was Vice President, Roosevelt spoke at the Pan-American Exposition in Buffalo. "The century upon which we have just entered must inevitably be one of tremendous triumph or of tremendous failure for the whole human race, because, to an infinitely greater extent than ever before, humanity is knit together in all its parts, for weal or woe." It is a wonderful sentence, exact in its prediction and in its vision.

Later in that speech, he said, "We all look forward to the day when there shall be a nearer approximation than there has ever yet been to the brotherhood of man and the peace of the world. More and more we are learning that to love one's country above all others is in no way incompatible with respecting and wishing well to all others, and that, as between man and man, so between nation and nation, there should live the great law of right." He continued, "No ability, no strength and force, no power of intellect or power of wealth, shall avail us, if we have not the root of right living in us."

In my interviews with World War II veterans, they sometimes tell me that the reason they fought was they had learned as children the difference between right and wrong and they didn't want to live in a world in which wrong prevailed, so they fought. Right there, I think, one hears the voice of Theodore Roosevelt ringing in the words of soldiers born after his death. It seems to me that perhaps our greatest strength is that American kids are brought up to know right from wrong. And of all our Presidents, the one who used the words "right" and "wrong" more than any other, who did the most to exalt right-doing, was Theodore Roosevelt.

He was a man who wanted to preserve as well as look forward. He wanted to keep as many historic sites as possible as monuments. At the Centennial Exercises at the Presbyterian Church in Washington, on November 16, 1903, he thanked the congregation for preserving the church and keeping unchanged the pew in which he was sitting. "I hope it will remain unchanged in this church as long as our country endures," he said. "A man would be a poor citizen of this country if he could sit in Abraham Lincoln's pew and not feel the solemn sense of the associations borne in upon him." Looking at a broader range, he said, "We have not too many monuments of the past; let us keep every little bit of association with that which is highest and best of the past as a reminder to us, equally of what we owe to those who have gone before and of how we should show our appreciation."

Then he concluded with a line that only he could have uttered: "This evening I sit in this pew of Abraham Lincoln's, together with Abraham Lincoln's private secretary, who, for my good fortune, now serves as Secretary of State in my Cabinet."

Just imagine being with Theodore Roosevelt and John Hay that day.

Roosevelt guided us in new directions — conservation; openness and tolerance; our rightful position in world affairs; a modernized armed force that could protect us from our enemies; a federal government that could regulate the great corporations and economic life in general, and protect the individual from tainted products; a spirit of teamwork mixed with just a bit of hubris.

On May 21, 1903, as President, he spoke in Portland, Oregon. It was the hundredth anniversary of the Lewis and Clark Expedition's setting out from St. Louis, and T.R. was in Portland for the laying of the cornerstone of a monument to

Lewis and Clark. He said, "We have met to commemorate a mighty pioneer feat, a feat of the old days, when men needed to call upon every ounce of courage and hardihood and manliness they possessed in order to make good our claim to this continent." That was a description of the past, true and succinct. In his next sentence, he spoke to the future: "Let us in our turn with equal courage, equal hardihood and manliness, carry on the task that our forefathers have intrusted to our hands; and let us resolve that we shall leave to our children and our children's children an even mightier heritage than we received in our time."

We did receive a mightier heritage, thanks in large part to the legacy of Theodore Roosevelt. That legacy does not include imperialism. For a half-century, Cuba has not been an American protectorate or colony. The government of Panama today owns and operates the canal. For sixty years the Philippines has been an independent democracy. Puerto Rico is still an American commonwealth, but the residents can at any time vote for independence or statehood or to remain as they are.

So not all that Roosevelt started has lasted. But because of him and his influence on his successors, our armed forces are the best in the world. He left us with a presidency that has become more powerful in a greatly expanded government, one that follows his lead in regulating American life in nearly all of its diverse forms. What marks him as a great man, one to whom we all owe our thanks and gratitude, is the direction he set the nation on to conserve national resources of all kinds and types. Of all his many triumphs, conservation stands first.

# Chapter Seven

# *Democracy, Eisenhower, and the War in Europe*

I was nine and a half when the Second World War ended in Europe. I had followed it avidly if not always accurately, from the radio, the newsreels, and the newspapers. What seemed clear to me was that America had won the war thanks to her incredible industrial production, in which my mother was a participant, working in a pea cannery in Whitewater, Wisconsin, six days a week, alongside German POWs captured in North Africa. I was aware that by the end of the war, over half the airplanes in the world had been produced in the United States, plus half the ships of war, artillery pieces, rifles, and more. I knew that the U.S. Army was the best equipped, the best fed, the best educated, with the highest mobility of any army. We won the war not because we outfought them but because we outproduced them.

We did so for many reasons, chief of which was that we did not have unlimited manpower. On many occasions, in many battles, the Germans outnumbered the Americans. And, of course, the Germans were fighting on their own continent. Even though they had Eastern, Western, and Southern fronts, they did not have to transport supplies and men anywhere near as far as the Americans had to. Germany had a total mobilization of 18 million; the U.S. armed forces numbered at the peak 16 million; the Soviet Union 13 million; Great Britain 6 million. But the total U.S. Army strength in northwest Europe was 3 million. The Russians had not only more men fighting the Germans, but more tanks.

That we had won the war on the drawing boards and in the factories rather than in the field was a commonplace attitude, which I had absorbed. No one meant to deny the glory of the achievements of the fighting men but what we did say, feel, believe was that without the American production of the tools of war the job could not have been done. That is perhaps so, maybe even probably so. But in the decades since 1960 I've been studying the war, I've learned that the essential part of the American victory was the men in its Army. Specifically, they gave it a special spirit, teamwork. Of course all armies try to instill such qualities as an elite status and teamwork into their infantry companies, but none do it as well as we do. And no other army emphasizes democracy as we do, because we have learned and know that democracies produce great armies.

The American Spirit was raring to go. Despite the political divisions over isolationism and interventionism, when the test came America was there. On the day Germany invaded Poland to begin World War II, Lieutenant Colonel Dwight D. Eisenhower, serving in the Philippines, wrote his brother Milton, "Hitler should beware the fury of an aroused democracy." He should have indeed, but he didn't, and on December 10, 1941, he declared war on the United States. If he had known what had happened here two days before, he might have ditched that declaration of war as a bad idea.

What happened on December 8, 1941, was this: The U.S. armed forces had more enlistments that day than on any other day in American history. Most of the youngsters who joined the military on December 8 and thereafter came from families who had endured the worst of the Great Depression. They had seen little of the promise and opportunity of America. Yet they were ready to fight when needed. Among them were African Americans and other minorities for whom the American promise was just words.

Eighty years earlier, the South had fought to keep African Americans in slavery. The Civil War gave blacks their freedom, but throughout the Second World War they remained segregated in the North as well as in the South. Their schools were inferior when they existed at all. Blacks were discriminated against in employment, in music, in the movies, in their lives.

Mexican Americans were treated like scum. The people of the small Japanese-American community were torn from their homes and sent into camps in the desert — and from those camps young men volunteered for the Army and fought in Italy and Southern France. One Japanese American, later Senator Daniel Inouye, of the 442nd "Go for Broke" regiment, received a Medal of Honor.

Women too struggled for their identity. In 1941 they could be housewives and not much more. For the most part, women who worked for wages were nurses, telephone switchboard operators, clerks, salespersons, or grade or high school teachers.

But they were all Americans. The war showed what the American spirit could accomplish, once we were unified and fighting as a team. And America began the overdue work of dealing with its sins and failures, racism and male chauvinism. It took too long to get there and the process is not yet completed, but after the war there was openness, the civil rights movement, women's liberation. Women had opportunities undreamed of by their mothers and grandmothers. Asian Americans, once excluded, even shunned, took their important place in society. People from other parts of the world, the Middle East, came and contributed. All this started with the way in which America fought the war, as an open, free society of people who volunteered.

"We are all in this together" was what we said.

I was in grade school but I heard that a thousand times. In 1944, at the height of the war, we had a national election to pick our leader — something no other nation did or would have dreamed of doing. My doctor dad, a staunch Republican, was stationed at a Navy hospital in the New Hebrides. He voted for Tom Dewey to be his commander-in-chief. Just imagine being on a base more than 5,000 miles from home and being able to vote for President.

The American Spirit began with George Washington at Valley Forge in the winter of 1777–78. Then what Meriwether Lewis and William Clark and the men of the Corps of Discovery demonstrated in 1803 is that there is nothing that men cannot do if they get themselves together. They had developed a bond, had become a band of brothers, and accomplished feats that we stand astonished at. There was more to the Corps of Discovery than teamwork, of course, as there has been to those who have fought well and successfully and have sometimes lost in the past two centuries. Yet the American Spirit they all exemplify includes the freedom to improvise, to make decisions and carry them out, for all to become leaders.

And in World War II, there was more to the U.S. Army in Europe than weapons, trucks, medical units, supplies, and all matériel an army requires. When Hitler declared war on the United States, he was betting that German soldiers, raised up in the Nazi Youth, would always outfight American soldiers, brought up in the Boy Scouts. He lost that bet. The Boy Scouts had been taught how to figure their way out of their own problems. The German soldiers, the Japanese soldiers were disciplined, fairly well armed, generally in good physical condition, with a strong, even fanatic commitment to their cause. But they could be, and often were, mean, cruel, barbaric. Not all American troops were compassionate, kind, lovers of children, respecters of life, but most were. They were also warriors. They were not just well equipped but well trained. They could fight as a team and rise to the occasion. In the German, Japanese, and Soviet armies, when the platoon leader, usually a lieutenant, got killed or wounded, the privates, corporals, and even sergeants waited for orders. This did not happen all the time, of course, but it did so often as to become characteristic of those armies. In the American Army, the natural leader among the enlisted men, whether a private or a sergeant, would step forward and say, "This is what we will do," and it was done.

In the Second World War, if you were going to be conquered and occupied by a foreign army, the last thing you wanted was for it to be the German, Japanese, or Red army. The first thing, around the world, was to hope it would be the American Army. This was because you would be better fed, receive better medical care, treated like a human being.

★ ★ ★

General Dwight D. Eisenhower's first biographer, Kenneth Davis, entitled his 1945 work *Soldier of Democracy*. It was apt. Eisenhower represented all that was best about democracy — he was honest, straightforward, able to listen to different points of view before making his own decisions, encouraging, responsible, imaginative, reasonable, and trustworthy.

He gave the war effort everything he had. From December 7, 1941, to May 8, 1945, he slept four hours per night, almost never eating in a restaurant; smoking four packs of cigarettes and drinking eight or more cups of coffee per day, always conferring, inspecting, studying, meeting — and giving orders. He was a man of keen observation. During the first invasion he led, in North Africa in November 1942, he learned this, he said: "Optimism and pessimism are infectious and they spread more rapidly from the head downward than in any other direction. Optimism has a most extraordinary effect upon all with whom the commander comes in contact. With this clear realization, I firmly determined that my mannerisms and speech in public would always reflect the cheerful certainty of victory — that any pessimism and discouragement I might ever feel would be reserved for my pillow."

On March 6, 1943, Eisenhower wrote General George Patton, "You must not retain for one instant any man in a responsible position where you have become doubtful of his ability to do the job. This matter frequently calls for more courage than any other thing you will have to do, but I expect you to be perfectly cold-blooded about it."

Ike wanted leadership from the noncommissioned officers (NCOs) and the junior officers, always. On June 3, 1943, he wrote his son John, a cadet at West Point, "The only quality that can be developed by studious reflection and practice is the leadership of men." Later he added, "The art of leadership is deciding what to do, and then getting men to want to do it."

To the graduating class at Sandhurst (Great Britain's West Point) in the spring of 1944, as the graduates were about to lead platoons into the Normandy invasion, Eisenhower delivered an impromptu address that ranks as one of his best. He spoke of the great issues that were at stake, and made each of the new officers aware that his own chance for a happy, decent life was directly tied up in the success of the invasion. He reminded them of the great traditions of Sandhurst. He told them they must be like fathers to their men, even when the men were twice their age, that they must keep the enlisted men out of trouble and stand up for them when they transgressed. Their companies, he said, returning to his favorite theme, must be like a big family, and they must be the head of the family, ensuring that the unit was cohesive, tough, well trained, well equipped, ready to go.

Eisenhower knew that he was fighting not for

his own glory or for conquest, but for democracy. In 1942 he had written his son John that he had "one earnest conviction" about the war: "It is that no other war in history has so definitely lined up the forces of arbitrary oppression and dictatorship against those of human rights and individual liberty." His single goal was to do his full duty in helping "to smash the disciples of Hitler."

In a letter to one of his subordinates written about the same time, he said that the Allied cause was an inspiring one, because it was "completely bound up with the rights and welfare of the common man." He ordered his commanders to make certain that every GI was made to realize that "the privileged life he has led . . . his right to engage in any profession of his own choosing, to belong to any religious denomination, to live in any locality where he can support himself and his family, and to be sure of fair treatment when he might be accused of any crime — all of these would disappear" if the Nazis won the war.

These were private letters, or extemporaneous talk, written or spoken before the invasion, and almost a full year before Eisenhower or anyone else serving in the European Theater knew fully what the Nazis were doing to Europe's Jews. The Holocaust was the most evil crime ever committed. The "Final Solution," the death and camps scattered across German-occupied Europe, were kept so secret that only when

Allied armies overran them did the full dimension become known. Even Eisenhower, the Supreme Commander of the Allied Expeditionary Force, was unaware that the Nazis had murdered millions of civilians. But he certainly did know who was fighting for democracy, and who was against it, and he had a superb way of expressing his own feelings about that.

One of the countless GIs who understood what his commander expressed was Lieutenant Thomas Meehan, the CO of Easy Company, 506th Parachute Infantry Regiment, 101st Airborne Division. On May 26, 1944, eleven days before Operation Overlord in Normandy, Meehan wrote to his wife. Among other things, he wrote, "We're fortunate in being Americans. At least we don't step on the underdog. I wonder if that's because there are no 'Americans' — only a stew of immigrants — or it's because the earth from which we exist has been so kind to us and our forefathers; or if it's because the 'American' is the offspring of the logical European who hated oppression and loved freedom beyond life? Those great mountains and the tall timber; the cool deep lakes and broad rivers; the green valleys and white farmhouses; the air, the sea and wind; the plains and great cities; the smell of living — all must be the cause of it.

"And yet, with all that, we can't get away from the rest. For every one of our millions who has that treasure in his hand there's another million crying for that victory of life. And for each of us who wants to live in happiness and give happiness, there's another different sort of person wanting to take it away.

"Those people always manage to have their say, and Mars is always close at hand. We know how to win wars. We must learn now to win peace. Make the world accept peace whether they damn well like it or not. Here is the dove, and here is the bayonet. If we ever have a son, I won't want him to go through this again, but I want him powerful enough that no one will be fool enough to touch him. He and America should be strong as hell and kind as Christ."

On the night of June 5, 1944, Lieutenant Meehan was sitting in his C-47, waiting to take off for France. He scribbled a short note to his wife: "Dearest Anne: In a few hours I'm going to take the best company of men in the world into France. We'll give the bastards hell. Strangely I'm not particularly scared but in my heart is a terrific longing to hold you in my arms.

"I love you Sweetheart — forever.

"Your Tom."

Over Normandy, just after midnight, his plane was shot down by German antiaircraft fire and he died. But Easy Company, now under the command of Lieutenant Richard Winters, went on to give the Germans hell, from June 6, 1944, to the end of the war. It was a small part of the mighty host the United States had put together to defeat the Nazis, all under the command of Dwight D. Eisenhower.

# Chapter Eight

# The War in the Pacific

It was the worst war that ever was. World War II in Europe involved more people and land area, but it was a different war. It did not have the ferocity and rage that defined the war in the Pacific. Whether it was Japanese-Chinese, or Japanese-Russian, or Japanese-Filipino, or Japanese-Indonesian, or Japanese-British, or Japanese-Korean, or Japanese-Vietnamese, the extent of the mutual hatred was higher than the tallest mountains and deeper than the bottom of the sea.

Highest and deepest of all was the hatred of the Japanese for the Americans, and of the Americans for the Japanese. It started in the nineteenth century and from 1941 to 1945 was fed by each government. Although the propaganda put out by Tokyo and Washington was vile, it was believed by the people in both nations. The men at the top, in command, embraced it. So did nearly everyone else, but none with the furor of the infantry. The men on the front lines, whether the U.S. Army and Marines, or the Japanese army, were extraordinarily young. They carried in their packs a heavy burden of racism. They fought to live or die, and did so because of the hatred they felt toward each other.

The outrages they committed are surpassed only by the Holocaust. In the Pacific, what the men asked of themselves went beyond the notion that there is a limit to human endurance. In an environment that always changed but could always be described as "hell," they did things never seen before or since. There are many contenders for the title of the Worst War That Ever Was, but a combination of factors give the Pacific War some claim.

The things the riflemen thought about the guys on the other side of the ridge are stupefying. Their misinformation about each other was nearly total. Almost everything they had been taught and absorbed about the nature of their enemy was designed to make them hate. Their experiences with each other, on islands stretching across the South and Central Pacific, ratcheted up their already orbiting hatred.

It was not just so in the European Theater of Operations. It could not be in an American Army that was nearly one-third of German-American heritage. Cousins were fighting cousins. They killed each other, abundantly, but they sang the same Christmas carols. They knew something about each other, often quite a lot. That meant nothing in a kill-or-be-killed situation, but it did to those who became prisoners of war.

In the Pacific War, almost no infantryman on either side became a POW. If the Japanese ever managed to capture a live Marine — which almost never happened — they tortured him to death. There were other differences between the two theaters. In the Central and South Pacific, it was hot; in Europe, 1944–45 was one of the coldest winters of the century. In Europe, whenever the GIs liberated or captured a village, there was wine in the cellars, women in the houses. That did not happen in the Pacific, where the Marines drank a concoction made of Aqua Velva aftershave and fruit juice (which could cause blindness), and as for sex, they had their hands and nothing more. When they ran out of ammunition, German squads would surrender. Not the Japanese. They fought with hand grenades, bayonets, even their teeth, to the end. Their aim was to kill ten Americans before they were killed themselves.

In the Pacific War, both the Japanese and Americans did things to each other that are unspeakable. Atrocities included routinely cutting off a dead man's private parts and sticking them in his mouth, extracting gold teeth, urinating in the open mouth of a dead man. They were encouraged, reveled in, casual. On the American side, many of the atrocities were spontaneous; on the Japanese side, they were policy. Whichever, one is stunned at what they did to one another. Only hatred as intense as the heat at the core of an active volcano could have caused that.

The differences between the war in Europe and the Pacific came about for many reasons, but chief among them was racism. The Japanese were different. A different color, different facial makeup, different height and weight, different culture and education. The Germans were sometimes called "Goons," or "Krauts," or "Huns." The Japanese were called lice, vermin, monkeys, cockroaches, or "Japs" or "Little Yellow Bastards." The Japanese used similar epithets for the Americans.

On both sides the men descended into hell, and not as visitors, but as participants. To these depths had the burden of racial hatred carried them. It also made them into fierce soldiers.

World War II continues to fascinate because it was so stupendous, because everyone's life changed as a result, because it was total. When nations fall into total war, as Japan and the United States did from 1941 to 1945, they put all they have into proving that their society is more efficient, competent, that it produces better strategists, better soldiers.

In most areas, American equipment and field skills far exceeded those of the Japanese. Certainly this was true of the engineers. When the Marines took the unfinished airfield at Guadalcanal, in August 1942, in the first offensive of the Pacific War, the Japanese engineers had been working on it for seventeen days and were far from finishing its 2,000-foot runway. Using captured Japanese trucks and other implements, the Americans finished what they called Henderson Field (a name it retains) in four days. Over the next week they extended the runways to 3,800 feet.

At Iwo Jima, the Japanese engineers worked for months to build a road up to the top of Mount Suribachi, but never got it done. The Marines came in on February 19, 1945, and in a few days had a road, still there, to the summit.

In 1941 and 1942, the Japanese torpedo was superior. So was the Japanese single-engine fighter airplane, the Zero. But the Japanese never improved theirs. By 1943 the Americans had the better weapons.

What everyone in command in Japan, from the Emperor to junior officers, relied upon was the Japanese code. They believed that their men's willingness to die for the Emperor made them better soldiers. In fact it made them better targets early in the war, but when they finally learned enough to abandon their suicidal banzai attacks, they went underground, in caves and tunnels, from where they could inflict great damage. But not win. The Japanese did many things well, some superbly, but they never mastered tactics. At a time when the U.S. Army and Navy and Marines were constantly studying their own and others' experience in the war, and making changes to correct mistakes, the Japanese believed to the end that the never-surrender code would lead to victory.

The Americans made their own mistakes. If the Japanese high command of the army and navy were in marked disagreement, so were their American counterparts. For each nation, the consequence was an absence of agreement on how to win the war. It was not until mid-1945, and the completion of the Okinawa campaign, that the United States committed itself to a plan for Japan's final defeat. All throughout the war, the Japanese military had no plan of any kind concerning how to defend the empire it had just gained. Insofar as they had a strategy, it was to force the price to be paid for victory so high that the Americans would tire of the war and negotiate a settlement that might leave Japan with many of her conquests.

Nothing like that happened, although it was getting closer after the Iwo Jima and Okinawa campaigns, when the American people began to worry about the terrible cost of the war. Nevertheless the American military went ahead on its plans to invade the home islands of Japan, in what would have been the biggest invasion armada ever, leading to the greatest battle never fought — the Battle of Tokyo.

American mistakes on the battlefront resulted from a hubris built on a belief in the racial superiority of Americans, and a conviction that American technology — airplanes, warships, bombs, and shells — would triumph at an acceptably low cost in American lives. But most of the high explosives made at such cost, shipped to the battlefront at an even higher cost, then dropped or fired by the biggest battleships and the largest, most modern bombers, or artillery batteries on the ground, were useless.

Twice in the last year my wife, Moira, and I and our son Hugh have gone to the Pacific to examine the battlefields. We went to Guam, Saipan, Tinian, Iwo Jima, Okinawa in the Central Pacific, and Guadalcanal, Australia, New Guinea, Peleliu, Bataan, Corregidor, Manila, Pearl Harbor. I have been visiting battlefields and studying them for almost four decades — Civil War, Revolutionary War, Indian battlefields in the United States; fields from wars all across Europe (almost every battle from Normandy to east of Berlin; from Italy north to Berlin; Moscow). None was as testing, as difficult, as dangerous, as shocking in the ordeal they presented to the Marines as Peleliu, Guadalcanal, Iwo Jima, Okinawa. I believe that no infantry force in the world could have done what the Marines did on those islands.

At Peleliu, Iwo Jima, Okinawa, and elsewhere, a complex network of trenches, galleries, caves, and tunnels protected the enemy as it provided them with the best possible firing positions and concealment. On every island, American reconnaissance had failed to uncover the nature and magnitude of the defenses, even the number of enemy, which it generally underestimated by 40 percent or more.

I believed when I was young that America won the war because of its manufacturing capability, its tremendous delivery of shells and bullets to the battlefront. Now I've learned different. For one example, take Okinawa. Against Kakazu Ridge on the island, 324 American artillery pieces fired 19,000 shells. Eighteen warships joined in the bombardment, along with 650 planes dropping bombs and napalm and firing rockets and machine guns. On Okinawa, the Army and Marine artillery fired 1,766,352 rounds. The carrier-based planes, plus the U.S. Army Air Forces, dropped 14 million tons of bombs. An incredible number of shells from the battleships, cruisers, and destroyers rained down on the Japanese defenses.

But all this tremendous tonnage of high explosives, roughly equal to the atomic bomb over Hiroshima, barely dented the enemy defense. Enemy soldiers, often terrified and without sufficient food or water, remained relatively safe, emerging when American infantrymen came within shooting or grenade range.

The Marines had to be better soldiers than the Japanese. Their shells and bombs and napalm were not going to defeat their foes. On Iwo Jima and elsewhere, the Marines had to move forward cave by cave, tunnel by tunnel, foxhole by foxhole. To get at the Japanese, they had to rely not on the big guns or the big planes but on their M-1s (through most of 1942 on their '03 Springfields), Browning automatic rifles

(BARs), machine guns, mortars, flamethrowers — in short, handheld weapons that they had to get close to the enemy to use.

The Americans had an optimism of ignorance. One cannot count how many times Marines going in for an island assault said to one another, as they watched the pre-invasion bombardment, that "nothing could live through that," only to discover when they hit the beach that the Japanese fortifications were intact and well manned. The Americans had underestimated the Japanese. This was caused, primarily, by an over-reliance on heavy weapons and by assumptions of racial superiority. What made up for those failures was the American Spirit.

The Marines were the best fighting men of World War II. The U.S. Army was second, and not far behind. These were the children of democracy, fighting for democracy.

Men living in caves, given enough water and food to sustain human life, pretty good weapons, and some ammunition, plus the resignation or determination that came from knowing they were all going to die and that Japan would not be able to hold the island, and expectation of a glorious afterlife having sacrificed themselves for the Emperor, make brave, determined, dangerous soldiers who were able to inflict great damage. This even after they were reduced to licking each other's sweat to slacken their thirst, eating raw insects for food. Still, after the bombardments, most of the Japanese in their caves, bunkers, tunnels, foxholes were secure, ready to fight.

Which they did, which led to another mistake by the Americans, who were so stirred by their hatred that they wanted to, and did, kill every Japanese soldier on the islands. This need not have been. On Iwo Jima, after Mount Suribachi and the two airfields to the north had been captured and were in use, there was no point in going after the remaining enemy on the northern half of the island. That enemy was cut off, was receiving no naval or air assistance, no reinforcements, no resupply. They had little ammunition, almost no food or water. Yet the Marines took almost half their losses digging out and killing this pitiful force.

On Okinawa, after the capture of the airfields in the middle of the island and the conquest of its northern half, the Japanese defenders — also without assistance, reinforcements, or supplies — withdrew to a prepared defensive line protecting the southern third of the island. They had no airfields, no radio or radar, little artillery. They posed no threat. The Americans nevertheless plunged forward, causing far more U.S. Army and Marine casualties, not to mention casualties among Okinawa's civilian population and virtually all of the Japanese army, than ever had to be. Almost 100,000 of Okinawa's civilian population of less than 500,000 was killed, by bombs, shells, and machine gun and rifle fire.

The invading force the United States was building in the Philippines and on Okinawa would be a part of the greatest armada ever put together. About half the men going ashore would be Army, while the other half or so would be Marine. Those Marines were like the GIs in Europe, American kids brought up as Boy Scouts and full of the American Spirit. But they were fighting a different war, against a different enemy, in a different way. E. B. Sledge, a teenage Marine in the 1st Division, wrote a memoir entitled *With the Old Breed at Peleliu and Okinawa* (1981), a book that many military historians, including me, think is the single best book on combat in World War II ever written.

Sledge writes that no account of the Marines in the war can be accurate if it leaves out the intense hatred all Marines felt for the Japanese. This was partly racism, partly a result of the Pearl Harbor attack, but mainly brought on by the way the Japanese fought. As one quick example: in Europe, the medics wore their red cross armband, counting on it that the Germans would not shoot at medics doing their duty. Generally, they did not. In the Pacific, the corpsmen quickly learned to get rid of their red cross armbands, because the Japanese made them prime targets. As another: the Japanese would emerge from a cave, hands up and dressed only in a loincloth. But when a Marine got close enough, the soldier would snatch a grenade from his crotch, pull the pin, and throw it.

The Marines reacted to Japanese atrocities as anyone would do, but the Marines had some special qualities going for them. Journalist Robert Sherrod, in his *On to Westward: War in the Central Pacific* (1945), writes that "Someday someone will write a book about the Marines which will adequately explain their superb *esprit de corps*," then points out that their "training included not only a thorough course in the use of weapons but also a stiff indoctrination in what *New York Times* military correspondent Hanson Baldwin called 'moral superiority.' "

Nowhere is the sense of belonging to a team and working as one done on a larger or more successful scale than in the U.S. Marine Corps. Every day in every way the recruits had instilled into them that they were part of a family. As is true of one's biological family, being a Marine is something that is always part of you. It cannot be escaped. There are no ex-Marines. Once a Marine, Semper Fi.

In World War II, in Korea, and in Vietnam, the Marines made its family believe that they were special. The Best Damn Fighting Men in the World! That is not strictly true, but it was close enough. Where they were the best, better than any of the other units, whether American or Allied or enemy, was in their love for each other. They would do anything for their buddies and expected them to do the same. How? Each Marine could look at every other Marine and know that the other guy had been through a similar boot camp. The bond created the biggest family in America, if not the world.

Captain Ron Drez, USMC, was a company commander in Vietnam. After he was discharged, he became a student of mine, later my assistant, then my partner. In the late 1980s we taught a course on Vietnam. There were some 300 students, literally sitting in the aisles. I described the politics of the war, especially on the home front; Ron taught the history of combat in Vietnam. He was spellbinding. He was in many firefights, lost some, won others, suffered many casualties, conducted himself throughout the way I'd want my company commander to act if I were in combat. I came to have a limitless admiration for him. Ron did not come out of the Naval Academy. He was a Tulane graduate, an NROTC student.

My older brother, Harry, was a Marine officer. Recently I asked him why he had joined the Marine Corps. I wanted to know what motivated him, and all those older than he who had joined up during World War II. A part of his reply:

During my senior year in high school the Inchon landing occurred [September 15, 1950, the beginning of the fall semester]. In June 1951, my best friend, Charlie Hill, enlisted in the USMC. He soon went to Korea and we corresponded actively. This got me interested in the Corps.

Upon graduation [in 1951] I matriculated at Dartmouth College as an NROTC regular midshipman. During my sophomore year I got to know Major John Lindsay, the Marine officer instructor. He strongly influenced me to take the Marine option, a decision which I have never regretted.

Under his tutelage we (there were five of us NROTC midshipmen in the Marine program) studied every major battle the Corps fought. He taught us to be drill instructors and gave us a lot of coaching on leadership, which was later amplified at Basic School. The most important lessons which still stick in my mind:

Always take care of your men first. Never eat until you are sure they have been fed.
Never retreat unless ordered to do so.
Never leave a wounded Marine behind; always carry him with you.
The best Marines are often the smallest in stature. Many of them volunteered to carry the BAR, which is a very demanding duty.
Always maintain eye contact during conversation and never reveal self-doubt to anyone.
Always be prepared to attack and pursue a retreating enemy vigorously.
Always be on the alert.

During our junior/senior summer cruise we were at Quantico. We lived in an enlisted barracks and went through a simulated boot camp. Our platoon sergeant was a World War II veteran. He was an outstanding teacher and disciplinarian. He had us cleaning the head with toothbrushes until midnight the day of our arrival. We rose at five A.M. every morning and fell out for rifle inspection soon after. We underwent the requisite three weeks of rifle training with dry firing exercises each weekday of the first two weeks, followed by five days of firing on the big range.

We could field-strip and clean our rifles in our sleep. We could recite the entire Tables of Organization by heart. The good old Marine Corps triangular concept of three rifle teams per squad, three squads per platoon, etc., was combined with tactics such as two up, one back.

I was commissioned in June 1955 along with about 200 other Dartmouth men who went into the Army, Navy, Air Force, and Marines. I immediately reported to Quantico for the six-month Basic School attended by all newly commissioned second lieutenants. Our platoon commander was Captain Bog Hall, a World War II and Korean War veteran. This was a continuation of the prior summer, as we lived in enlisted barracks, carried a rifle, stood frequent inspections, and marched to chow. We learned the basics of infantry, artillery, amphibious and helicopter techniques, communications, etc. with classroom lectures and field exercises our usual daily experience.

By the time Harry got his commission, the Korean War had been over for two years. He went from Basic School to Communications Officers Schools. His active duty ended in 1958 after a year as communications watch officer at Headquarters, USMC, in Arlington, Virginia.

Harry concluded his letter: "I have always been very proud of my Marine affiliation. The leadership training I received has been invaluable to me as a businessman and volunteer."

The men who joined up for World War II were mostly teenagers. Some of them lied about their age and got into the Corps at fifteen years old, even more at sixteen, a whole lot at seventeen. They were younger than the Army recruits, in better physical shape, more eager to be shaped up and to prove themselves. They knew the Corps was going to be tough — that is why they joined — and that they would be going through an experience that few of their age-mates would ever know. They knew their drill instructors would put them through tasks that they had never imagined, and that in civilian life would be deemed humiliating or worse — such as Harry's cleaning the head with a toothbrush until midnight on his first night. They would learn to obey every order, without question or hesitation.

Most of all, they knew they would be bonded with a team and a family, that they would be plunged into combat — which was what they wanted — and be fighting with the best.

The Japanese presentation of the war to its children runs something like this: one day, for no reason we ever understood, the Americans started dropping atomic bombs on us. A book on the Rape of Nanking, in China, from December 1937 to March 1938, is banned in Japan. The atrocities against civilians in Korea, Manchuria, China, the Philippines, the Marianas, New Guinea, Guadalcanal, Indonesia, Indochina, Thailand, elsewhere are ignored, forgotten. As to the victims, no apologies, no reparations. American servicemen unfortunate enough to have been captured on Bataan worked as slave labor for Japanese corporations for two or three years — and have received nothing. No apology.

My wife and I were in Bataan when the Battered Bastards of Bataan were having a reunion and we joined them for a few days. Their accounts of what the Japanese did to them are scarcely creditable, except that they happened. One of them said that while most Americans during the war thought of the Japanese as beasts, they really were not. "A beast," he said, "is an animal, and animals kill only to eat. The Japs killed for fun."

Thirty years ago, here is the way I used to teach about Hiroshima. By the summer of 1945, Japan was defeated. She had almost no surface fleet left. Her air force had been reduced to kamikazes. Her army was spread across Manchuria, Korea, China, parts of Indonesia, Indochina. Because American submarines had all but eliminated Japan's transports, Japan could not bring her army home to defend the home islands. The Japanese were a rational people who knew that the time to surrender had come. But they had a single demand — that they be allowed to keep the Emperor — i.e., that he would not be arrested, tried, much less executed, that he remain the titular leader of Japan.

In July 1945, meeting at Potsdam, Germany, the Big Three — Churchill, Stalin, and the new American President, Truman — issued the Potsdam Declaration, calling for unconditional surrender by Japan on pain of great destruction (the atomic bomb was operational, as Truman learned during the conference). They also agreed to retain the Emperor after the Japanese surrender, but would refuse to let the Japanese know this.

Japan rejected the Potsdam Declaration, as it contained no guarantee on the Emperor. On his way back to the United States, Truman gave the order to drop the bomb.

Why the hurry? The invasion of the home islands was not scheduled until November 1, so there was time to see what effect the anticipated Russian declaration of war (scheduled for August 8) on Japan would have. Even so, the proposed invasion made the use of the bomb imperative to the Truman circle, because they later claimed they feared as many as 800,000 American casualties in what would have been a gigantic invasion launched out of Okinawa.

Truman's critics, including me, charged that the sequence of events demonstrated that the use of the bomb was the first act of the Cold War, rather than the last act of World War II. Truman used the bomb not so much to force a Japanese surrender as to show the Russians what we had, and that we were not afraid to use it. We critics also believed that the potential American casualty figures were grossly inflated. According to us, there were other motives. There was a fear of the kamikazes. There was a desire to punish the Japanese for Pearl Harbor.

There were those in Congress, the Cabinet, and the military at the time who said that dropping the bomb was the only way to justify to the people the expenditure of $2 billion to produce it. Life had become cheap in the world of 1945. To kill a few more of the enemy seemed natural enough. The racial element in the decision cannot be ignored. The British military writer B. H. Liddell Hart later said the United States would never have used the bomb in Berlin.

The bomb over Hiroshima was dropped on August 6. It did not bring an immediate Japanese response. The Soviet Union declared war on August 8 and the Red Army moved into Manchuria and southern Sakhalin. The Japanese Manchurian army surrendered. To prod the Japanese, the United States on August 9 dropped a second bomb, on Nagasaki. Even after Nagasaki, the Japanese insisted on a guarantee about Emperor Hirohito's safety. The United States made the required promise and Japan surrendered on September 2, 1945. Since Truman and Churchill and Stalin had already decided to do that anyway, the President was not giving anything away.

Here is what I've learned since. The Japanese government was by no means rational or ready to surrender. There were logical, sensible people in Japan, but they were not allowed a say in decision making. No scientist, professor, lawyer, nor even politician had an influence. They were dictated to by Hirohito and the military, who believed they could inflict enough casualties to force the Americans to negotiate. That might leave them with some of their wartime gains. They were ready to fight to the last Japanese. They were training women and children in the use of sharpened bamboo stakes, to meet the Marines at the beach. They were preparing the most elaborate defenses, using what they had learned in Iwo Jima and Okinawa. They had hundreds, perhaps even thousands, of kamikaze planes, hidden in caves or in forests. They had kamikaze powerboats, loaded with explosives, ready to hit the American fleet. They had men trained with explosive backpacks ready to crawl under American tanks. To surrender on American terms would be a humiliation for the Japanese military, who were pledged to fight for the Emperor to the last man. They were ready to sacrifice the whole nation to preserve their personal honor.

As to the projected American casualties, they could have been higher than 800,000. I know an Army rifle-company commander who after the war was awarded a 90 percent disability pension for life, but in the summer of 1945, scarcely able to walk, was listed as fit to go, to lead his company ashore on Japan. Colonel Andrew Goodpaster was in the War Department at the time, having been wounded in Italy, and was in charge of projecting probable casualties. I asked him how he arrived at his figure. He said the Japanese had 2 million soldiers on the home islands. He had taken the total Japanese ground forces in Okinawa and looked at what they had done. A bit more than 100,000 had inflicted losses of 40,000 Marines and Army on the islands. So he multiplied the casualties on Okinawa by a factor of 20 and came up with 800,000-plus.

The need to end the war was overwhelming. The Japanese were starving and killing American POWs, mainly fliers who had been shot down over Japan. Meanwhile thousands or more civilians in the Japanese-held territories in Asia and the offshore islands were dying every day because of Japanese mistreatment.

So, today, I tell my students, Thank God for Harry Truman. For his courage and decisiveness.

# Chapter Nine

# *The Legacy of World War II*

In 1945, there were more people killed, more buildings destroyed, more high explosives set off, more fires burning than before or since. In 1945, the sight of a group of teenage German, or Japanese, or Red Army troops, in uniform, armed, brought terror to civilians in France, Belgium, Holland, Korea, the Philippines, China, Germany, Poland, elsewhere. Those squads of teenage soldiers meant, for certain, rape, pillage, looting, wanton murder, senseless destruction. There was an exception. A squad of teenage American soldiers meant candy, C rations, cigarettes, freedom. It was true in France, Belgium, Italy, the Philippines, China, even Germany and, after August 1945, Japan.

A bright image of the legacy of World War II came to me from a veteran. He told me that he felt he had done his part in helping change the twentieth century from darkness to light. In 1945, it was difficult to believe in human progress. The two world wars had made a mockery of the Enlightenment idea of progress. In 1945, one had to believe that the outcome of the scientific and technological revolution that had inspired the idea of progress would be a world destroyed in a nuclear holocaust.

But slowly, surely, the spirit of those GIs handing out candy and helping bring democracy to their former enemies spread, and by the beginning of this century it is democracy, not dictatorship, that is on the march. Today, one can believe again in progress. This is thanks to the GIs — along with the millions of others who helped liberate Germany and Japan from their evil rulers, then stood up to Stalin and his successors. That generation has done more to spread freedom and prosperity around the globe than any previous generation.

That this triumph was accomplished in the second half of the twentieth century depended first of all on the victory of the American Spirit in the Second World War. Today, we are the world's only superpower, and around the world — even in Russia — there is nearly virtual agreement that if there is to be only one superpower then thank God Almighty that it is the United States.

The first American Century turned out even better than Henry Luce dared imagine.

I don't know if this is the best of all possible outcomes, but I do know it is the one we have got, and America can be proud of what it has accomplished. More people enjoy more products and more liberty, around the world, than ever before. There are many reasons, and the credit needs to be shared, quite obviously, but the one that stands out is that generation of Americans born between 1890 and 1930. It fell to them to defeat the triple towers of barbarism, the totalitarian empires of Nazi Germany, Imperial Japan, and Soviet Russia, and to throw them where they belong, in the ashcan of history.

America is the first democratic nation-state, now more than two and a quarter centuries old. Our greatest triumphs are the eighteenth-century creation of our democratic republic, the nineteenth-century abolishment of slavery and the holding together of our Union, and our twentieth-century crushing of totalitarianism.

In the nineteenth century, our best minds labored to discover and describe nature — Lewis and Clark come to mind. In the twentieth century our best minds labored to conquer nature — Henry Ford, the Wright brothers, many others, but most of all those who invented, developed, and produced better methods to kill more effectively and cheaply — Enrico Fermi, J. Robert Oppenheimer, and many others who made the atomic bomb. Those who created the weapons were engaged in the most critical of all tasks, because it was the worst century in the whole history of mankind, with the greatest issue at stake. It was, simply put, a contest over what system could best implement and use the Industrial Revolution to run the world: totalitarianism or democracy?

Critical to the victory in 1945 were the other democracies, especially Britain, Canada, and Australia, as well as the Soviet Union, which fought the Nazi invasion of its country. Because we won the war, at great sacrifice, we opened the way. The Soviet Union is gone today, replaced by struggling democracies. The Chinese and Cuban communist systems will shortly be history.

On September 1, 1939, when Nazi Germany invaded Poland, Lieutenant Colonel Dwight Eisenhower, serving as an aide to General Douglas MacArthur in the Philippines, wrote his younger brother, Milton. He said it scarcely seemed possible "that people that proudly refer to themselves as intelligent could let this situation come about." He blamed Hitler, "a power-drunk egocentric, one of the criminally insane, the absolute ruler of eighty-nine million people." That is when he made the prophecy I have already quoted, "Hitler should beware the fury of an aroused democracy." Eisenhower was born in Texas in 1890. He grew up in Abilene, Kansas, almost in the exact center of the lower forty-eight states. His father was a foreman in the local creamery. He went to public grade and high school, then got a free college education at West Point. From 1915 on he was a professional soldier. He served on posts across the United States, in Europe, in Panama, in the Philippines.

In the summer of 1945, following the German surrender, Eisenhower was commander of the American Zone in occupied Germany. He told his staff officers then that "the success or failure of this occupation can only be judged fifty years from now. If by then the Germans had a flourishing, stable democracy, we will have succeeded."

One of Eisenhower's first acts was to call the members of the German press corps into his headquarters. He told them that Germany had to have a free press if it was going to become a democracy, and specifically that if he did something they disagreed with he wanted them to criticize him in their newspapers. The reporters were astonished. They had been working for the Nazis for twelve years; here was their conqueror telling them to be critical of him.

He called in the leaders of the German labor unions and told them that their job was to represent their workers, not the government. They had been working for the Nazis for twelve years, they were also astonished. Next he called in the schoolteachers and told them to encourage their students to think for themselves.

Eisenhower meant what he said about the need for democracy in Germany. In 1959, to his Secretary of State, Christian Herter, who had just told him that the Christian Democrats in West Germany were afraid of reunification with East Germany because they feared that the Socialists in West Germany would combine with the communists in East Germany to defeat the Christian Democrats in a free election, he replied, "If they get a true free unification, then they have to take their chances on politics."

His response was perfect. I think of something a German student said to me in 1980, at the University of Munich: "You Americans sometimes seem to forget, you liberated us too." A Japanese student might say the same thing.

None of this was foreordained. In September 1944, as U.S. troops first reached Germany, Eisenhower issued orders forbidding fraternization between Germans and Americans. He put photographs of GIs and Germans together on the censored list. In April 1945, he received his operating instructions as head of the occupation in a document called JCS 1067 (Joint Chiefs of Staff Paper No. 1067). It forbade any fraternization. And Eisenhower was prepared to enforce it. After a month trying to enforce JCS 1067, Ike wrote to Army Chief of Staff George C. Marshall that it was impossible to maintain the nonfraternization rules in the case of small children. He said he knew it was simply silly to forbid American soldiers to talk to or give candy bars or chewing gum to German children. And it was absurd to try to keep GIs from dating — not raping, but dating — German women.

In 1919, at Versailles, the Allies, led by France and England, set out to punish the defeated Germans by taking away their colonies, severely reducing the size of their army, keeping them from occupying the Rhineland. What the world got out of this was Hitler. But we learned, and from 1945 on, the victors worked to make Germany into a modern democracy. They succeeded.

What America, with its Allies, did in West Germany and throughout Western Europe in the aftermath of the Second World War was generous and wise. America's young men had gone to Europe not to conquer, not to enslave, not to destroy, but to liberate, and no country in the world had the resources of spirit to do what America did. America turned West Germany from a Nazi dictatorship into a democratic state, then made it into a model that all the Central European countries occupied by the Soviet Union, including East Germany, envied. When the chance came to overthrow their communist rulers and embrace freedom and democracy, they did so.

It sounds too good to be true. It happened. While the Soviets were looting, raping, pillaging in eastern Germany, Poland, and elsewhere, the Americans were feeding, rebuilding, restoring. In 1948, while the Soviets were attempting to blockade West Berlin into starvation and submission, the United States was feeding and supplying the city through the Berlin Air Lift. The Marshall Plan was just what Winston Churchill said of it, the most generous act in human history.

President Harry Truman's Secretary of State Dean Acheson titled his memoirs of the years after the war *Present at the Creation*. That caught it exactly. After playing a leading role in the defeat of Nazi Germany and the principal role in the defeat of Imperial Japan, the United States set out to create a new world. A democratic Germany. A democratic Japan. A democratic South Korea. The Berlin Air Lift. The Marshall Plan. The recognition of Israel. The formation of the North Atlantic Treaty Organization. All these came into being a half-century ago, under the sponsorship and leadership of the United States. It is impossible to imagine what the world would be like today without them. And it was the American Spirit, more than American productive power, that made it so.

A second great legacy of the victory was the crushing of imperialism. That didn't come about all at once, of course, but it happened because of the war's outcome. The Japanese drove the British, the Dutch, the French, and the Americans out of their colonies in Asia, only to establish their own empire, which in early 1942 stretched from the Central and South Pacific deep into China, Burma in the east, north to the Aleutian Islands (the westernmost part of North America), south to New Guinea — the largest empire in history. And they ran their colonies in the most brutal fashion imaginable, but never effectively. By September 1945, they had been driven out and their empire came to its never-mourned end.

By 1942, the Germans had established their own empire, stretching from the English Channel on the west to as far north as Norway, as far east as Moscow, as far south as Libya and Egypt. After they were driven back to their prewar boundaries, the Germans lost all their empire in Central and Eastern Europe to the Soviet Union, and their eastern quarter of Germany to East Germany — all a communist system of imperialism. This too ultimately failed, thanks to American perseverance during the Cold War.

America led the way in the defeat of imperialism, not only by doing so much to defeat Japan and Germany, but by repudiating its own imperialism. Even before World War II in the Pacific began, the United States had promised independence to the Philippines by July 4, 1946. After driving the Japanese out of the Philippines in 1945, we kept our promise. The Filipinos did not have to wage a war of national liberation to gain their freedom; the Americans acknowledged their mistake of 1898 and recognized their independence.

America's role in this flush of freedom includes not only the victory in the war, but the example the United States set in the postwar years. Much of this can be directly credited to Dwight Eisenhower. Two examples will suffice. In 1956, when the British and French were attacking Egypt to maintain their control of the

Suez Canal, and asked for their wartime ally America to help them, Eisenhower, running for reelection, declared in a campaign speech that his country would never do that. "We cannot subscribe to one law for the weak, another law for the strong; one law for those opposing us, another for those allied with us. There can be only one law — or there shall be no peace." A year later, Vice President Richard Nixon, just returned from a trip to North Africa, told President Eisenhower that Algeria was not ready for independence. The Algerians would be better ruled by the French, make more progress, and live more prosperously than if they ran the country themselves. Eisenhower replied, "The United States could not possibly maintain that freedom — independence — liberty — were necessary to us, but not to others."

A third legacy of the Second World War was the atomic bomb. It is possible that had there been no war there would have been no atomic bomb. Unless its very survival was at risk, no nation would have spent so much money, time, and effort, not to mention creative genius, on such a risky proposition as making the bomb. And of all the threats to peace and democracy today, the worst is atomic weapons in the hands of madmen.

Still there is a positive side. The making of the bomb showed that there is almost nothing mankind cannot do, especially when a government gets behind the project and money is unlimited.

Despite the shortcomings that plague every government everywhere, scientific progress is possible with government support. Most of the great projects since 1945 have come about because of that awareness. And many of them got going during the war, including medical advances across the spectrum, radar, computers, jet airplanes, missiles, and much else.

When he was President of the United States, Eisenhower met with a group of congressmen who urged him to destroy the Soviet menace with an atomic attack, a first strike, thus eliminating the communist threat. He replied that he would never do such a thing, then informed the congressmen that despite their desire to reduce or even end the Cold War, it should never be done through a first strike. "This is a continuous crisis that the United States has to live with. Our most realistic policy is holding the line until the Soviets manage to educate their people." He said that if they wanted to keep up with the United States — "and they do" — they would have to educate their people. "By doing so, they will sow the seeds of destruction of Communism as a virulent power." That seems to me to be exactly what had happened by the time Mikhail Gorbachev rose to power.

The generation who fought World War II has done more to spread freedom and prosperity around the globe than any preceding generation. Sergeant Henry Halsted, who was one of them and a winner of a Bronze Star, participated after the war in an American-conceived and sponsored program that brought together college-age Germans, Frenchmen, and Americans in Munich. The idea was to teach through contact and example. Years later, a French participant in the program wrote to Halsted, "In the immediate postwar years, France was in ruins. I saw only a world marked by war, by destruction, by the shadow of war, and by fear. I believed it was not finished, that there would be a next war. I did not think it would be possible to build a life, to have a family. Then came your group of young Americans, attractive, idealistic, optimistic, protected, believing and acting as though anything was possible. It was a transforming experience for me."

In 1997, Halsted got a Christmas card from a German participant: "I think often of our meetings and mutual ideals. Indeed, the program and everything connected with it was the most important, decisive event for me. Influenced my life deeply!"

That spirit — we can do it, we can rebuild Europe and hold back the Red Army and avoid World War III — was the great gift of the New World to the Old World.

In his Farewell Address to the American people, Eisenhower spoke to the best instincts of the American Spirit. "We pray that peoples of all faiths, all races, all nations, may have their great human needs satisfied; that those now denied opportunity shall come to enjoy it to the full;

that all who yearn for freedom may experience its spiritual blessings; that those who have freedom will understand, also, its heavy responsibilities; that all who are insensitive to the needs of others will learn charity; that the scourges of poverty, disease, and ignorance will be made to disappear from the earth, and that, in the goodness of time, all peoples will come to live together in a peace guaranteed by the binding force of mutual respect and love."

After the Germans and Japanese had surrendered, America extended its hand to its former enemies. At the beginning of the twenty-first century it is believed by some that nation building will never work. But it did, in Germany and Japan. For twelve years Germany had lived under the totalitarian rule of Hitler and his Nazis, but with American guidance and help, it became a democracy. Japan was a feudal society, dominated by its Emperor and its military. But after September 1945, America guided Japan, giving Japanese women their rights, for the first time, abolishing the feudal system, establishing schools, and creating a democracy.

Immediately after the German surrender, Lieutenant (later Senator) George McGovern and his fellow B-24 pilots, who had just completed their thirty-five missions bombing the enemy, began flying the planes to northern Italy, Austria, and Germany, carrying food to the defeated foes. In 1948 the United States committed vast amounts of its resources to restore the economies of former foes and former allies alike. The stable democracies of Western Europe and Japan owe their existence in no small part to the Marshall Plan.

# Chapter Ten

## *Vietnam*

America's war in Vietnam ended more than a quarter of a century ago. It continues to divide us, especially those who lived through it. Unlike World War II, when Americans were united, Vietnam split us apart. Even families. My brothers, Harry and Bill, were hawks, while I was a dove. Up to 1965, when the war began, we had a good relationship, talking often over the phone, seeing each other in the summer, getting together for Christmas. But by 1966 we were arguing about the war almost always, and by 1967 we were so furious with each other that we stopped talking. Not until 1974, after the war ended, did we begin to repair our relationship.

We were not alone. And thirty years after the war, the American people continue to disagree over who was responsible, whether it was a good cause or not, how it was fought, what could have been done. Almost no one, certainly not I, emerged unscathed. In the high command there were no heroes. Not the commander-in-chief, not the Secretary of Defense, not the generals and admirals in the Pentagon, not the commanders at sea, in the air, and on the ground in Vietnam. All had their reputations tarnished, in some cases besmirched. Any heroes we had emerged from the ranks of the junior officers and enlisted men, and from the prisoners of war, mainly pilots.

In one way or another it continues to affect all of us today. My brothers and I get along fine nowadays, but only because we never talk about the war. Each side learned something different. The doves can say that it is possible for the United States to live in peace with a unified, communist-run Vietnam; that neither the Chinese nor the Soviet Union could control a communist Vietnam; that the world is not divided into two blocs. The hawks were persuaded that if America is going to fight a war, do it. We should have sent in more troops and firepower, though it is impossible to imagine more bombs, and we should have invaded North Vietnam, Cambodia, and Laos. If the United States had stayed in the struggle and prevailed, South Vietnam would be a far better place today — an apt comparison, the hawks say, is North Korea and South Korea. They believe the war effort was undermined by the dissenters at home.

The war taught many military lessons, such as firepower does not always prevail. The Americans and their South Vietnamese allies had far more firepower than the Vietcong and the North Vietnamese army, firepower from the air, from the sea, on the ground, but it was not enough.

We also learned that the power to destroy is not the power to control. And the wisdom of one of Eisenhower's favorite maxims: Never send a battalion to take a hill if you have a regiment available. That was the lesson applied by President George H. W. Bush in Operation Desert Storm.

In 1945, the Vietminh under their leader, Ho Chi Minh, were fighting for their independence from the French. Ho told the Americans he wanted independence within five to ten years, land reform, a democracy based on universal suffrage, and national purchase of French holdings. He had worked closely with American agents during the Second World War and had copied the Vietnamese Declaration of Independence from the American document. But the French insisted on their right to return and take up their colonial master role. And the French were crucial to the anti-Soviet alliance the United States was creating in Europe to fight the Cold War. So to appease the French, the Americans helped them try to regain their rule in Vietnam. It was Truman's decision and he was wrong on that one. It got worse. Beginning in 1952, as the Vietminh went into open revolt against the French, the United States paid as much as 90 percent of the cost of the war to the French.

When he became President in 1953, Eisenhower told the French they absolutely must promise the Vietnamese that at the conclusion of hostilities, they would get complete independence. Although they could not prevail, the French would not make the promise. Instead they put their best troops into an isolated garrison north of Hanoi, called Dien Bien Phu, and dared the Vietminh to come after them. They did and the French were soon on the brink of catastrophe. The Eisenhower administration called into the White House eight congressional leaders and asked if they would support a resolution authorizing American entry into the war. The congressmen, including Senator Lyndon B. Johnson, were aghast. They remembered all too well the difficulties of the Korean War, especially after the Chinese came into it.

On April 7, 1954, with Dien Bien Phu about to fall, Eisenhower was asked at a press conference what was so important about Vietnam. He replied that all Southeast Asia was like a row of dominoes. If you knocked over the first one, what would happen to the last one was "the certainty that it would go over very quickly."

A week later, Vice President Richard M. Nixon said that "if to avoid further Communist expansion in Asia and Indochina, we must take the risk now by putting our boys in, I think the Executive has to take the politically unpopular decision and do it." A storm of congressional protest followed the speech and the talk about putting in "our boys" came to an end.

At the time I was a sophomore in college. The United States had just signed an armistice with

North Korea, bringing one Asian war to an end. Now it looked as if we would soon be involved in another, and that it would be my generation that would do the fighting. All of us had been in grade school during the Second World War and had been brought up to do whatever our country told us to do — and we certainly would have. Still, I had a difficult time seeing the dominoes falling and was baffled by the link between Vietnam and the Cold War. To me, the Cold War was about Europe. But what did I know?

On May 7, 1954, Dien Bien Phu fell. On July 20 and 21, the French and Vietminh signed the Geneva Accords. The parties agreed to a truce and to a temporary partition of Vietnam at the seventeenth parallel, with the French withdrawing south of that line, while Ho Chi Minh's Vietminh would hold the north. Neither party would make a military alliance with an outside party. Within two years there would be elections to unify the country. There would be no war.

But Secretary of State John Foster Dulles would not let go. In September, he persuaded Britain, Australia, New Zealand, France, Thailand, Pakistan, and the Philippines to join the Southeast Asia Treaty Organization (SEATO), an Asian NATO. In a separate protocol, SEATO extended its protection to Cambodia, Laos, and South Vietnam. Thus did the United States violate the Geneva agreements by bringing South Vietnam into an alliance system. It did so again when it approved the seizure of power from the French by a South Vietnamese leader named Ngo Dinh Diem. Eisenhower tried to require social and economic reforms from Diem, but it was generally true that Diem could do as he wished as long as he remained firmly anticommunist.

American economic aid began to come into Diem's hands. But that did not deal with the fuzzy legal situation. Under the 1954 Geneva Accords, South Vietnam was not a nation but a territory, to be administered by the French until elections were held in 1956. And neither side was to allow the introduction of foreign troops into their territories. But the United States redefined the agreements, deliberately creating the fiction that Geneva Accords had set up two Vietnams, North and South.

They had not. And in 1956 Diem refused to allow the scheduled, nationwide elections to take place (most observers agreed that Ho Chi Minh's communists would have won easily). For some years thereafter, the North Vietnamese concentrated their resources on rebuilding their half of the country, and installing socialism. The Vietminh in the South felt abandoned and grew restive. They started a campaign to assassinate village chiefs and thus destroy Diem's hold on the South Vietnam countryside. Diem reacted by going after his enemies.

In 1960 John F. Kennedy defeated Richard Nixon for President, barely. He had some wonderful prose and some unmatchable rhetoric in his Inaugural Address, but he could not possibly have meant what he said, nor expected the nation to live up to it. "We shall pay any price, bear any burden, meet any hardship, support any friend, oppose any foes, in order to assure the survival and success of liberty. This much we pledge — and more."

What "and more" could there be after paying any price, bearing any burden? And if Kennedy meant the whole "free world," and most specifically South Vietnam, how high could the price go? I felt at the time it would be a terrible mistake to pay any price, etc., in support of the two-bit dictator Diem and his corrupt government. To stop Hitler from conquering Great Britain, yes. To stop Ho Chi Minh from unifying his own country under his rule, no. But Kennedy and the men around him had been impatient with Ike's leadership. They wanted to spend more, do more.

Kennedy and Eisenhower did agree on the largest point of all. Both believed and said that American policy should be to wait. Eisenhower explained to a congressional delegation that the Cold War was going to take a long time. But if the communists wanted to keep up with the free world they would have to educate their own people. In the process they would sow the seeds of their own destruction. It was a rotten system sure to collapse someday.

In his 1961 State of the Union address, Kennedy told Americans to expect a long, slow process of evolution "away from Communism and toward national independence and freedom." In one of the best of his many memorable lines, he added: "Without having a nuclear war, we want to permit what Thomas Jefferson called 'the disease of liberty' to be caught in areas which are now held by the Communists."

I thought then that both Presidents were right, and that was the way I taught it to my students. But Kennedy had taken office at a time when America's hubris was very high. IIis goals, in short, were almost as boundless as his pledges about paying any price and bearing any burden. Most Americans agreed with him. That was not what I believed and I criticized it, then and now.

In 1960, the Vietcong had gone into full-scale revolt. Many Americans urged negotiations, I among them. But shortly after Kennedy's inauguration, Secretary of State Dean Rusk replied that negotiations would introduce the dangers of a Far East Munich, thereby equating Ho Chi Minh with Hitler, and raising the dreaded specter of appeasement. Kennedy decided to send in much greater quantities of military aid to South Vietnam, with the idea that the South Vietnamese could do their own fighting. America could continue its policy of the containment of communism without casualties. "South Vietnam will supply the necessary men," he said.

The policy seemed to be working. In June 1962, Secretary of Defense Robert McNamara visited Vietnam and reported, "Every quantitative measurement we have shows we're winning the war." A year later, Rusk declared that the struggle against the Vietcong had "turned an important corner" and was nearly over. These were damnable lies, lies from the government about policy and performance. They turned many more against the war and gathered in few adherents.

In November 1963, South Vietnamese generals carried out a coup. They captured and killed Diem. A military regime took over. Three weeks after Diem's death, Kennedy himself was assassinated and Lyndon Johnson became President.

These events and others left us dizzy, confused, groping. I had many friends in the military, some of them in Vietnam. Eisenhower was still alive and would never disagree with the President on a war situation, so he said nothing. But I had to believe that he still believed what he had said back in 1954, after Dien Bien Phu — that it would be a terrible mistake to send American soldiers into Vietnam because the jungles would just swallow them up in division-sized units.

Between 1964 and 1969 I was teaching at Johns Hopkins University and working on the Eisenhower Papers there, and writing a biography of Ike. President Johnson gradually and steadily increased the American commitment to South Vietnam. He felt he had no choice, that he had to continue the policies of Truman, Eisenhower, and Kennedy, that America's position in the Cold War was threatened, and that the United States would prevail at an acceptable cost. He was wrong on all of these, and more. And the lies he told the American people about why we were becoming engaged in Vietnam, and how well we were doing there, came from the same man who told the American people the truth about Jim Crow and segregation. I felt and said, and still do, that he was at once simultaneously the best President of the century, and the worst.

In the presidential campaign of 1964, Republican candidate Barry Goldwater advocated all-out war in Vietnam. Johnson presented himself as the man who could be trusted to be prudent. But in August he pushed through Congress the Gulf of Tonkin Resolution, based on reports that American destroyers had been attacked by North Vietnamese torpedo boats in the Gulf of Tonkin. Congress, by a vote of 416 to 0 in the House, 88 to 2 in the Senate (Wayne Morse and Ernest Gruening dissenting), authorized the President to use "all necessary measures to repel any armed attack" against American forces, and to "prevent further aggression" by taking "all necessary steps" to protect South Vietnam.

In February 1965, the Vietcong attacked the American air base at Pleiku, South Vietnam. Johnson ordered retaliation. The American Air Force began bombing North Vietnam. With some fits and starts, this air offensive continued and grew over the next four years. The sheer magnitude of the effort was staggering. First, headlines proclaimed that America had dropped more bombs on tiny Vietnam than in the entire Pacific Theater in World War II. By 1967 it was more bombs than in the European Theater. Then more than in the whole of World War II. Finally, by 1969, more bombs had been dropped on Vietnam, North and South, than on all targets in the whole of human history.

In my weekly interviews with Eisenhower at Gettysburg during this period, I never brought up Vietnam. I don't know what he might have said had I done so. I know what I felt, based on what I was learning from him about the Second World War.

First, that America would never win the war through airpower, for many reasons but most of all because the industrial base for the enemy was not in North Vietnam but in China and the Soviet Union. Second, this fighting to defend South Vietnam was self-defeating. It left the initiative to the enemy. Any time his losses became too heavy he could simply withdraw to come back again next month or next year. Third, the way to win was to greatly strengthen the American ground forces and invade North Vietnam and occupy Hanoi. If we were not willing to do that, and every indication was that we were not, then we should pull out. Now.

The decision not to invade North Vietnam had many roots, but chief among them was the memory of what happened in North Korea. America's armed forces had invaded the North and driven up almost to the Yalu River, but then the Chinese entered the war. Whatever else, no one in Washington was prepared to fight a ground war in Vietnam with the Chinese.

How Eisenhower would have responded to such arguments I do not know. In one way I wish very much I had asked him, but then I got so much information and so many stories from him about World War II that my time with him was priceless.

It was a terrible time to be a professor, even at the elite school of Johns Hopkins. The students began to question everything, to protest against anything. There were antiwar demonstrations and riots on campus, there were protests against air and water pollution, for or against women's rights. Students burned their draft cards. As the American commitment mounted, from $10 billion to $20 billion to $30 billion per year, as the level of ground troops in Vietnam escalated from 150,000 to 300,000 to 500,000, as the casualties mounted, as the bombs rained down on the people of both North and South Vietnam, the students began to question not just the involvement in Vietnam but the overall policy of containment of communism. And to ask, What kind of a society can support such a war? This led to an examination of all aspects of American life.

Some students came to believe that they lived in an evil, repressive society that exploited not only foreigners but Americans as well.

For my part, where could I turn for a beacon of light in a country that had seemingly gone mad? Where was there a manifestation of the American spirit? I was just a kid professor. Where were my leaders?

They were there. Older men with a stake in the society and a commitment to preserving it. Many of them came to believe that containment, and the specific expression of that policy in Vietnam, was not saving America but destroying it. They returned to an older version of America, best expressed by Lincoln at Gettysburg, which saw America's mission as one of setting an example for the world. Walter Lippmann wrote, "America can exert its greatest influence in the outer world by demonstrating at home that the largest and most complex modern society can solve the problems of modernity. Then, what all the world is struggling with will be shown to be soluble. Example, and not intervention and firepower, has been the historic instrument of American influence on mankind, and never has it been more necessary and more urgent to realize this truth once more."

To Lippmann's words, Senator J. William Fulbright added, "The world has no need, in this age of nationalism and nuclear weapons, for a new imperial power, but there is a great need of moral leadership — by which I mean the leadership of decent example." These men, plus George McGovern, Robert Kennedy, Wayne Morse, Ernest Gruening, and many others, inspired me, gave me hope, helped me keep my faith in my country.

Johnson's frustration over Vietnam mounted as he sent in more troops. In public, he was upbeat. So were his generals and admirals, his secretaries of state and of defense, a sizable majority of the media, many of the troops in the field. But in private, Johnson bemoaned "this bitch of a war." He claimed that he could have been the greatest President ever, even ahead of Franklin D. Roosevelt, had it not been for Vietnam. He claimed that Truman, Eisenhower, and Kennedy had committed him to the defense of South Vietnam, that America had a moral commitment not to allow the South to fall to the communists. So, hating it but feeling forced, he sent in more troops, even as he confessed to his advisors and some senators that he had no idea how to win this war, nor any idea of how to get out.

I had students fighting in Vietnam, some ROTC graduates, some men who enlisted midway in their college careers, some who got drafted after graduating. From them I got a sense of the war that I was not getting from the news reports, how hopeless it appeared to those on the spot doing the fighting. To them I gave encouragement and praise for what they were doing, plus a sense that they had not been forgotten, and a promise that there was an academic world at home ready to further educate them.

In late January 1968, the brave words from the Johnson administration were blown apart as the enemy launched a brutal and surprise attack on the Vietnamese religious holiday of Tet. The communists drove the Americans and the South Vietnamese army out of parts of the countryside and into the cities, and even took some of the cities. In Saigon, a Vietcong suicide squad took temporary possession of the American embassy grounds. The American answer to the offensive was firepower. When the Vietcong took control of the ancient cultural capital of Hue, David Douglas Duncan, a combat photographer with long experience in war, was appalled by the American method of freeing the city. "The Americans pounded the Citadel almost to dust with air strikes, napalm runs, artillery and naval gunfire, and the direct cannon fire from tanks — a total effort to root out and kill every enemy soldier. The mind reels at the carnage, cost, and ruthlessness of it all." It was an artillery officer who explained to Duncan, "We had to destroy the city to save it."

On March 31, 1968, stung by the worldwide criticism of the American tactics, Johnson announced that he was stopping the bombing on Hanoi. Then to everyone's astonishment, he withdrew from the upcoming presidential race.

It was a humiliating end. Johnson had been the most powerful man in the world, and quite possibly he had the strongest will, yet the North Vietnamese and the Vietcong had resisted, overcome his power, broken his will. Johnson had overreached himself. He had wanted to bring democracy and prosperity to Southeast Asia but he had brought only death and destruction.

Vice President Hubert Humphrey was the Democratic nominee in the 1968 presidential campaign and Richard Nixon was again the Republican candidate. Humphrey and the Johnson administration implied that peace was at hand. But the President, and presumably Vice President Humphrey, knew that the South Vietnamese government had not agreed to the proposed peace formula, and that the North Vietnamese had not agreed to settle for something short of victory. In its quest for votes, the administration treated the American people with cynical contempt. It would take years, and many violent storms with hurricane-force winds, to clear the air of the loathsome stench of the last week of the 1968 campaign.

Nixon won, barely.

A change had to be made. After reviewing his options, President Nixon decided he was not going to invade North Vietnam or otherwise escalate the war. He would not use nuclear weapons. He had to cut the casualties and the numbers of men in Vietnam, but he could not lose the war. He therefore decided on a policy he called Vietnamization, which was a return to the policy Kennedy had originally advocated — the United States would provide the military weapons, the South Vietnamese the troops.

By lowering the draft calls and making them fairer, by reducing the number of American troops in the war zone, by letting young men know at age seventeen or eighteen whether or not they would be called up, he defused the antiwar demonstrations. He had begun the long, slow, painful but necessary process of deescalating, or withdrawing.

I tried to understand what Nixon hoped to accomplish. I knew he could not just bring all the men home, at once, without setting off an even worse series of protests, marches, condemnation. It might even approach a civil war. And perhaps, maybe, who knew? Leaving behind the guns and equipment for the South Vietnamese as the American commitment shrank might work. As Vietnamization put something of a lid on the antiwar movement, throughout 1969 and into 1970, the American government regularly released figures to prove that it was working. The Army of the Republic of Vietnam (ARVN, the South Vietnamese) could "hack it." Enemy body counts were higher than ever. ARVN had more troops, more and better leaders and equipment.

Then on April 30, 1970, Nixon made a surprise announcement that a large force of U.S. troops, supported by major air strikes and backed by a big ARVN force, had invaded Cambodia. That was something I and many others had urged some years earlier (along with an invasion of North Vietnam and Laos, dropping the fiction that the only war going on was in South Vietnam and thus only there could the U.S. Army operate). But by 1970 it was almost surely too late, and anyway Nixon said his purpose was to gain time for the American withdrawal. In other words, he was attacking to cover a retreat. But the invasion accomplished little, except to turn Cambodia into a battleground and then a slaughterhouse, and eventually prompted a successful communist insurgency there, thereby making the domino theory come true.

The Cambodian invasion revived the antiwar movement at home. There were demonstrations on campuses across the country. On May 4, four students were shot dead by the Ohio National Guard at Kent State University.

Nixon issued a statement: "When dissent turns to violence, it invites tragedy." He had not a word of sympathy for the dead students, or their families, or the eight wounded students, most of whom were merely changing classes. They were kids going about their business, shot down by other American kids in the Ohio Guard. Kent State sent the campuses into an uproar such as had not been seen before, and pray God never will be again. Four hundred fifty colleges and universities went on strike. In California, Governor Ronald Reagan closed down the entire state system. Across the country copies of the Constitution were buried, to the sound of taps.

As the campuses shut down, antiwar protest rallies sometimes turned into riots. Students marched through the streets, chanting, throwing rocks, breaking windows, burning down buildings. The baby boomers were on a rampage. Their activities shocked and frightened older Americans as much as Kent State had shocked and frightened the college kids. In the view of the older folks, these kids should have been grateful for their privileges; in the view of the college students, the older Americans should have been ashamed of themselves for supporting Richard Nixon.

In the fall of 1970 I had started my duties at Kansas State University as the Eisenhower Professor of War and Peace. A couple of weeks into the new semester, President Nixon came to the university to deliver the Landon Lecture, named for Alf Landon of Kansas, the Republican nominee for President in 1936. This was the first time a President had been on a college campus since LBJ spoke at Johns Hopkins in 1965 (I was there for that speech, in which LBJ called for a Tennessee Valley Authority–type of program in South Vietnam). Nixon used the occasion not to urge reconciliation between the hawks and the doves, or the students and their parents, but to denounce the perpetrators of violence on college campuses. "The time has come for us to recognize that violence and terror have no place in a free society," he said. As he continued, a small group of forty or so hecklers in the back of the auditorium began calling out, "What about Kent State?" or "Stop the war." Nixon plunged on: "Those who bomb universities, ambush policemen . . . share in common a contempt for human life."

My wife and I were seated in the front row of the faculty section, not too far from Nixon. That morning the *Kansas City Star* had carried a headline, "New Record Tonnage of Bombs Dropped." To hear Nixon condemn "those who would choose violence or intimidation to get what they wanted" was more than we could take. Moira and I began calling out what reporters at the speech called "obscenities." Perhaps they were; in any event, our heckling consisted of "Napalm," or "Free Fire Zones," or "Body Count." As we began to draw hostile stares, I told Moira we had to leave, and less than halfway through the speech we walked out.

An hour or so later, I was on a panel of six faculty members discussing the President's speech. Some panelists supported what he had said, others were not so sure. When my turn came, my anger overwhelmed me and I said, "I'll be goddamned if I'll let that SOB lecture to me on violence." The few doves in the audience cheered.

Most were shocked. Some hung their heads in shame. For my part, I wish I'd never said it. It was inappropriate, demeaning, offensive to use curse words to describe a President, most of all one who had been invited to the campus and was KSU's guest. But I said it, and I can't change that.

The incident surely did change my life. A persistent rumor in the academic world to the contrary, the KSU administration did not fire me. Indeed, I've been back to the university to speak on a number of occasions, most notably in 2001 to deliver the Landon Lecture. But the university administration made it clear that KSU would be much happier if I could find employment elsewhere. In the small community of Manhattan, Kansas, meanwhile, Moira and I were just about read out of polite society. Before the Nixon speech, the town leaders had welcomed us, or at least my credentials — Johns Hopkins University, the Naval War College, Eisenhower's biographer. And now I had pissed in their soup. So I took Moira down to New Orleans, and found that the chancellor of Louisiana State University in New Orleans (LSUNO), Homer Hitt, would be delighted if I came back. (I'm not sure if he had heard of my performance at the Nixon lecture.) It was Moira's first visit to the Crescent City and she found much of it to be strange or foreign. But as she likes to remind me, I told her "there's one thing about New Orleans."

"What is that?" she asked.

"Down here you can be as eccentric as you choose and no one will ever mind." That hooked her, as it always has me, so it was back to New Orleans.

In the fall of 1971 I began to teach at Louisiana State University in New Orleans. It was painful to see how much the war had divided our students, who were mainly working-class, over the most important issue of the day. What hurt the most was the way returning veterans were treated. You could spot them immediately on campus, because they still had crew-cut hair. Some of the hippies — even in New Orleans, there were many hippies — despised them. Once I saw a woman student with long hair, wearing a T-shirt with no bra, go up to a discharged veteran, spit in his face, and ask, "How many children did you kill over there?"

Nixon was of great help on this one. He had judged, correctly if cynically, that the heart of the antiwar movement was male college students threatened with the draft. On May 19, 1969, less than five months after he took office, he had asked Congress to change the Selective Service System. He wanted to go from an oldest-first to a youngest-first order of call, meaning nineteen-year-olds first, along with a reduction in the period of prime draft vulnerability from seven years to one year. The net effect was that twenty-year-olds and up were no longer threatened by

213

the draft and, just as Nixon hoped and expected, most of them stopped marching for peace and started getting on with their lives. That was good not only for them but for those of us on the faculty as well. We could get back to teaching. For the nineteen-year-olds, a lottery system would let them know where they stood (a consistent and loudly uttered and quite justifiable complaint by the youngsters was that they never knew if and when they would be called to service).

Before Nixon changed the draft system, it was commonly charged that Vietnam was a rich man's war and a poor man's fight. Rich kids could often find some way to avoid the draft, or if not to get assigned to Germany or the Pentagon or at least to get themselves onto somebody's staff.

Meanwhile, by 1971 I was the father of five children, three of them sons who would soon be entering high school and after that subject to the draft. I was a teacher in extensive contact with students who were vehemently, sometimes violently, opposed to the war. Many of them blamed the professional soldiers and sailors and airmen for getting us into this war and keeping us there.

I never agreed with that view. I was opposed to the war because it seemed to me then, and does now, that Johnson's administration had told the military to do something it could not — win an unpopular war with inadequate resources. Neither Johnson nor his party nor the government as a whole were willing to raise, train, equip, and then send to Vietnam sufficient manpower to do the job. It was as if the government believed we must prevail but we can't — won't — pay the price.

Other doves blamed the American system, a view so shallow that it made no impression on me. A minority were able to get a few people to decide that we were fighting on the wrong side. They glorified Ho Chi Minh and the North Vietnamese communists. That was a view so far removed from the reality of the situation as to be absurd — or so I thought then and still do now. Meanwhile, they vilified the South Vietnamese government, in its various phases, as antidemocratic, dictatorial, to be despised. There was some truth in that, and there wasn't much that the Johnson, later the Richard Nixon, administration could or would do about it.

When we moved to New Orleans in 1971, I had become as much a foreign policy scholar as a military historian and had published a book entitled *Rise to Globalism: American Foreign Policy Since 1938*. In that book, as in my American history survey classes, I praised the country for its role in World War II and the Cold War. I had some special words of thanks to Franklin Roosevelt for having dumped Henry Wallace as Vice President in 1944 and replacing him with Senator Harry Truman. By the time of the Democratic convention in 1944, Roosevelt was a sick man who apparently knew he was going to die before finishing his fourth term, and he knew better than to hand over the presidency to the muddle-headed Wallace. Why he settled on Truman was something of a mystery to me. Apparently Roosevelt thought he needed the Democratic bosses, who were backing Truman, to win the election. America, and the whole world, benefited from his choice.

Almost everything President Truman did in foreign affairs I approve of. The Truman Doctrine of containment of Communism, the Berlin Air Lift, the Marshall Plan, NATO, the recognition of and support for Israel, the integration of American armed forces, rearming the American military, standing up to Senator Joseph McCarthy and his charges that the administration was riddled with communists, going to the support of South Korea when the nation was attacked by the communist North, firing General Douglas MacArthur when he wanted to take the war north of the Yalu River and attack the Chinese — all these and other Truman decisions and actions were criticized, in some cases denounced, and always aroused the opposition. He stuck to them. How lucky we were.

In Vietnam, American policy was to subordinate that country's politics and aspirations to the much larger Cold War context. More than American hubris, American racism, American attitudes toward former European colonies in

Asia, the key element in the American tragedy in Vietnam was in treating that country as a pawn of the Cold War. That began in 1945 and did not end until 1973.

In a 1970 press conference, Nixon was told by a reporter that some Americans believed the country was headed for revolution, while others thought that the violent demonstrations were leading to an era of repression. What did the President think?

Nixon was calm and reassuring: "This country is not headed for revolution." The right to dissent was being exercised across the country. With regard to repression, "That is nonsense . . . I do not see that the critics of my policies are repressed."

As a thirty-four-year-old professor, I agreed with both sides. This meant I was of no use in handing out advice or in attempting to get things to calm down. I wanted us out of Vietnam but not at the price of domestic peace and tranquillity, or of our freedoms. So I watched, helplessly. It was an awful feeling. It was an awful time.

When Pat Moynihan left Nixon's Cabinet on December 21, 1970, he praised Nixon for his "singular courage and compassion. To have seen him late into the night struggling with the most awful complexities, doing so because he cared, trying to comprehend what is right, and trying to make other men see it, above all caring." Eighteen years later I was interviewing Moynihan and Nixon speechwriter Bill Safire. I asked Senator Moynihan if he still regarded Nixon as good and honest and decent. He replied that what impressed him most about Nixon's leadership was what did not happen. The country was in danger of falling into something approaching anarchy, or civil war, when Nixon took office, according to Moynihan. Nixon, provoked though he was, stayed calm and managed to ride out the crisis. I asked Moynihan if he was exaggerating the threat to the Republic. He insisted that if anything he was understating it. Safire agreed.

This is an aspect of Nixon that few have seen, and even fewer have cared to. On January 4, 1971, Nixon was on a televised interview with representatives from the networks. Nancy Dickerson reminded him of his 1968 campaign call for "the lift of a driving dream." She wondered what had happened to that goal. He replied, "Before we can really get the lift of a driving dream we have to get rid of some of the nightmares we inherited. . . . If we can get this country thinking not of how to fight a war, but how to win a peace — if we can get this country thinking of clean air, clean water, open spaces, of a welfare reform program that will provide a floor under the income of every family with children in America, a new approach to government, reform of education, reform of health, if those things begin to happen, people can think of these positive things, and then we will have the lift of a driving dream. But it takes some time to get rid of the nightmares. You can't be having a driving dream when you are in the midst of a nightmare."

Nixon said he was ending the war. Many had a difficult time seeing how he was doing that. He could not win the war; he would not end the war; he refused to lose the war. He had put himself in the position of fighting a war while retreating from it without attempting to win it but refusing to admit that his country had lost it.

Three months later, on a radio interview, Nixon was asked about charges being made by prominent Americans that the country was in danger of becoming a police state. "Let me say I have been in police states," Nixon commented, "and the idea that this is a police state is just pure nonsense." He pointed out that in a real police state, "You can't talk in your bedroom. You can't talk in your sitting room. You don't talk on the telephone. You don't talk in the bathroom. You can't even talk in front a shrub. That is the way it works."

Of course he was right. The United States, during his presidency, could in no way be described as a police state. There was freedom to demonstrate, freedom of expression, freedom to work for a change in government. Sometimes not all of us recognized that, and not enough of us spoke up about the spirit of America, but it was true.

However — there is always a "however" when you are talking about Dick Nixon — it was also true that during his presidency you couldn't talk without being secretly tape-recorded in the Oval Office, or in the Executive Office Building (EOB), or in the Cabinet Room, or over the White House telephones.

In Vietnam, Nixon continued all-out support for the ARVN. He increased the number of American air strikes in the North, as he pulled out American ground troops. By November 1972 he had managed to reduce the American ground forces commitment from 550,000 to 20,000. More than any other single factor, it ensured his reelection.

Secret talks, meanwhile, had been going on between Secretary of State Henry Kissinger and North Vietnamese representative Le Duc Tho. After much wrangling, they finally agreed on a cease-fire document. On October 26, 1972, just in time for the election, Kissinger announced that "Peace is at hand." Nixon claimed that his policies had brought "peace with honor." Democratic candidate George McGovern's call for an immediate end to the war was undercut. More than 60 percent of the voters chose Nixon, the greatest victory in modern American electoral history.

Immediately after the election, the cease-fire was off. Nixon raised the price for peace. He demanded an ironclad guarantee that North Vietnam would not attack South Vietnam. Le Duc Tho refused and the North Vietnamese said they would not turn over the POWs they held so long as there was no agreement. Nixon responded with the so-called Christmas bombing campaign against Hanoi (actually there were no bombings on Christmas week). Hanoi quickly became the most heavily bombed city in the history of warfare. But for the Americans too, the price of war had gone up. The Air Force had fifteen B-52s and eleven fighter-bombers shot down by Soviet surface-to-air missiles. And there was worldwide condemnation of the bombing.

In January, in Washington, a new Congress was coming to office. The Democrats were in control, despite Nixon's big victory, and there were more doves than hawks. Nixon knew that the new Congress was going to cut off all funds for bombing. He therefore agreed to sign the original cease-fire, and it was done. On January 23, 1973, all active American participation in the war in Vietnam ended.

Nixon had ended up doing in Vietnam what McGovern had been advocating throughout the campaign — just get out.

The cease-fire in Vietnam quickly broke down. The battle raged on between North and South for two more years, until April 30, 1975, when the South Vietnamese government surrendered unconditionally. Johnson's and Nixon's (and Eisenhower's and Kennedy's) dire predictions about all the dominoes that were going to fall when Vietnam fell proved to be wrong. Within a year communist Vietnam was at war with communist Cambodia; by 1978 it was at war with China. But any doves who believed that the communists were agrarian reformers who only wanted to redistribute the land were in for a terrible shock. The Khmer Rouge communists instituted in Cambodia one of the most murderous regimes in the world's history; it was so bad, in fact, that Senator McGovern advocated military action by the United Nations in order to stop what was going on in Cambodia.

In Vietnam, meanwhile, tens of thousands tried desperately to get out, by any means possible. For all the faults of the Diem and Thieu regimes in Saigon, the city was a veritable paradise of free speech and assembly while they were in charge, as compared to what was happening under the communists. As Nixon noted with some satisfaction in 1978, no one was trying to break into communist Vietnam.

By 1975, America's long relationship with Asia, begun with the acquisition of the Philippines three quarters of a century earlier, had reached a divide. America had been involved in war in Asia for twenty-two of the thirty-four years between 1941 and 1975. Over 120,000 American men had died in combat there (41,000 in World War II, 33,000 in Korea, 46,000 in Vietnam) and 530,000 were wounded (130,000 in World War II, 100,000 in Korea, 300,000 in Vietnam). The ratio of combat deaths to wounds was much lower in Vietnam thanks to helicopter evacuation of the wounded and to magnificent progress in field medical techniques.

Americans had brought a lot of death and destruction to themselves and to the people of the Pacific world. The twentieth century began with much promise for the Americanizing mission in the Pacific; it ended with a mixed record of failure in Southeast Asia, but success elsewhere. Modern Japan is in many ways shaped and influenced by the American presence. On the Korean peninsula in the mid-1950s and after, the United States made South Korea a far more desirable place than North Korea — to paraphrase Nixon, no one since 1953 has ever tried to escape into North Korea. Civilians in Japan and South Korea paid an appallingly high price for their country's gains, but thanks to America's aid in restructuring their economies and politics they live free and prosperous lives today. Democracy is spreading elsewhere in Asia, and China is going capitalist in its economy.

# Chapter Eleven

## *Writing in and About America*

My first piece of historical writing never got published. It came about during my junior year at the University of Wisconsin, when Professor Hesseltine, in his course on the Civil War, told his students that we would not be doing a term paper, summarizing what we had read in four or five books. Instead, we would do a biography of a prominent Civil War Wisconsin resident — whether a soldier, doctor, teacher, farmer, businessman, lawyer, politician, whatever — that would be placed in the Wisconsin State Historical Society in a collection of Wisconsin biographies. We would, Hesseltine went on, not be repeating what others had discovered but instead making our own contribution to knowledge.

The words caught me up. I was nineteen. It had never occurred to me that I could make a contribution to knowledge. I picked Charles A. Billinghurst as my subject. Billinghurst was a two-term Republican representative in Congress, just before the Civil War. He was primarily interested in getting a railroad from Milwaukee to Minneapolis (which was done). He did nothing else of any note. I read his speeches in the newspapers; I read his letters in the State Historical Society; I wrote a twelve-page biography. When I handed it in, I had an immense feeling of pride. I knew more about Charles A. Billinghurst than anyone else alive! Then I realized that was because no one else wished to know. But then I further realized that if I could tell his story right, I could make them want to know.

Reading Billinghurst's letters in the Historical Society got me interested in other Civil War letters. Among those I read, the letters of James K. Newton stood out. Newton was the kind of person I admired in the war, a man I would have hoped to have been like. A schoolteacher, eighteen years old when the war began, he enlisted in the 14th Wisconsin Volunteer Infantry and stayed in the service until 1865, rising from private to lieutenant, fighting at Shiloh, Vicksburg, on the Red River, at Mobile, and elsewhere, traveling more than 5,000 miles. After the war he entered Ripon Academy in Wisconsin, then studied at Oberlin College in Ohio, where he remained as professor of French and German until 1888. In 1961 the University of Wisconsin Press published my edited version of his letters. The title was *A Wisconsin Boy in Dixie*.

It was my first book, even if only edited rather

than written, with a title that was prophetic. It was about an enlisted man who rose to be a junior officer. From Newton I began to learn what mattered to the common soldier. Personal and family matters, first of all — gossip from home, how are the crops doing, what is sister Sue up to, and so on. His own health, a subject of great importance to the Civil War soldier (sickness and disease claimed more lives than did bullets). The weather — and the incoming mail, or lack thereof — always subjects of the greatest importance to soldiers.

In my senior year at Madison, Hesseltine let me into his seminar. As this was his seminar for his Ph.D. candidates, getting into it as an undergraduate was a privilege and involved much hard work. The seminar met every Monday afternoon — I had to persuade the football coaches to excuse me from Monday practice so I could attend — and consisted of one student submitting a paper, usually a chapter, from his dissertation. Everyone else would read it, then criticize it at the seminar. Hesseltine encouraged us to go after each other like cats and dogs. He wrote his comments on our papers, using red ink usually. His remarks were sometimes humorous, usually insightful, frequently helpful, often scathing. Many times it seemed he wrote more in the way of comments than we had written in the paper.

First, I had to have a subject. All the others were well launched on their dissertations. I needed one that no one else had written about, and I wanted a biography, mainly because biography was Hesseltine's first choice for a subject. Always he lectured on people — his major undergraduate course was entitled "Representative Americans" — and he insisted that what interested people most was other people. What they did, in what circumstances, with what effect. He suggested Henry Wager Halleck, an 1839 graduate of West Point who had been Lincoln's chief of staff. What appealed to me most of all was that there was no biography of Halleck. I went to work, which consisted primarily of going through the *War of the Rebellion, Official Records of the Union and Confederate Armies*, a 128-volume government publication that contained the telegrams, reports, and other documents of both armies. I consulted many secondary sources, books by Civil War scholars, and newspapers and magazines and various manuscript collections of Halleck and his associates, but mainly I did my work in what is called the *O.R.*, or *Official Records*. This was pretty heavy stuff for a twenty-year-old undergraduate, but I stayed with it because it was heady. I was doing what no one had done, studying Halleck.

Following graduation, I went to Louisiana State University in Baton Rouge to study under T. Harry Williams and earn an M.A. in history. Williams had been Hesseltine's first Ph.D. student and had published *Lincoln and His Generals* (1952), which was a huge success and made him into one of the nation's top Civil War historians.

In his book, Williams had discussed the Union "command structure," which Hesseltine thought was a fraud. I had heard the two of them arguing about it and had wanted to participate, which was the biggest reason I had jumped at the chance to write about Halleck. I had heard Hesseltine's belief that to talk about a Civil War "command structure" was to impose World War II terminology and practice on the Civil War. Now I wanted to listen to Professor Williams. I continued my work on Halleck and argued with Williams, pressing Hesseltine's ideas, never convincing him. After a year at LSU, having completed my work on Halleck and earned my M.A. degree, I returned to Wisconsin.

Williams wanted me to stay at LSU for my Ph.D., and I was tempted. It was a much smaller department with far fewer graduate students. But I wanted to compete with the best, and the best were the graduate students in Madison, and I wanted to study with the best, and the best teachers (except Williams) were in Madison. All of the history graduate students thought Wisconsin was better than anyplace else, at least in American history, better than Harvard, Yale, Princeton, Michigan, Berkeley, wherever. We had Hesseltine, and they did not. We had Merrill Jensen, Howard Beale, many others, and in European history George Mosse, Mike Petrovich, and others. We had the Wisconsin State Historical Society Library, jammed with manuscript collections and documents, and a library of books to rival the Library of Congress. So it was back to Madison, where I stayed for two years, got my Halleck manuscript in shape to be submitted for publication, and worked on my dissertation topic, General Emory Upton, the second youngest Union general, and after the war the Army's leading intellectual.

Hesseltine's seminar was small, ten students, and, we at least believed, the most rigorous not only at Wisconsin but in the country. He was a famous mentor, but the number who earned their Ph.D. under his direction was tiny — one every two years. This was because he demanded that before he granted the degree, the student have his or her dissertation ready to send into the publisher.

Hesseltine made his system work. Those who received their Ph.D.'s from him invariably had their dissertations published within a year or so. Most of his students went on to receive the Pulitzer Prize for their second or third historical work. I was not one of them, but T. Harry Williams was, along with Kenneth Stamp, Frank Freidel, Benjamin Quarles, and others.

He was a great teacher of writing. He insisted on solid research, having something new to say, thinking through your topic, mastering the literature on the subject, and more, but above all else he insisted on good writing. He wasn't all that good a writer himself — acceptable, but not outstanding. Once, when he blasted my writing, I found a review of his book on Ulysses S. Grant's presidency that criticized his writing, brought it to his office, and asked, "What about this? How can you demand that I do better than you?"

He took his curved pipe out of his mouth, blew a smoke ring, swung his feet up on his desktop, patted himself on his fat tummy, chuckled, and said: "My boy, you have a better teacher than I did."

On another occasion I handed in the first chapter of my dissertation on Upton. I was Hesseltine's assistant, teaching what were called "quiz sections" and grading papers for his "Representative Americans" course, so I was in his office every day. Each day I would expect him to tell me that he had read my chapter and liked it so much that he had sent it off to the editor of the *American Historical Review*, telling him it should be the lead article in the next issue. But he said nothing.

After a week, I could take it no more, so I asked, "What about my chapter? Have you read it?" He chuckled and said yes. "Well?" I demanded.

"My boy," he began, "do you know that when I was on the farm back in Virginia, and a snake would sneak into the henhouse to eat some eggs, why I'd be sent to kill that snake. Then I would skin it and hang the skin on the henhouse door, to scare away all other snakes."

A long pause. What the hell did this have to do with my chapter on Upton? After a bit, he smiled again, pointed to the back of his office door, and said, "Look."

There was my chapter, nailed up on the door. Written sideways, scribbled across the pages, on the back of the pages, at the bottom and top, were his comments, all of which he summed up as, "Let that be a warning to you. Don't ever hand in a chapter like this again."

In 1960 I got a job at the fledgling Louisiana State University in New Orleans, as an instructor without Ph.D. — what I had was called an "ABD," or "all but dissertation," meaning I had passed all my examinations and completed the required course work but still had to have the dissertation completed and accepted. I continued to work on Upton, taught classes, began a family life. I would mail chapters of Upton to Hesseltine, and to Harry Williams, who served as my unofficial and much appreciated mentor. Hesseltine sent them back, full of his scathing comments. Williams sent his back, demanding better writing and more research. Even at the time I realized how lucky I was — a twenty five-year-old student with two of the greatest Civil War historians in America as my teachers.

I sent my M.A. thesis on Halleck to LSU Press in Baton Rouge; they sent the script around for expert reader's opinion; it passed, and in 1962 my first real book, not an edited collection, appeared as *Halleck: Lincoln's Chief of Staff*. It got some fair reviews, with some faint praise and a bit of criticism. It won no prizes and had a limited, at best, readership. But one of the readers made up for the absence of a prize or of a front-page, or any page, *New York Times Book Review* notice. He was Dwight D. Eisenhower. Two years after publication, he called me to Gettysburg to ask me to work on his papers, to be published by Johns Hopkins University. He said not a word about *Halleck*. I went to meet him and we talked for a few days about what would be involved in editing his papers. At one point, General Eisenhower said, "Son, you must have a lot of questions."

"Yes sir, I sure do," I replied. "But first of all, why me?" I was then twenty-eight years old.

He replied, "I read your book on *Halleck*."

So my first book was the book that changed my life. At the time I had finished Upton and had my degree, and was beginning to work on a history of West Point during the Civil War, fully intending to be a Civil War scholar for my career. But Eisenhower's invitation brought me overnight into World War II, and it came because of Halleck.

I was flattered that he had read the book, of course, but puzzled. I asked him why. He replied that he had been thinking of writing something about General George C. Marshall, the chief of staff in World War II, the same position Halleck held under Lincoln, because he was afraid that Marshall, who had held no field command, would be forgotten. So he had asked David Herbert Donald, a leading Civil War scholar, if there was a book on Halleck for him to read as he thought about doing something on Marshall (Forrest Pogue's magisterial biography of Marshall had not yet appeared). Donald recommended my book. Eisenhower told me that what had impressed him most, and led him to ask me to work on his papers, was its fairness.

I learned fairness from Hesseltine. He pounded into us, Do Not Write Editorials. Leave the editorials to the newspaper editors. An editorial is meant to persuade. In its way it is like a political speech. History is not. It is an account of what happened, and why, in a context that contains many different points of view. History is conflict, and you cannot have conflict without varying legitimate perspectives. So I've always tried to be fair to my subjects. That is easy enough when they are as likable and admirable as Lewis and Clark, or Eisenhower; it becomes more difficult when they are as disparate as Crazy Horse and Custer, or as hard to like as Richard Nixon. Anyway, what mattered in 1964 was that Eisenhower thought I had been fair to Halleck in my treatment of his role in the Civil War.

The first sentence of the book is my own, but the thought of having a dramatic or at least a striking opening came from Hesseltine, who insisted that you must grab your reader right away. It reads, "His story is the story of the Civil War." That stretches things a bit and I doubt that I would write it quite that way again, but the text goes on to explain: "His hand shaped strategy in every theater of the war. No man on either side took part in more campaigns." I then quote some of his admirers — most of all Ulysses S. Grant, who said, "He is a man of gigantic intellect and well studied in the profession of arms." Then I quote his detractors, such as Secretary of the Navy Gideon Welles, who wrote in his diary that "his [Halleck's] being at Headquarters is a national misfortune," and another general who characterized him as "heavy headed, originates nothing, anticipates nothing, takes no responsibility, plans nothing, suggests nothing, is good for nothing."

What could I learn from such a man? Quite a lot, actually. He was called "Old Brains" because he was the Army's leading intellectual, the author of *Elements of Military Art and Science* (1841), used as a textbook at West Point. President Lincoln read it during the Civil War and it was widely distributed to amateur officers. Through Halleck, I learned about Civil War strategy, how it was made and how carried out. I also learned about the growth of a national, professional army at the expense of the state militia systems, and about the beginnings of a modern command system.

Halleck held only one field command, and then only for a couple of months. He fought no battles. Hesseltine rather liked this about Halleck. Williams was impatient; he wanted generals who got out there and fought, and that wasn't Halleck. In his seminar at LSU Williams would chide me on Halleck, who never seemed to do anything. Once he queried me sharply, "And what did Halleck do?" I began to reply: "He wrote a telegram to Lincoln —" Williams pounced: "That's all he ever did, write. He never fought."

Although he was scornful, that was a good description of Williams. He had been in the Illinois National Guard before World War II, but due to physical problems he was not in combat. Neither was Hesseltine, come to that; he was too young for World War I, too old for the next war. It was also true of me — I was too young for Korea and too old for Vietnam. Our attraction to military history did not flow from our experience, but from our feeling that the key events in American history were military. Winning the Revolutionary War, or the Civil War, or World War II were the turning points in our history, the sine qua non of our forward progress, and we felt that understanding how victory was achieved was the most important thing we could know.

Personality clashes, not just between my professors, but between the generals, were a central feature of my Halleck study. It was a lesson I carried with me in all subsequent books, whether about soldiers or politicians or businessmen. At one point in 1862 Halleck saved William T. Sherman from being discharged from the Army. At another point he almost got Ulysses S. Grant dismissed, when on March 4, 1862, he telegraphed Washington, "A rumor has just reached

235

me that since the taking of Fort Donelson General Grant has resumed his former bad habits." That meant just one thing — Grant was drinking again. But Halleck relented and kept Grant in command. Grant was in charge at Shiloh. Secretary of War Edwin Stanton told Halleck after the battle that Grant had been drunk and was thus the cause of the Confederate surprise and the consequent heavy Union casualties. Halleck stood up for Grant, replying: "A great battle cannot be fought or a victory gained without many casualties. The enemy suffered more than we did."

In World War II, George Marshall had Halleck's Civil War position, much expanded but still with many similarities. They had charge of logistics, the movements of armies, and strategy. It was also their task to explain elementary tactics and military maneuvers to the civilians, and to keep the generals fighting on the same side rather than against each other. Because he had had to keep Field Marshal Bernard Law Montgomery and General George S. Patton on the rails and working together, Eisenhower found he could identify with Halleck and his problems.

My first book was not very well written, about a general who was far from the action, managing rather than leading. Still, Halleck played a critical role. From studying and writing about him, I learned there is much more to war than shouting "Charge!" or "Follow me!" And, in what still seems to me to be a miracle of sorts, I managed to impress General Eisenhower.

I completed my dissertation in 1963 and it met Hesseltine's standards. LSU Press published it in 1964 with the title of *Upton and the Army*. Unfortunately, Hesseltine died that year from a heart attack — a blow to his colleagues; his students, graduates and undergraduates; and his readers.

Upton, an 1861 graduate of West Point, was a combat veteran who covered himself with honors, rising by the age of twenty-five to major general. After the Civil War, he remained in the Army, where he served as Commandant of Cadets at West Point. He went to Europe as an observer of the Franco-Prussian War, then on a tour of Asia. He called his first book *The Armies of Asia and Europe* (1878). He wrote other military books, including Infantry Tactics, which was adopted at West Point and by the state militias and brought in $3,000 a year in royalties, and *The Military Policy of the United States*, which he did not finish before his death in 1881 but which was finally published by Secretary of War Elihu Root in 1904. Root used Upton's work as the basis for his sweeping reforms in the War Department, bringing it into the twentieth century. In a sense Upton was Halleck's successor as the Army's intellectual.

Upton appealed to me for that reason, and for his fighting record in the Civil War. Another reason was that he had attended Oberlin College before his appointment to West Point, when Oberlin was the only integrated college in the country. He was a cadet at the time of John Brown's raid. The incident caused much disruption in the cadet corps. Wade Hampton Gibbes of South Carolina made some offensive remarks about Upton's supposed intimate association with Negroes at Oberlin. Upton demanded an explanation. Gibbes refused to give one. They had a duel, with swords, that night — Upton suffered a facial cut that left a permanent scar on his upper right cheek.

My opening sentence of my second book read, "He was the epitome of a professional soldier." I went on: "Courageous to the point of recklessness, Emory Upton always went into battle at the head of his column. Devoted to his duty . . . dedicated to his profession . . . a reformer." Those are characteristics I've found in many Army officers and all the best ones.

Upton committed suicide at forty-two years of age. Two years after my biography appeared in print, my wife, the former Judy Dorlester, whom I had met and married in Madison, committed suicide. She left me with two children, Stephenie and Barry, ages seven and five. By then I was working at Johns Hopkins University in the History Department and as associate editor of the Eisenhower Papers. Shortly after Judy's death, I met Moira Buckley. She lived down the street and had three children, Andrew, Grace, and

Hugh. Andy was four years old, Grace two, and Hugh an infant. Her husband had just left her.

We took one look and fell in love. Moira got a divorce and we married. I adopted her kids, she adopted mine. For thirty-five years we have lived happily together, raised our kids, enjoyed each other, our family, and life.

At Hopkins, I taught two courses, the American history survey and the Civil War, put in three full days a week editing the Eisenhower Papers under the direction of Dr. Alfred DuPont Chandler, and worked the remainder of my time on my own book, a history of West Point. By this time I had done research in libraries scattered across the country and thus a special appeal of West Point was that I could do most of the research in documentary sources close to Baltimore, either in Washington at the Library of Congress and the National Archives or at West Point in the library there.

There was another factor. Although my Ph.D. was in American history, my first two books were about Civil War generals and I was being labeled a military historian. I didn't mind that, in fact was rather pleased by it, but I knew that most of my fellow academic historians were scornful of military history. They thought that all military historians did in their research and writing was "bang-bang," that we were all hopeless right-wingers, that in no way should we be taken seriously in a profession that emphasized politics, science, business, education, labor history, and other serious matters. I thought that by doing a history of West Point, I could keep my hand in on military history while getting involved in educational history. So I decided to study West Point in order to become respectable in my profession.

I asked General Eisenhower to write a foreword to my book. He agreed. What he emphasized was that "West Point gives its graduates something that far transcends the techniques and knowledge involved in developing, training, and leading an army. It helps them build character, integrity." This is also what I found to be true of West Point — character is its overriding concern. It is not like that in civilian colleges, certainly not the ones I attended. I have written about many West Point graduates, and know many more. The quality they all have in common is character.

On completion of *Duty, Honor, Country: A History of West Point* (1966), I went to work full-time on editing Eisenhower's papers and writing about his life. With some breaks to do shorter books, my research and writing about Eisenhower continued for more than two decades.

In my first meeting with Eisenhower, when he told me he had selected me to work on his papers because of the Halleck book, he added, "Son, you ought to get some articles out of this work." I had not anticipated that he would say anything like that, but he had been a university president (at Columbia) after all, and he knew what made things buzz in the academic world. Obviously privileged access to Dwight Eisenhower's wartime papers, and the opportunity to interview him about them, would provide material for scores of articles.

I had been reading Eisenhower's memoirs of the war. What struck me most was his quoting his parents, who always told him, he wrote, that "America is the land of opportunity. Reach out and seize it."

I figured this was my chance, so when Eisenhower said there were many potential article subjects in his career, I didn't stop to think but just blurted out, "General, I'm hoping to write your biography, not just a couple of articles."

He smiled and said he would help me in every way he could. And so I went at his papers and began gathering material for his biography.

In the first decade of my Eisenhower work, 1964–1973, the Vietnam War was raging. I thank God that I was where I was. I was antiwar to such a degree that without the balance of Eisenhower and his associates I might well have slipped into the pit that many doves fell into — blaming the United States for everything that went wrong here and abroad. But it was impossible to be with Eisenhower, often on a weekly basis, for the first five years of the war without learning to respect and honor our country. I learned, too, from his associates, when he was in the Army and when he was President.

I interviewed General Andrew Jackson Goodpaster, who was Eisenhower's staff secretary in the White House, when he was Superintendent at West Point and later. He was about as fine a man as anyone could ever know. So too Omar Bradley and many others, including Alfred D. Chandler, an outstanding historian. He taught me a lot about my craft. Most of all, these men and others made me aware of what great men America had, how much of themselves they gave to the nation, what they did to make their nation what it is. Without the calm, steadying influence of the men who worked with Eisenhower, I don't like to think of what might have happened to me during the Vietnam War.

From that first meeting in 1964 down to today, I thought Dwight Eisenhower was a great and good man. All those who knew him, including some of the most powerful men in the world, liked him immensely, some to the point of adulation.

He had the clearest blue eyes. He would fix them on you. I was a youngster. In my every interview with him, he would lock his eyes on to mine and keep them there for the two-three-four-hour interview. He concentrated on what I wanted to talk about. He would laugh that big, gutsy laugh, twinkle, grin, frown, get red in the face when he got mad, tell me anecdotes about this man or that event. We never discussed politics.

He worried about me. Where would I eat on

the drive from Baltimore to Gettysburg? I would mumble something, but he stayed with it. He warned me against this or that restaurant, saying that he had stopped there and could not recommend it. One diner where he went for breakfast had this short-order cook. He sat at the counter (this was before JFK's assassination so the former President Eisenhower had no Secret Service guards). The cook had a cold, and as she prepared his scrambled eggs, she was dripping from her nose onto the eggs. So don't go there, he warned.

As I interviewed him we had maps — North Africa, Italy, England, France, and Northwest Europe — spread in front of us. He cursed like the lifetime soldier he was — never sexual words, but damn, hell, Christ Almighty, sometimes a goddamn. I mentioned this to historian Forrest Pogue once, and Forrest said, "That shows he trusts you. He knows you will clean up his language." After that, I always did.

One afternoon, when four P.M. came, an aide came into his office to say that the editors from Doubleday were there, to go over his White House memoirs with him. He had his tie down, his jacket off, his shirtsleeves rolled up. We were deep into the Battle of Kasserine Pass (February 1943) and his talk was full of colorful expletives. "Tell them they will just have to wait," he said without taking his eyes off the map.

Ten minutes later, the same scene. Twenty minutes later, he told me I would have to go. I nodded and began packing up my tape recorder, gathering the maps. The Doubleday editors walked in. As they did so, I saw Eisenhower pull up his tie, button his top shirt button, roll down and button his sleeves, and slip on his jacket. He began talking to the editors and to my astonishment all the curse words disappeared from his vocabulary. In front of my eyes, he had changed from being a soldier caught in the mud of North Africa to President of the United States.

I wrote a book entitled *Eisenhower and Berlin, 1945* about Eisenhower's 1945 decision to halt at the Elbe River instead of continuing east to capture Berlin. It was the most controversial decision he made during the war. Pretty much forgotten today, with Germany united and the Wall torn down, it was constantly cited and criticized from the late 1940s to the late 1960s. If Eisenhower had taken Berlin, the argument ran, the city would not have been divided, there might not have been a division of Germany into East and West, and the Cold War in Europe would have taken a different course. All this was nonsense, I knew from my daily, weekly, monthly immersion in Eisenhower's papers, so I welcomed the chance to set the story straight. It was a small book (119 pages) on an important subject and it had an impact. Eisenhower read and approved of it.

What I said — that Eisenhower could not have gotten to Berlin before the Red Army, that Franklin Roosevelt, who according to some of his critics was a communist, did not order Eisenhower to bypass Berlin so that the Soviets could take it, that what Eisenhower did when he sent his armies north to the Danish border and south into Austria was a correct decision — has been generally accepted today by most people.

For the next three years I annotated Eisenhower's wartime letters, telegrams, directives, memos, speeches — the kind of thing an editor does. Meanwhile I was writing my account of his war years — not a biography but an examination of Eisenhower from December 1941 to May 1945. *The Supreme Commander: The War Years of General Dwight D. Eisenhower* was a big book — 732 pages, with more than 2,000 footnotes. I opened it thus: "This is the story of a soldier. It is told in his terms. . . . My hope is that it conveys some sense of the magnitude of the task Eisenhower undertook and met, a feeling for the extraordinary charm and deep integrity of the man, a conception of the way in which he operated, a recognition of the manner in which he weighed alternatives, made decisions, and saw to the enforcement of his orders, and some understanding as to the way his decisions affected the outcome of the war."

I had the best help any World War II historian could ever desire. Chandler to start with, then Forrest Pogue, who read the entire manuscript and gave me the benefit of his great knowledge, and Sir Ian Jacob of the British Chiefs of Staff, who read the manuscript and allowed me to use his diary. That is something I've always encountered in my writing: that the people who were associated with your subject or are knowledgeable about him or it are not just willing but eager to help. Scholarship, at its best, knows no jealousies. Scholars do not try to hide what they have discovered — they want other people, especially their fellow scholars, to know it too. People like Chandler or Pogue do not become scholars to make money. Their goal is to learn and share. That is just as true of Hesseltine and Williams and many others. I've made such men my models.

My two-volume biography of Eisenhower was different from *The Supreme Commander*, because in it I discussed his personal life, his relationship with his parents, his brothers, his friends, Mamie and his son John, his associates. None of them had seemed important to me when I was covering his war career, but they were to him and thus became so to me. Even more, I learned how to write in scenes because he was involved in, usually at the center of, many events. They did not happen all at once. Some of them, such as his relationship with other generals; or with the British; or with the Army Air Force; or with his secretary, Kay Summersby; or John Eisenhower; or George Marshall; and so many others, happened over long stretches of time and had to be split up.

This was even more true of his presidency. Relations with foreign powers stretched over all eight years. Elections happened every two years. Race relations were always important, always changing. They too had to be written in scenes. In presenting what happened in a chronological manner, I learned about the demands made on a five-star general in a world war, or on an American President during the Cold War. It was a process of discovery.

Eisenhower had maxims that he often quoted and lived by. He said he learned early on in the war to save all his doubts about forthcoming operations for his pillow. He wrote his son John, then at West Point, "The only quality that can be developed by studious reflection and practice is the leadership of men." He asserted, "Never question another man's motives. His wisdom, yes, but not his motives." In his view, "Extremes to the right and to the left of any political dispute are always wrong." In his Farewell Address as President, he asserted, "We — you and I, and our government — must avoid plundering for our own ease and convenience, the precious resources of tomorrow. We cannot mortgage the material assets of our grandchildren without risking the loss also of their political and spiritual heritage. We want democracy to survive for all ages to come."

It is for these and other reasons that Eisenhower is my choice as the American of the twentieth century. Of all the men I've studied and written about, he is the brightest and the best.

# Chapter Twelve

## *War Stories*

## Crazy Horse and Custer
## and Pegasus Bridge

I spent the academic year 1969–70 at the Naval War College in Newport, Rhode Island, where I was the Ernest J. King Professor of Maritime History. This was the height of the Vietnam War. Many of the students — generally Navy commanders and captains, Army and Air Force majors and colonels — were just back from Vietnam, the others were on their way. (One of them was Major John M. Shalikashvili, who wrote his thesis under my direction and went on to become U.S. Army Chief of Staff.) I learned from them far more than I taught about the modern American military in general and the war in Vietnam in particular.

I taught a class, conducted a seminar, gave lectures to the entire student body, and wrote *Rise to Globalism: American Foreign Policy Since 1938*. It was the ideal place to write a book on World

War II and the Cold War, both because of the outstanding library and because the men of the faculty and student body had been in one or both of the wars. My early condemnation of American policy at the beginning of the Cold War, in Korea, and in Vietnam gave way to a more realistic appraisal of what the Soviet Union was up to and the behavior and consequences of international communism. Over the years I've done several updates, and find that each time, I praise the United States more, and find even less excuse for Soviet behavior. By the 1970s I was calling the Soviet leaders the heads of a criminal conspiracy, this before Ronald Reagan was calling the Soviet Union, correctly, an evil empire.

I was late to the conclusion, far behind most political and some intellectual leaders, but ahead of many of my fellow professors. In 1970 I was a speaker at a banquet for the Navy War College students. I talked about Eisenhower and the Second World War. Time for questions from the audience. The first man stood up. He was an Army officer. He said, "I'd just like to thank you. It's grand to know that there still is at least one professor in the United States who is patriotic." I blushed, then said that there were many more than me.

Years later, I had to wonder. In 1996 I taught a course on World War II at the University of Wisconsin. The auditorium was filled with students sitting in the aisles. At the conclusion of the course, some forty lectures long, a young woman student came up to me to say, "You are the first professor I've had in four years in Madison to teach me the meaning and value of patriotism." I like to think that Ike would have nodded his approval.

In 1971, I spent the summer in the Black Hills of South Dakota with my family, which led to a book entitled *Crazy Horse and Custer: The Parallel Lives of Two American Warriors*. It was an exhilarating book to write, and relatively easy, as I already knew something about Custer's childhood in Ohio, not that much different from mine in Wisconsin a century later, and about Custer's West Point training and about his Civil War role and his professional life in the Army after the war. Crazy Horse I had to learn about, but there were some good books out on him and the Sioux, and I could camp with my family at his campgrounds, ride over his battle sites, and otherwise do my best to get in touch with him.

Fort Abraham Lincoln is across the Missouri River from Bismarck, North Dakota, where Custer had his headquarters and where he set off in 1876 to go after Crazy Horse (there is a sign at the North Dakota–Montana border that reads, "Custer Was Healthy When He Left North Dakota"). Pompeys Pillar, downstream on the Yellowstone River, outside Billings, Montana, is where Crazy Horse and Custer stood and fought a skirmish; Crazy Horse failed in his attempt to lure Custer into an ambush. The Fort Fetterman battle site is in Wyoming. Camp Robinson, Nebraska, is where Crazy Horse was killed. We camped at various Indian reservations and pow-wows, and for long stretches at the Little Big Horn.

My children helped me look for Crazy Horse and Custer. At the end of every day of writing I made Moira stop what she was doing at six P.M. and sit back and listen as I read aloud that day's outpouring.

The book brought the finest praise I've ever received. Indians, some of them in prison after the incident at Wounded Knee, North Dakota, wrote to tell me that no one had ever written so honestly about a Plains Indian. White men, Custer buffs of all kinds and types and ages who are devoted to Custer, wrote to tell me that I had got him right.

It forced me to deal with a question, Which man would I rather have been? I never came up with a satisfactory answer, mainly because I liked each man, in his own way, almost without stint. Their lives appealed to my romantic impulses. Life on the Great Plains, or in the Indian-fighting Army, had its obvious appeal — unlimited horseback riding across the unfenced prairie, leading men into battle, an unchecked male chauvinism, hunting to their heart's content.

But there were profound differences. The culture Custer came from was inventive and progressive. Never satisfied with the present, it lived for the future. It had an almost manic desire to reach out and overwhelm nature, to force it to submit, to exploit it. When Custer looked on a virgin forest, he envisioned sawmills, planks rolling out of them, houses being built, farms cleared of trees, carefully cultivated. Crazy Horse saw the trees as they were at that moment, noting an immediate use for the saplings as lodge or travois poles, casting a practiced eye over the scene to calculate what animals lived where in that particular forest.

Custer saw history sequentially, events marching forward in a recognizable order, with cause and effect being known and understood, leading ever onward and upward. Crazy Horse saw history as integrated in the present, incorporated into daily life. Custer had dead heroes. Crazy Horse had only live ones.

Crazy Horse believed that he was connected to all that there was, the earth, the sky, the sun and moon, the plants and animals, even the insects, and his ancestors, known not in any collective detail but present nevertheless — everything was part of *Wakan Tanka*, the Great Spirit. Custer saw himself as distinct from, and superior to, everything — most of all, the animals and even some of his fellow human beings, namely blacks and Indians.

An important difference between the two men was their mood. Custer was never satisfied with where he was. He always aimed to go on to the next higher station in his society, always in a state of *becoming*. Crazy Horse accepted the situations he found himself in and aimed only to be a brave and respected Sioux warrior, which by the time he was a young adult he had been, was then, and would be. He was in a state of *being*.

As to which of these guys I would rather be, I can't say.

In 1981 I began leading an annual two-week tour called "In Eisenhower's Footsteps from D-Day to the Rhine." Forrest and Christine Pogue came with us, along with many other veterans, sons and grandsons of veterans, interested people, about forty altogether. We stopped at Pegasus Bridge, over the Orne River canal outside Caen in Normandy, where British gliders landed shortly after midnight on June 6, 1944, to begin the battle. We examined the bridge, still intact, studied the landing places of the gliders, looked around, and began boarding up for the drive to Paris, with a stop at La Roche-Guyon, German Commander Erwin Rommel's headquarters. We were late, as usual, so I was hurrying people. When they were all on board, I began to climb into the bus. A white-haired man, leaning on a cane, stopped me and asked, "I say, are any of you chaps from the British 6th Airborne Division?"

"No, sir," I replied, "we're all Americans on this bus."

"Oh, I'm sorry," he said.

"Don't be sorry," I answered. "We're all rather proud to be Americans. Were you in the 6th Airborne?"

"I was indeed," he replied. "I'm Major John Howard."

I knew that John Howard had commanded the glider-borne company that had seized the bridge where we were standing, that he had performed one of the great feats of arms of the Second World War. I shook his hand vigorously and expressed something of the thrill and honor I felt at meeting him.

"Would your chaps like to hear a word or two about what happened here?" he asked.

Indeed we would. I got "my chaps," their wives and children, off the bus. We gathered around Major Howard, who stood on the embankment, his back to the bridge. He told his story so well that we were all overwhelmed. The next year he came back at my invitation, and again in 1983. As the bus pulled out that year, en route to Paris, he stood in front of the Gondree Café, the first building in France to be liberated, and snapped into a salute. I was standing in the aisle, next to Forrest Pogue. I asked Forrest if anyone had ever written up the story of Pegasus Bridge. "No," he replied. "Why don't you do it?"

I had a sabbatical coming that fall and Moira and I spent the semester in London, interviewing John and a couple dozen of his veterans. Among other things I got to know England and

Wales, traveling on railroads. At John's invitation we went to Normandy and rented a car, then drove to Hamburg to interview Hans von Luck, the man who had commanded the opposing forces. I didn't want to do it — I told John I did not want to meet German officers. He said he and Hans had become good friends. At the bridge they got together each year to talk about the action. They visited each other in their homes.

Hans came to my hotel in Hamburg. Our appointed meeting time was four P.M. As he was a Prussian officer I knew he would come at precisely the time agreed upon, and at four P.M., not a second earlier or a second later, there was a knock at the door. He was seventy-two years old, with a weathered face, deeply lined. Although he wore a business suit, it took only the slightest imagination to see him in his uniform, buttoned to the high stiff collar, his Knight's Cross around his neck, a German officer's hat set back on his head, his goggles in place, the dust of North Africa covering him.

He had maps and reports. We ordered coffee brought to the room. He lit up a Marlboro Light cigarette, which I discovered he chain-smoked. He began talking immediately and the next time I looked at my watch it was seven P.M. We went out to dinner, then began again in the morning — a twelve-hour session — and the next morning, and the next. Hans had led his reconnaissance battalion to the English Channel in 1940, under Rommel's command. Then he led the way into Russia in 1941, actually going farther east than any other German officer, across the Leningrad–Moscow canal. Then to North Africa, then posted back to France to set up defenses, under Rommel, in Normandy. He fought the Americans throughout France, then was sent to the Eastern Front, where he was captured in May 1945. Off to a slave labor camp in the Caucasus until 1950, when he was allowed to come home.

It wasn't just how amazing his wartime career had been; it was the way he told of his adventures that left me stunned. He wasn't making any of it up; he just wanted to get his actions down on paper. He spoke with great modesty. He was an old-world aristocrat, his manner and bearing impeccable. In twenty-five years of interviewing veterans of World War II, I had never heard war stories so well told.

I urged him to write his memoirs. He thought there would not be much of a market in Germany for any book of World War II memoirs. I convinced him to write in English, certain there was a market in the United States. He did and the book got such rave reviews that he translated it into German (he is one of the few men I've known who could do that), where it was also successful.

German generals march through his pages — including Albert Kesselring, Alfred Jodl, Heinz Guderian. The dominant personality is Field

Marshal Erwin Rommel. But the real hero of the book is the German soldier. Hans's troops never let him down. They were remarkable for their endurance, tenacity, boldness, comradeship, and loyalty.

Before meeting Hans I knew no German officers and did not want to know any; he changed my mind. Hans and I became close friends. Over the next two decades we visited each other at our homes in the States and in Germany, at Pegasus Bridge and in Paris. I got him to spend a summer in Innsbruck, Austria, at the University of New Orleans summer school; the students reacted to Hans as I had.

John Howard came to Innsbruck for a week and together with my class we took a Thursday afternoon train to Paris, then on to Normandy on Saturday morning. John and Hans talked to the students at Pegasus Bridge. That night we ended up in a cheap wine bar, knocking back Calvados, exchanging stories, getting drunk. One of the female students midway through the drinking session came up to Hans to say, "God how I wish you were twenty years younger!" A couple of drinks later, she came again: "God how I wish you were ten years younger!" At the end of the Calvados, she grabbed him to say, "I don't care how old you are!" and planted a big kiss on him. John Howard suffered through an almost identical scene.

It was 1988. Hans had completed his manuscript of his wartime memoirs, and brought it with him so that we could go over it together. "He writes just the way he talks," was Moira's final judgment. Hans called it *Panzer Commander: The Memoirs of Colonel Hans von Luck* in English; in German he named it *Gefangener meiner Zeit: Ein Stuck Weges mit Rommel* (*A Prisoner of My Time*). The Military Book Club made it an immediate main selection.

My book that came out of all these interviews was called *Pegasus Bridge: June 6, 1944*. It was based on interviews with John Howard, Hans von Luck, a couple dozen British veterans of John's company, plus three or four of his superiors; and ten or so German veterans who fought with Hans, plus a few of his superiors. In British Columbia I spent three days interviewing John's glider pilot, Sergeant Jim Wallwork. According to Air Chief Marshal Trafford Leigh-Mallory, Wallwork was the man who performed "the greatest feat of flying in World War II." I met all sorts of British characters — Corporal Wally Parr, for one, a Cockney with a split-your-sides sense of humor, and many others. I met German characters — farmers from Bavaria, city youngsters from Berlin. It was my introduction to the British and German armies in World War II. My respect for all of them shot up. My respect for the American fighting men did not go down, but I did realize that other countries could also produce superb fighting men.

I was a sort of Boswell to the two old soldiers, John and Hans. I was almost twenty years younger, young enough to have been their son. I had no combat experience. They told me what I needed to know. They liked that I cared and paid attention. I liked that they wanted to share their experiences with me.

# Chapter Thirteen

# Writing About Nixon

Richard Milhous Nixon had been involved in national politics since 1946, when he was elected as a representative to Congress from Orange County, California. In 1950 he won election to the United States Senate. In 1952 he was the successful Republican candidate for Vice President, again in 1956. In 1960 he was the Republican candidate for President, when he was defeated by John Kennedy. In 1962 he ran for Governor of California, against Democratic incumbent Pat Brown, and lost. In 1968 he was the Republican candidate for the presidency, which he won, and won again in 1972. He resigned his office in 1974. So the year I turned ten years old, he went into Congress, and except for 1961 to 1968, he held elected office in Washington until 1974, when I turned thirty-eight.

If you lived in California from 1946 to 1972, you almost always had a chance to vote for Nixon, and millions did, in the elections of 1946, 1948, 1950, 1952, 1956, 1960, 1962, 1968, and 1972. He was nominated by the Republican Party for national office on five occasions ('52, '56, '60, '68, '72) and he won four of those elections. An astonishing, even breathtaking, record. In four elections, Franklin D. Roosevelt got 103.3 million votes; in five elections, twice as vice presidential candidate, Richard M. Nixon got 178.4 million votes. Despite being the all-time champion in getting people to vote for him for President or Vice President, Nixon regarded himself as having been cheated by life.

He never got my vote. I was too young in 1952 and 1956. By 1960 I had turned against him. He appeared to me to be a politician who would always lie to advance his personal cause, a man who believed in nothing but himself. As I felt more or less the same about his opponent, Senator John Kennedy, in 1960 I could not bring myself to vote.

In the summer of 1983, when I was at our cabin in the wilds of northernmost Wisconsin writing the last chapter of my Eisenhower biography, my editor at Simon & Schuster called. This was kind of amazing by itself, as until that July we had never had a telephone at the cabin. If I absolutely had to contact somebody, I'd drive or bike to the local sportsman's bar, Trout Haven, some six or seven miles away, and call from the pay phone. This being Wisconsin it was awfully noisy, between the fishermen lying about their catch, the pool sharks shooting pool, the jukebox playing so couples could dance. But just before the S&S editor called, we had installed a telephone at our cabin, and added electric lights, a radio, and an honest-to-God refrigerator, not an icebox.

Her call may have been the first one on that phone. In any event it was exciting. I grabbed the receiver, went outside to close the door on the cord and shut out the noise of the radio (all country music), and said yes, this was indeed me, and what did she want?

She said that for my next book she wanted me to write a biography of Richard Nixon.

"Oh, I can't do that," I exclaimed immediately. "He is such a despicable person. It was about nine or ten years ago that we all felt we had finally gotten him out of our lives, and here you want me to write about him."

"Indeed," she said.

"I don't even like the guy. How on earth do you expect me to spend five, seven, eight years with someone I don't like? Get somebody else."

"We want you to do it."

"I can't and won't. I've got lots of books I want to write. Nixon isn't one of them."

She threw out her net, began to pull it in, and caught me. "Where else," she asked, "can you find a bigger challenge?"

I wasn't so much hooked as trapped. So I went to work.

I went into the project convinced that every American either hated or loved Nixon, that there was no neutral ground. Even before Watergate and his resignation, Nixon had inspired conflicting and passionate emotions. I recall one occasion in the summer of 1970. A middle-aged man and I got into a discussion of politics. He said something admiring about President Nixon. I replied that I thought Nixon was the worst President we had ever had, save only perhaps Andrew Johnson. He said he thought Nixon was the best President ever. We did not know each other, we were not trying to sell anything, we just felt a need to express our feelings. After we had done so we turned and walked angrily away from each other. In 1973 Watergate exacerbated those feelings to a remarkable degree.

On August 8, 1974, Moira and I were visiting my father in Whitewater, Wisconsin. That evening Richard Nixon came on national radio and television. We anticipated a resignation announcement. The expectation made it impossible for my father and me to be together, as we had such different feelings about the man. My father was a strong Nixon supporter and had been since the Alger Hiss case. Moira had worked for Nixon in the 1960 campaign but after 1968 she had withdrawn her support because of his failure to end the Vietnam War. I was and had been for twenty-eight years a Nixon critic. So that evening, and again the following morning as Nixon said good-bye to his Cabinet and staff, I went out in the driveway to listen on the car radio, while Moira listened on the kitchen radio, and Dad watched on the television in the living room.

Nine years later, to my own surprise, I embarked on a biography of Richard Nixon. Simon & Schuster thought they were going to get a one-volume biography, but when I said I couldn't possibly do justice to Nixon in one volume, the firm reluctantly agreed to two volumes. When I finally informed my publisher that it would have to be three volumes, as he was in the center stage of national and world politics for almost three decades, had been involved in so many earth-shaking events, that I needed more room, the firm even more reluctantly agreed. My editor told me that the first volume would outsell the two that followed, by quite a bit. I said I didn't care; if I was going to do Nixon I wanted to make it as good a book as I could, and that required space.

*Nixon* is by quite a bit the longest book I've ever written and it took the longest time — almost a full decade. But it is not my best book. How could it be, given the subject? It wasn't that he was a prince, or pure evil. Historian Richard Reeves, in his fine book *President Nixon: Alone in the White House*, calls him brilliant but severely handicapped. Many people saw him one way or another, but in life he was so full of contradictions that it would take a Shakespeare to understand him. I can't make a man who does strange things into either a hero or a villain. I can, and do, tell readers what he did, with what effect, but most of the time I'm damned if I can tell why he did it. I hope this approach makes for good history; I know it does not make for compelling biography.

I completed the manuscript for volume one in 1986, two years after signing a contract. I often get asked, How on earth do you write such big books so fast? (*Nixon: The Education of a Politician, 1913–1962*, is 752 pages long, with some 2,320 footnotes.) There is no secret. You do it by working hard, six to ten hours per day, six or seven days a week. The book, whatever the subject, consumes you. I get up in the morning and can't wait to get back to the typewriter (or later, the computer) to pick up the story again. Only from the documents that I find in my research (letters, reports, and newspapers, to name a few) can I figure out what happened next, and why, with what results.

Although I never shook hands with my subject and of course never interviewed him, I learned a great deal in my time working on him, not only about Nixon and/or the Republican Party, but about my country. When I was working on Eisenhower in the 1960s and 1970s, I did a great deal of interviewing, first of all with the general and then with most of the men who had been his subordinates or assistants. They were men about my father's age, born around the turn of the century or close to it. They wore three-piece suits, usually dark, with a tie, highly polished shoes, garter belts, a handkerchief in the breast pocket. Except in an all-male locker room atmosphere, they never cursed. They were what we used to call "rock-ribbed Republicans." So was my dad. They told the truth, always, even when it hurt. They had an iron will. They guided America through the Second World War and in the 1950s into the modern age. That was Eisenhower's world, one that I was privileged to see as a citizen and then get to know as an historian interviewing them.

Nixon and the people around him seemed different. Born during or immediately after World War I, they were the junior officers in World War II. Their dress was more casual than that of their predecessors in the highest ranks of government. Some of them, at least, could curse quite a lot. They were Republicans, but Nixon men first, and would lie for him if it seemed necessary. Quite a few of them went to prison for what they had done while in the White House.

When Eisenhower was President I was a college student, following the news closely but not avidly. In Nixon's case I was a teacher, trying to convey what was happening in Washington and the world to my students, reading the newspapers, the magazines, and watching the TV news every day. I knew a great deal about Nixon's associates — but then so did everyone else. For all those born before 1950, the names of Chuck Colson, Ron Ziegler, Robert Finch, Elliot Richardson, Egil Krogh, Ray Price, John Dean, Henry Kissinger, H. R. Haldeman, John Ehrlichman, Maurice Stans, Jeb Magruder,

Spiro Agnew, John and Martha Mitchell, and so many others are so well known as to be enshrined in the American political hall of notables. The media vilified them, made many of them appear as monsters out to destroy the American system of government, all in the name of Richard Nixon, the chief villain of all. I went into my interviews with these men fearful that they would eat me alive, or at least chew me up. In fact what I found was that some of them would have blended in well with the Eisenhower administration types. What they wanted was what I wanted, what was best for our country.

In the fall of 1987, Steve Hess invited me to a small dinner party at his Washington home. The other guests were Pat Moynihan, Bill Safire, and Mort Allin. We talked about Nixon for nearly six hours. Of course I learned a great deal, but it was the overall impression I took away that had the biggest impact on me.

Steve Hess, by this time, was at the Brookings Institution. Moynihan was a Democratic senator from New York. Safire, who had been a Nixon speechwriter, was a senior columnist for the *New York Times*. Allin, younger than the others, was still rising in the federal government; he was just back from an extended tour in Russia with the United States Information Agency. All four men were at (or almost at) the absolute top in their professions. None of them owed anything to Richard Nixon, and there was nothing Nixon could do for or to any one of them. Each had reason to feel that Nixon had let him down.

The four men represented four very different political perspectives. Their ideas are strongly held and strongly stated. There is little that they agree on, but they agreed that Nixon was a kind man, a considerate man, a rewarding man to work for, and a good if not great President. As noted in Chapter Ten, Moynihan and Safire believed that Nixon had kept the country from falling into something approaching anarchy. That Nixon could so impress these men, who had worked with him so closely, naturally impressed me. Although in the course of doing my research and writing, I seldom found the man they talked about so positively, I kept their feelings in mind when writing about him.

In the fall of 1987, Hofstra University on Long Island, New York, sponsored a conference on Nixon's administration. More than two dozen members of that administration came, including Henry Kissinger, H. R. Haldeman, John Ehrlichman, Maurice Stans, Charles Colson, and Ron Ziegler. The conference gave me an opportunity to hear these men speak in a formal, academic setting about their experiences, and a chance to meet with them informally and ask questions.

In January 1988, I held the Nixon Chair at Whittier College. I taught a seminar on the Nixon administration, and was fortunate enough to have Haldeman, Robert Finch, and Stans visit the seminar to answer questions from the students and from me. Haldeman gave generously of his time and knowledge. He read the entire manuscript of my book and made hundreds of comments. He provided a needed corrective in perspective. He remained as completely loyal to the former President as he was from 1968 to 1974. I adopted many of the changes he suggested and rejected as many more. He strongly, vigorously, and bluntly disagreed with many of my interpretations, most especially on the role and importance of the media, on the Watergate break-in and subsequent attempts to cover up or contain the scandal, and on the character of Richard Nixon.

I never met the man himself, nor his family. Nor did I have a chance to talk to the person outside the family who perhaps knew him best, his secretary Rose Mary Woods. I had gotten much precious information from Eisenhower's personal secretary, Ann Whitman, who, when I finished that biography, wrote me to say that although there were some mistakes in it, overall I had gotten it right — which is about as good as a compliment gets.[*]

[*] Ms. Whitman also came up with the line that inspired this book. In 1959, Khrushchev came to America. In a press conference just before he arrived, a reporter wanted to know what Eisenhower wanted Khrushchev to see. After listing housing, suburbs, roads, schools, and more, Eisenhower said that most of all, "I want him to see a happy people. I want him to see a free peo-

I asked Ms. Whitman if she would ask Ms. Woods to see me. She did. I was later told that Ms. Woods referred the request to Nixon, who said no. In any case, I got a letter from Ms. Whitman saying it would not be possible.

I wrote Nixon on a number of occasions, asking him this or that question or requesting an interview, but got no reply. To my knowledge he spoke about me only once. He was on the Charlie Rose TV show, promoting his 1990 book *In the Arena: A Memoir of Victory, Defeat and Renewal*. Rose asked him what he thought of what I had written about this or that subject.

"I never read Ambrose," Nixon shot back.

"What?" Rose exclaimed. "You never read Ambrose?"

Nixon replied, "He is just another left-wing historian."

I've always loved that line because in quoting it I can add, "Eisenhower didn't think so." Plus which, it is so Nixonian. He doesn't just stick in the knife: once he has it buried, he gives it a little twist. If he wanted to call me a left-wing historian, that is his right. Goodness knows I call him lots of names. To add that "just another" to the characterization was twisting the knife.

---

ple, doing exactly as they choose, within the limits that they must not transgress the rights of others." Whitman, in her notes, called Eisenhower's reply a "love song to America."

★ ★ ★

I published my first book a quarter of a century before volume one of the Nixon biography. Here I need to note how much more efficiently one can research and write history today as opposed to the early 1960s. This is because of technology and the skills of the archivists and librarians of the nation. When I began writing, working in a manuscript collection meant taking notes from the documents by hand. It was terribly time-consuming. One used what shortcuts one could — paraphrasing from a letter, summarizing, shorthand — but at the risk of serious error or overlooking a key phrase. Today, I can skim a letter in the archives, decide I want it, for a pittance purchase a copy that is full, complete, and exact. By a rough estimate, the copying machines — and the staff that so carefully make the copies for me — have reduced my research time by a factor of thirty.

Having a big family of smart kids also helps. Each one of the five has done research for me. Our oldest daughter, Stephenie Ambrose Tubbs, has an M.A. in history from the University of Montana. She went through sixteen years of the *New York Times*, the *Los Angeles Times*, and the *San Francisco Chronicle*, plus other California newspapers, copying Nixon items for me. She also found and copied the Nixon speeches and remarks in the *Congressional Record* for 1947 to 1953.

Moira Buckley Ambrose sat beside me in

archives in the Eisenhower Library, Abilene, Kansas, and at Laguna Niguel, going through the Nixon Vice Presidential Papers, one by one, making selections. On the average, one out of one hundred documents was worth copying, and about one out of every twenty copied were used in the final manuscript. This makes for long, dull hours of reading from letters, memos on trivial subjects, innumerable bread-and-butter notes, countless letters regretfully turning down invitations to make a speech, and so forth. But Moira never complained — although she did insist on taking an apartment overlooking the surf at Laguna Beach — and indeed would become as pleased as could be on finding a revealing document.

At the conclusion of my introduction to volume one, I wrote, "Without Stephenie and Moira, I would be today still stuck in the research phase of Nixon's first fifty years, instead of looking forward to beginning the research on his resurrection, triumph, and fall."

For volume two, my sons, Barry, Andy, and Hugh, pitched in on the research, as did Barry's wife, Celeste. So too our second daughter, Grace, who went through the *Washington Post* getting copies of Nixon items. Like her older sister, Stephenie, she has a sense of humor. Stephenie would make handwritten comments on the newspaper or magazine articles she copied for me. They were often sarcastic, but sometimes right on the mark. As one example, somewhere she found a piece entitled "Richard Nixon's Favorite Bird." She made a copy, then scribbled beside the headline, "The Phoenix."

Grace went through, among much else, the "Style" section of the *Washington Post*, about the last place I would look for Nixon material. But in the February 25, 1969, edition, Grace found a story by Myra MacPherson with the headline "Watergate, Where Republicans Gather." The Johnson administration was moving out, the Nixon administration was moving in, and Grace recognizes gold when she sees it. She copied it for me and I used it as the first sentence of my account of the Nixon administration in volume two. That book, entitled *Nixon: The Triumph of a Politician, 1962–1972*, was 736 pages long, with some 2,240 footnotes. The third volume, *Nixon: Ruin and Recovery, 1973–1990*, was 667 pages long with 1,400 footnotes.

Clearly a lot of research was involved. As for the children, who did nearly all the newspaper and magazine research, I paid them for their work — not handsomely enough, in their view; too generous, in mine. In the archives, located from the East Coast to the West Coast, Moira and I did the research. She never got paid — but she had me. Plus I try to think of something original and true to say of her in my acknowledgments (when I'm not dedicating the book to her, which I do often).

In volume two, I wrote: "Without Moira, I could never get through any book; for Moira, this one has been especially difficult, because of her passionate opposition to the war in Vietnam. Although she supported Nixon in 1960, his Vietnam policy set her teeth on edge. Often when I finished reading to her a section dealing with Nixon and Vietnam, she would spit out the words, 'Oh, how he's disappointed me!'

"Sometimes I would respond, 'Honey, it was as much Lyndon's fault as it was Dick's.'

"Other times I would say, 'How can you, a writer's wife, say such a thing when he is giving me all this great material to work with?' "

In the acknowledgments to volume three, I wrote that our already mixed feelings toward Nixon continued "but became more complex and mixed after 1982, when we embarked on an eight-year voyage of discovery seeking to understand and evaluate the man." I went on to describe the work she did and to acknowledge "first of all that I could not possibly have begun, much less completed, this voyage without her.

"The funny thing is, the more she got to know Richard Nixon, the less she liked him, while as for me, well, in volume one I developed a grudging admiration for the man. . . . In volume two I came to have a quite genuine and deep admiration for many of his policies. . . . And in volume three I found, to my astonishment, that I had developed almost a liking for him."

I've never agreed fully with all the decisions any President has to make — not even Jefferson was always right, nor Lincoln, nor Eisenhower

— but in Nixon's case I was a part of that broad group of Americans who thought of themselves, and were labeled by others, as Nixon-haters. For me, that meant that whatever decision he made, whether on détente with the Soviet Union or the opening to China, on clean air and water, on welfare reform, on revenue sharing, or anything else, was always characterized by hypocrisy. If Dick Nixon wanted it, worked for it, struggled to get it adopted, I was against "it," because I was certain the "it" was self-serving. But you can't go through nearly a decade of your life, living daily with a man, studying his every action and trying to figure out the causes of his doing what he was doing, and remain constantly negative.

When I finished the three volumes, I did not claim to have attained a position of indifference or neutrality. What I do claim is to have made my best possible effort to be an objective, careful, honest, and fascinated observer of the life of Richard Nixon. As my editor said when the project began, where else could I find such a challenge?

Much if not most of the reason I changed my mind about Nixon was the result of his own record. He did what he did. I wrote at the end of volume three, "He never gives up and is always true to himself. Of course, many of the qualities that make him what he is are negative — his self-centeredness, his partisanship, his anything-to-win methods, his anger, among others — but he is being himself as he acts them out.

"So my second acknowledgment goes to Richard Nixon [Moira got the first one]. I have lived with him for up to ten hours per day, almost every day, for almost a decade, and never once got bored."

To my astonishment, when I got to the last line of my three-volume biography (I was at my computer at the desk where I sit now, trying to sum up what I had learned after writing 2,155 pages on Dick Nixon), I wrote: "When Nixon resigned, we lost more than we gained." That was my conclusion.

Perhaps my all-time favorite line in a review of one of my books came from the Cleveland *Plain Dealer*, which concluded with the statement, "This book is one sentence too long."

I have not only the participants who allowed me to interview them to thank. I need also to thank my readers who took the time and went to the trouble to write me about the first or second volume of the biography. They gave me a much-needed boost. I have spent at least five and often eight hours a day, six and sometimes seven days a week, at the computer. This is a lonely way to live. As I got to page 500, or 700, or 800 of the manuscript, I would wonder, Who on earth is going to read all this stuff? Can there be any living person who wants to know this much about Richard Nixon?

Time and again, just when those feelings of loneliness and "nobody will ever read this anyway" got almost unbearable, a letter would arrive from a reader who said he or she could not wait for the next volume. There is nothing like that to keep a writer going.

Writing that biography was an exhausting process. More often than not I'd get no exercise in the course of a day — and there were altogether 2,920 days I devoted to the project. I spent probably a sixth of them, or about 500 days, writing, an average of five pages per day. The other days I was reading memoirs, documents, newspaper articles, all the material that goes into a big book. Sometimes — it can't be as long as it seems in retrospect — I was just sitting, thinking about who had done what, or said what, or why. This was especially true of a day with the transcribed Watergate tapes. I would read them, with their many garbled passages and deletions for "expletives," and try to figure out what was going on. In many cases, I knew perfectly well that Nixon already knew the answer to the question he was posing. So why was he asking? To confuse? To cover up? To find out what the other guy — Haldeman, Ehrlichman, Colson, Mitchell, or whoever — knew? To see if they knew what he knew?

I am a hunter, a fisherman seeking elusive game. I have spent much time in my canoe, on rough water, trying to read the water. I've been an historian all my adult life, trying to fathom what is frequently unfathomable. This is especially true of Nixon. After a full day of searching for him or trying to discern his motives, I come away exhausted — and too many times hardly enlightened at all.

I am, or used to be, a jogger, five to ten miles a day. In writing about Nixon, I had to say so long to all physical activities. But whereas I would get by with six or seven hours of sleep per night on my regular schedule, when writing about Nixon I needed nine or ten hours. So I would go to bed at eight P.M. at the latest, get up at six A.M., and take a nap in the middle of the day.

All this was done in pursuit of Nixon. Was it worth it? I can't say I got close to him, or that I understood him. But I had the satisfaction that only a writer of biography can experience — that I did my best. So did my family. So did the team at Simon & Schuster. So did all the men and women who worked with Nixon when I interviewed them. None of us ever got to where we could see him whole, but we all caught a glimpse of him, the real Richard Nixon. None of us would ever say that as individuals we understand the man, but collectively we come as close as possible.

I have written 2,155 pages on Dick Nixon. There are some mistakes. There are some insights, some discoveries. Anyway, I did it, and emerged a better writer and perhaps a better historian, with a better understanding of the Republican Party and of Richard Nixon. Was it worth it? You are damned right.

# Chapter Fourteen

## Writing About Men in Action, 1992–2001

I am often asked what is my favorite book of my own. And I always say, the one I'm working on. I'm a writer by profession. If the one I'm writing isn't better than those that went before I'd better find a new way to earn a living.

The next question is, "Tell me the secret to being a successful author." Hard work is the answer. You have got to have an insatiable curiosity, be an avid reader, have a memory that allows you to retain what you have read. Teaching is a great help here. For almost four decades I taught the American history survey course, three courses per semester at first, but even by the end of my career, when I could pick what I wanted to teach, I did the survey course at least once each semester. I got so adept at it that if you dropped in a coin and selected Teddy Roosevelt and the acquisition of the Panama Canal, I could give you a polished lecture on the subject. Or on the strategies of World War II. Or on American entry into World War I. Or on

America's Indian wars. By no means the whole of American history, which only a very few historians can do, but enough. To be a good writer of American history you have to know what you are talking about.

That doesn't seem like much of an answer, some tell me. "What is the real secret?" So I offer the few rules that my teacher Mr. Hesseltine pounded into me almost a half-century ago. Keep your narration in chronological order, as that is the way it happened. Don't anticipate. Don't tell your reader what is going to happen by the end of the book. Keep your reader guessing, on the edge of the seat, which is just the way it was for Dwight Eisenhower on the morning of D-Day, 1944, or for Richard Nixon the day the Watergate story broke. Do your level best to avoid all words ending in "ly." Leave out adjectives — as many as possible. Start your sentence, or your paragraph, with a time and place clause — events happened here or there on this or that date. Never use the passive voice. "Abraham Lincoln was shot dead Washington, D.C., at Ford's Theatre, on April 14, 1865" is a bad sentence. "On April 14, 1865, at Ford's Theatre in Washington, D.C., John Wilkes Booth assassinated Abraham Lincoln" is better.

Hesseltine used to say that a good sentence is like a good play — the reader wants to know where and when the action is taking place, then who is responsible for the action, then the result. There are many rules of good writing, and the best way to find them is to be a good reader. Know what you are writing about, whether it is history or travel or political analysis. Choose a good editor. It helps a lot if you show some promise as a writer, because there are many more want-to-be writers out there than there are good editors. Still, if you practice your craft and write often and as well as you can, you will locate a good editor who will take you on. When that happens, never let go. Never. No matter how angry you get. No matter how unreasonable his or her demands may be. And learn to write for your editor.

But the number one secret of being a successful writer is this: marry an English major. Moira did her graduate studies in English, has taught English in high school, is extremely well read, has a marvelous memory, and is never afraid to speak up. At the end of each day of writing, for the past four decades, I've read aloud to her whatever I've written that day.

Reading your own material aloud forces you to listen. If you stumble, if the words come out awkwardly, if you lose your place, if there is no flow, you had best go back and try again. Moira will tell me that this word doesn't work, that this phrase is out of place, that she can't understand what I'm getting at here, that she has had rather too much of this subject. She has a great ear and a marvelous imagination. I could give hundreds of examples, but if I did so my critics would accuse me of stealing her words and presenting them as my own (which I do), so let one example suffice.

In *Citizen Soldiers*, I had quoted a passage from Ernest Hemingway. It was terribly self-centered, mainly about how he and a member of the French Resistance liberated Paris, apparently by themselves. I read it to Moira. She nodded, then said, "When Hemingway sat down to write, he was the only person in view." It is a wonderful line. I laughed, scribbled the line in, and followed it up with, "Ernie Pyle didn't see the war that way, which is why he is read a half-century later, and Hemingway isn't."

Anyway, over the past decade, from 1992 through 2001, together we have produced seven books. They are all history. All heavily foot-noted. Six have been number one on the Nonfiction Best Seller list of the *New York Times Book Review* for at least a few weeks. They are *Band of Brothers: E Company, 506th Regiment, 101st Airborne from Normandy to Hitler's Eagle's Nest* (1992); *D-Day: June 6, 1944* (1994); *Undaunted Courage: Meriwether Lewis, Thomas Jefferson, and the Opening of the American West* (1996); *Citizen Soldiers: The U.S. Army from the Normandy Beaches to the Bulge to the Surrender of Germany* (1997); *Comrades: Brothers, Fathers, Heroes, Sons, Pals* (1999); *Nothing Like It in the World: The Men Who Built the Transcontinental Railroad, 1863–1869* (2000); and *The Wild Blue: The Men and Boys Who Flew the B-24s over Germany* (2001).

These are all substantial books with great chunks of footnotes, whether from memoirs, diaries, official histories, newspapers, archives. How do you do it? Hard work, I reply, by me and all those who are part of the team — starting with Moira, my son Hugh, my editor and her staff at Simon & Schuster, my family, friends like Doug Brinkley or Nick Mueller, many others. My favorite book is the last one printed, which is always better than those that were published earlier.

Which is why the one you are reading right now is the best.

In the fall of 1988 the veterans of Easy Company, 506th Parachute Infantry Regiment, 101st Airborne Division, held a reunion in New Orleans. My assistant Ron Drez and I went to their hotel to interview them on their D-Day experiences. When Major Richard Winters read the transcript, he wanted to set a couple of things straight. He was coming from Pennsylvania to see my friend Walter Gordon, also an Easy Company veteran, and wanted to know if he could come to my office. With him came Gordon, Sergeant (later Lieutenant) Carwood Lipton, and Sergeant Forrest Guth. We talked all afternoon with maps spread out over the floor. I invited them to dinner; they accepted. Moira, who has her own special way with the veterans and was as excited as I was, made her best roast beef dinner. We talked about the war, about what they did when they got home. They had all read *Pegasus Bridge*, which the Eisenhower Center always gave to every veteran who did an interview with us. Winters suggested that a history of Easy Company might make a good subject for a book.

I did not need persuading. I was just then finishing volume three of the Nixon biography and very much wanted my next book to be about men in combat, junior officers and enlisted men. I was planning a book on D-Day but not until we got closer to the fiftieth anniversary. I wanted to write about a unit that was special, and Easy Company was surely that — airborne troopers who had leapt into the battle in the middle of the night, they had an outstanding combat record. What appealed most was a closeness that lasted over the next fifty years. These guys knew each other well, knew each other's children and grandchildren, their problems, successes. I wondered about this remarkable closeness.

In May 1990, Drez attended the company's reunion in Orlando, Florida, where he videotaped eight hours of group interview. That same month I did three days of interviewing with Gordon. In July, I went to Winters's farm in Pennsylvania, where I did a couple of weeks of interviewing. On the last day, a half-dozen men from the company who were living on the East Coast drove to the farm for a group interview. Later in 1990 I spent a weekend at Carwood Lipton's home in Southern Pines, North

Carolina, where Bill Guarnere joined us. I flew to Oregon to spend another weekend with Don Malarkey and other West Coast residents. I interviewed a dozen other company members over the telephone and have had an extensive correspondence with nearly all living members of the company.

In November 1990, Moira and I toured Easy's battle sites in Normandy and Belgium. I interviewed Frenchmen from the area the company had fought over. In July 1991, we visited the scenes of Easy's battle throughout Europe with Winters, Lipton, and Malarkey. Winters, Moira, and I spent an afternoon with Baron Colonel Frederick von der Heydte, the German paratroop commander at Normandy, at his home near Munich.

I circulated the manuscript of the book to the men of Easy Company and I received a great many criticisms, corrections, and suggestions. The book, *Band of Brothers*, is very much a group effort.

Almost a decade after its publication, Tom Hanks and Steven Spielberg decided to make a ten-part miniseries for television out of the story. I worked with them. Hanks and Spielberg and the actors and cameramen and makeup artists and others had regular contact with the surviving members of Easy Company. HBO, which broadcast the series, had a premiere at Utah Beach in Normandy, along with a week of festivities for the veterans in Paris. It was about as good a time as I've ever had, or can ever expect to enjoy.

And just to assure all those who might be wondering, "Is *Band of Brothers* on the TV what actually happened?" I recommend that they read the book.

The year *Band of Brothers* was published, 1992, I was already embarked on my book on D-Day. It was something I had long wanted to do — the story of the invasion of Europe by the Americans, British, and Canadians, told primarily from the point of view of the junior officers and enlisted men. Of course I planned to have some reference to Generals Omar Bradley, Bernard Law Montgomery, and others, most of all Eisenhower, but it was the men on the beaches, where the action was, that held me. How did they do it? I wanted their stories, told in their words. So from 1989 onward, the Eisenhower Center at the University of New Orleans began collecting the oral histories of the men of D-Day. This was done in person, at a veteran's home or during conventions, by telephone, or by men speaking their reminiscences into a tape recorder. We located the veterans through the VFW or the American Legion magazine, or in their divisional association newsletter, or by getting their names and addresses from their buddies.

By 1992 the Eisenhower Center had collected 1,380 accounts of personal experiences. This was the most extensive first-person, I-was-there collection of memoirs of a single battle in existence. Since 1994 we have continued to collect such histories, not only those from D-Day but those who served throughout Northwest Europe. We now have more than 4,000 accounts. Student workers at the Eisenhower Center, under the direction of Ms. Kathi Jones and later Annie Wedekind, transcribed the material. I also got D-Day oral histories from the Imperial War Museum, London; from André Heintz from the Battle of Normandy Museum in Caen; from the U.S. Army Military Institute at Carlisle Barracks, Pennsylvania; from Phil Jutras, director of the Parachute Museum in Stc.-Mère-Eglise.

There is a vast literature on D-Day and although I could not read all of it, I did read most of the accounts. I'm especially eager to thank Dr. Forrest Pogue and his colleagues of the Army's Historical Section, who did interviews in the field with combat veterans, then wrote *The U.S. Army in World War II* (known as the Green Books from the color of the bindings), scores of volumes known worldwide for accuracy and thoroughness.

I visited the battlefields, from southern England on to Normandy, more than ten times. I persuaded veterans, ranging in rank from general officer to private, to come with me, to give me their on-site accounts of their D-Day experiences. Every one of the hundreds of veterans Moira has met will attest that she has a wonderful way with them, putting them at their ease, making them comfortable, enjoying being with them, fascinated by their stories, providing a soft, sensitive woman's touch to our meals, meetings, tramps over the battlefields, and airplane hassles.

*D-Day* too was very much a team effort. I like to think that General Eisenhower would have approved of it. From the moment he took up his responsibilities as Supreme Commander, Allied Expeditionary Force until the German surrender, Ike insisted on teamwork. Of all his outstanding characteristics as leader of the multination, multiservice crusade in Europe, his insistence on teamwork was key to victory.

D-Day was the pivot point of the twentieth century. Everything that went before it can be said to have led up to it; all that followed came about because of what happened that day. I've been studying it for two decades and more, and am still in awe. What I do best is quote others. Here are two of my favorites from June 6, 1944.

Captain Robert Walker at Omaha Beach recorded in his oral history that the scene brought to his mind Tennyson's lines in "The Charge of the Light Brigade," especially "Cannon to right of them/Cannon to left of them/Cannon in front of them/Volley'd and thunder'd. . . . /Theirs not to reason why/Theirs but to do and die. . . . /When can their glory fade?/O the wild charge they made!/All the world wondered./Honor the charge they made!"

In 1964, on D-Day plus twenty years, Eisenhower was interviewed on Omaha Beach by Walter Cronkite. The general said, "It's a wonderful thing to remember what those fellows were fighting for and sacrificing for, what they did to preserve our way of life. Not to conquer any territory, not for any ambitions of our own. But to make sure that Hitler could not destroy freedom in the world.

"I think it's just overwhelming. To think of the lives that were given for that principle paying a terrible price on this beach alone, on that one day, 2,000 casualties. But they did it so that the world could be free. It just shows what free men will do rather than be slaves."

On the fiftieth anniversary of D-Day, June 6, 1994, Moira and I spent much of the day and the weeks preceding and following it in England, Normandy, and Paris. When we returned to the States, I got started on my next book, *Undaunted Courage: Meriwether Lewis, Thomas Jefferson, and the Opening of the American West*, which would be published in 1996.

Ever since 1975, when I first read the journals of Lewis and Clark, the family had been spending at least a part of each summer following their trail across the western two thirds of the continent. They did it by foot, by canoe, by pirogue, by keelboat, by horseback, without any maps. With no idea of what lay ahead, they marched across a land inhabited by strange and presumably hostile Indians. How did they do it? I knew the only way I could find out was by following their trail, camping at their camp sites, reading their journals closely.

For two decades we followed Lewis and Clark, always with at least a few friends along on the trip, sometimes as many as a couple of dozen. For twenty years we were obsessed with Lewis and Clark, and still are. Three of our children and three of our grandchildren live in Montana, as do we in the summertime. We have canoed almost the entire Missouri River and much of the Columbia. On July 4, 1976, we camped with a group of my students from the University of New Orleans at Lemhi Pass, on the Idaho-Montana border. It is unchanged since Lewis and Clark camped there. Around the campfire we took turns enumerating the reasons we loved our country (not so easy to do with young people in 1976, in the wake of Richard Nixon's resignation and the fall of Saigon, but we did it with great success). We sang songs. We indulged ourselves in an outpouring of patriotism.

On our first backpack over the Lolo Trail through the Bitterroot Mountains, we were hiking over the trail, stepping in Lewis's and Clark's footprints. Behind me on the narrow trail, Moira said, "It makes my feet tingle." You can camp at their sites, swim at a hot spring where they swam, see sights first, and best, as they described them. Writing the book was a labor of love. I suppose that is true of all my books, but none quite so much as *Undaunted Courage*. We have endured summer snowstorms (at Lemhi Pass on July 4, 1986), terrible thunderstorms in canoes on the Missouri and Columbia rivers, soaking rains on the Lolo, and innumerable moments of exhilaration on the trail. The Lewis and Clark experience has brought us together so many times in so many places that we cannot measure or express what it has meant to our marriage and our family.

Moira and I owe so much to those who have shared the trials, tribulations, and triumphs of the trail with us, but most of all to our children and grandchildren, whose enthusiasm never flags. They make us so proud and give meaning to our lives. Together we have followed in the footsteps of Crazy Horse and Custer, Lewis and Clark in the best years of our lives. Without our children there would be no book on the Lewis and Clark Trail.

It is our dream that someday they will be taking their grandchildren on horseback over the Lolo, or by canoe down the Missouri, or camping at Lemhi on the Fourth of July, and that for them it will be as it has been for us, the greatest experience of all, one that draws their families together as it has ours.

*Citizen Soldiers* (1997) was a sequel to *D-Day*. It is about the GIs, the junior officers, and enlisted men of the European Theater of Operations — who they were, how they fought, why

291

they fought, what they endured, how they tri-
umphed, what they can teach us.

I make my living by reading other people's
mail, listening to their stories, reading their
memoirs. My job is to pick out the best and most
representative, the ones that illuminate common
themes or illustrate typical actions. Long ago I
learned from Professors Hesseltine and Williams
to let my characters speak for themselves. They
were there. I wasn't. They saw with their own
eyes, they put their own lives on the line. I
didn't. They speak with an authenticity no one
else can match. Their phrases, their word
choices, their slang are unique, naturally
enough, as their experiences were unique.

My sources were the men I interviewed for
*D-Day*, plus many new voices of those who came
into the campaign in Northwest Europe from
June 7 onward. I did many of the interviews. Ron
Drez did hundreds of them. In addition, the fiftieth anniversaries of D-Day, the Battle of the
Bulge, the crossing of the Rhine, and V-E Day
brought forth a flood of books by veterans about
their own experiences. I didn't read all of each
one of them, but I read plenty.

On May 7 and 8, 1995, the Eisenhower
Center sponsored a conference on the war in
Europe. Among those who participated were
Andy Rooney, Kurt Vonnegut, and Joe Heller.
Rooney gave me a front-line reporter's view of
the war (he flew missions in a B-17). Vonnegut
and Heller gave me a novelist's view. The funny

thing was none of these funny guys was funny when he talked about his personal experiences in the war. They were moving and vivid.

In the fall semester of 1996, as I was finishing the book, I was a visiting professor at the University of Wisconsin, teaching a course on World War II to some 350 students. They were dumbstruck by the descriptions of what it was like to be on the front lines. They were more amazed by the responsibilities carried by junior officers and NCOs who were then as young as they were now. Like all of us who have never been in combat, they wondered if they could have done it. Even more, they wondered how *anyone* could have done it.

There is a vast literature on the last question. In general, in assessing the motivation of the GIs, there is agreement that patriotism or any other form of idealism had little if anything to do with it. The GIs fought because they had to. What held them together was not country and flag, but unit cohesion. It has been my experience, through four decades of interviewing ex-GIs, that such generalizations are true to a point.

There is something more. Although the GIs were and are embarrassed to talk or write about the cause they fought for, they were the children of democracy and they did more to help spread democracy around the world than any other generation in history.

At the core, the American citizen soldiers —

unlike those from Germany or the Soviet Union or Japan or elsewhere — knew the difference between right and wrong, and they didn't want to live in a world in which wrong prevailed. So they fought, and won, and we all of us, living and yet to be born, must be forever profoundly grateful.

*Comrades: Brothers, Fathers, Heroes, Sons, Pals* (1999) came about because I had fainted a year or so earlier in a restaurant in Madison, Wisconsin, fell back, cracked my head against a granite floor, and spent the next ten days or so in intensive care. I can't remember any of that, except that I desperately wanted to get out, go home, and have a cigarette. When I was finally discharged I was in pretty awful shape. I could not see out of my left eye. My brain had scrambled and there had been some internal bleeding. I had no memory of things that had just happened to me. Moira tells me that all our kids came to visit but I can't recall. I could not remember our street address nor our phone number.

Moira tells me I was more or less impossible to live with during this period, something I doubt very much, but she had her senses about her and I didn't. But it absolutely cannot be that I said to her during an argument, "I don't love you anymore." She says I did.

My dear college friend John Holcomb came to Mississippi to help care for me. So did some others. Once a week I went to the LSU Medical Center in Slidell for rehabilitation treatments, which started off as children's games — making words out of various letters, simple mathematics, trying to memorize the objects in a drawing or a photograph — all of which seemed to help. I took long walks on the sandy beach of the Mississippi Sound at Bay St. Louis, twisting my head around for exercise and to learn to see with my left eye. After a couple of months it got so I could take my hand away from my left eye and read the morning newspaper with both eyes. Most helpful of all, I got an intense urge to write.

I placed a table at our bay window looking out on the beach, put my computer on it, and began. I discovered immediately that I could not do a research project, as I could not read well enough. Nor could I write about events that had just happened because I couldn't remember them. But I did find that my memory was sharp on the events of thirty or forty years ago, good enough so that with the help of one of the books on my desk I could recall what Eisenhower had done in 1942, or Crazy Horse in 1875, or Richard Nixon in 1970. Not policy so much, nor decision making, but who their friends were and how they got along.

I put myself into it, a bit, especially the first chapter, on "The Ambrose Boys"; Chapter Seven, "A Lifetime of Friends," on my college friends; Chapter Eight, on my "Dearest Friend," Nick Mueller; and the last chapter, on my relationship with my father. The remainder of the book was about people I had written about earlier who had friendships that seemed to me to be worth discussing. Lewis and Clark, obviously; the men of Easy Company; the Eisenhower boys; the Custer boys; Crazy Horse and his intimate friend He Dog; Richard Nixon (who had no friends); Eisenhower and Patton.

The book turned out to be an essential part of my rehabilitation and some people said some very nice things about it.

In the summer of 1999, just as I finished the manuscript for *Nothing Like It in the World*, my son Hugh and I had a picnic dinner in the Bitterroot Mountains at the Idaho-Montana state line, with George and Eleanor McGovern. The McGoverns live in Stevensville, Montana, in the summer, not too far from our home in Helena.

George said he had done some interviews recently with reporter Michael Takiff, who was interested in writing a book on McGovern's World War II career as a bomber pilot. I said that was a fine idea and told McGovern to tell Takiff that he could open with the story of the bomb McGovern's B-24 dropped on a farmhouse in Austria.

McGovern said that he wished I were writing the book. I hesitated, not out of any lack of interest but because Takiff had already begun his work. McGovern urged me to talk to Takiff to see if he would yield to me. Takiff agreed.

And so to work. I was enormously respectful of McGovern and his crew. I wanted to understand how a son of South Dakota became, at age twenty-two, a bomber pilot. I was interested in how American designers and workers and the industrial plants created the world's greatest air force, almost from scratch. I wanted to learn about the strategic air campaign, how it was planned and carried out. I desired to tell readers the story of how the leading opponent of the Vietnam War was, in World War II, a hero bomber pilot who was awarded the Distinguished Flying Cross.

I did a lot of reading. Hugh and I did a lot of interviewing, especially of McGovern and his crew. Together we rode in a B-17 and a B-24 — an extraordinary experience. We called the book *The Wild Blue*.

Writing is not the easiest way to make a living — you work long hours, usually all by yourself. It is not a way to make money — good businessmen make far more money than most good writers. Nor is it the quickest way to have an impact on your life and times — politicians are much better at that than are writers. Except for a very few, you almost never become an immediately recognizable face — that goes to the movie and music stars.

What you do get is an opportunity to work at what interests you, for as long as you wish. You get to write about ordinary men and women caught up in extraordinary circumstances — what they did, how they did it, with what effect. I know of no better way to make your own contribution.

# Chapter Fifteen

# *The National D-Day Museum*

In my first meeting with General Eisenhower, in 1964, at his office in Gettysburg, Pennsylvania, he said he noticed that I lived in New Orleans and asked if I ever knew Andrew Higgins.

"No, sir," I replied. "I didn't move to New Orleans until 1959 and Mr. Higgins died just before I got there."

"That's too bad," Eisenhower said. "You know he is the man who won the war for us."

I was astonished and my face showed it. Eisenhower noticed. "That's right," he said. "If Andy Higgins had not designed and then built those landing craft, we never could have gone in over an open beach. The whole strategy of the war would have been changed."

He was talking about the Landing Craft Vehicle Personnel, or LCVP, often called a Higgins Boat. In New Orleans, Higgins built 20,000 of them. He had 30,000 employees. Hitler called him the "American Noah." But despite his achievements, in 1968 there was nothing in New

Orleans to honor him. Not a street named for him, not an elementary school, not a statue, nothing. I came away from that meeting determined someday to do something in New Orleans in recognition of what Higgins and his workers had accomplished.

Over the next two decades, I traveled across Western Europe, researching Eisenhower and his men in the European Theater of Operations. I went to every World War II museum I could — in London, Portsmouth, elsewhere in Great Britain; in Caen, Ste.-Mère-Eglise, St. Lô, Arromanches, Paris, on the Maginot Line, elsewhere in France; in Arnhem, Holland; in Berlin; in Moscow. In war museums, I learn about this or that weapon, or item of clothing, or vehicle, or artillery piece, or airplane. In addition, I did interviews, first with the high command — Eisenhower, Omar Bradley, others — then with the junior officers and enlisted men.

The interviews were conducted, primarily, by me and my staff at the Eisenhower Center, which I had founded early in the 1980s to sponsor conferences and collect documents from and oral histories of World War II. The center grew fast enough so that in 1985 we held the first big conference, on the fortieth anniversary of the end of the war in Europe. We had a glittering array of speakers and participants. Forrest Pogue was there, along with Russell Weigley, Martin Blumenson, Michael Beschloss, and myself — all well-known

American historians.

M. R. D. Foot was there, plus Pierre Bertaux — the heads of Intelligence for Britain and France in the war. Colonel Hans von Luck of the German army and his opponent on D-Day, Major John Howard (along with two of his men, Sergeant Jim Wallwork and Private Wally Parr), also participated. Our banquet speakers were General John Frost, the British airborne commander who took the "bridge too far" at Arnhem in 1944; Viscount Montgomery, son of the Field Marshal; and General William Westmoreland, the American commander in Vietnam and former U.S. Army Chief of Staff. Former U.S. Senator George McGovern, the bomber pilot, presided.

The conference was a success. How could it have failed? We could not have had a more glittering array of speakers in 1985 than we did. It helped spread the name and reputation of the Eisenhower Center. We kept having other conferences on different subjects, World War II and international affairs.

By then, I was fully involved with the interviews with the men, preparing to write a big book on D-Day in time for the fiftieth anniversary, coming in 1994. I was also trying to establish something in New Orleans that would remind older people, and teach the youngsters, of what the city had contributed to D-Day.

In 1985, sitting in my backyard one afternoon after work, with my dearest friend Gordon

"Nick" Mueller, sipping sherry, we were engaging in fantasias. Nick, who was a vice chancellor at the University of New Orleans (UNO), had started a summer school in Europe on the campus of the University of Innsbruck, called UNO-Innsbruck. It already had the largest student body of any American summer school in Europe, and he wanted to expand it. I wanted to expand the activities of the Eisenhower Center, and to lead tour groups on a two-week trip through American battlefields in Europe.

But most of all, I wanted to honor Andrew Higgins, Higgins Industries. A statue? A plaque? A street? Possibly even a small museum, displaying the assembly line where the LCVPs were made. I told Nick we could build such a museum on the UNO campus, at the site where Higgins tested his boats, on Lake Pontchartrain, for about $1 million. Nick said the cost would be more like $4 million and we had better find a site near the French Quarter and thus the tourists.

To get started, he suggested a reunion of the Higgins employees. I thought we ought to get Al Hirt to come play his trumpet. Hirt, fifteen years old in 1944, had his first job at Higgins Industries and played in the Higgins band. Hirt agreed and we put a notice in the *Times-Picayune*. A thousand or so former employees showed up. Hirt played, I made a speech, a couple of the foremen and engineers from Higgins Industries gave a talk. People could visit the Eisenhower Center and listen to our tapes. Most agreed that a museum was a good idea and wished us luck. Some of them paid $25 to become members of the Eisenhower Center.

We had no money, no plan, only an idea. For three years, nothing happened except that a couple of junior professors sat around talking about what might be. Then I got a call from New York. Peter Kalikow, owner of the *New York Post* and a number of buildings in Manhattan, wanted to spend a day with me, talking about World War II. We went to New York. Kalikow knew a lot about the war. He asked me if I needed money for any of my projects.

I thought about asking for a substantial contribution to a fund to support conferences for the Eisenhower Center. But I said I needed seed money to plan for a museum in New Orleans dedicated to Andy Higgins and the Normandy invasion.

How much? he asked.

I gulped and said $50,000. Fine, he said, and pulled out his checkbook. It took me a while to realize that fund-raising would never again be that easy.

Nick and I agreed to use the money to bring the directors of the Truman, the Johnson, and the Eisenhower museums to New Orleans for a weekend of wisdom. We wanted to know how you go about building a museum. Have an idea, raise money, get a site, get a designer, most of all get a board. First, the board. We got a local realtor, Lee Schlesinger, to head it and a dozen or so business and professional men to serve on it. That was enough for me and Lee to go see Louisiana Congressman Robert Livingston, chairman of the House Appropriation Committee, spread out designs for him, and ask for $4 million. To our delight he agreed to appropriate the money to the Eisenhower Center at the University of New Orleans. We were off.

But not quite. Senator Sam Nunn had learned that Stanford University had received a grant and used it to purchase a sailboat that the top officials in the university could use for fund-raising events, football parties, and so on. Nunn was furious. He swore there would be no more appropriations to universities. Among others, that meant us.

We changed the name to the National D-Day Museum Foundation and split it from the university. We put together a fairly new board. We got the $4 million. We were ready to go.

First we needed a designer and a moviemaker. Arthur Davis, New Orleans's leading architect, was on our board. He suggested Jack Masey of Metaform, New York, as the designer — he had worked with Jack in the construction of the Louisiana Pavilion at the 1984 World's Fair. And Davis suggested Charley Guggenheim as the documentary filmmaker. They were veterans of the European Theater, which appealed to me. Moira and I flew to New York to meet with Masey. He showed us some of the many museums he had done in the city, including the

Ellis Island Museum, which is superb. What caught me the most was a small glass case, sitting on a pedestal smack dab in the middle of a room. It contained a pair of baby shoes. It was explained in a description that they had come across from Hamburg and been lost.

"You see," Jack said, gripping my arm. "In a museum, smaller is better."

At that moment I wanted Jack to be our designer, and he has been ever since.

We met with Guggenheim and were as impressed by his work as everyone else is. Together, Lee, Moira, Jack, Charley, and I flew to Normandy for ten days. I showed them what had happened here, there, everywhere. We talked about the operation and how to portray the battle in a museum. We agreed we had to have hedgerows, dunes, artifacts of all kinds (I already had many small ones given to me by veterans), an understanding of how America came from sixteenth in the world in the size of her armed forces to the gigantic armada that invaded Normandy on June 6, 1944, the planes, the ships, the landing craft, the men. D-Day, 1944, was the biggest undertaking of the war and it had to be shown that way.

Where to build the museum? Nick and I wanted it on the lakefront at the campus of the university, and we hired architects to design it. Months went by. Years. Nobody liked it but Nick and me. Eventually the board, now headed by Bob Howson, the CEO of McDermott Corporation, picked and bought an abandoned brewery in the warehouse district, near the Convention Center on the river and the French Quarter, with museums like the Children's Museum, the Contemporary Arts Center, the Confederate Museum, the Southern Arts Museum all around it. I was opposed, but Jack Masey loved it because it had big, thick masonry walls and no windows (museum designers hate windows, I learned). The board and Jack were right. I was wrong.

Charley was working on his documentary. Jack was collecting artifacts and making his designs. Bob Howson persuaded McDermott to put up the money to buy intact the contents of the St. Lô Museum in Normandy. It was going out of business — too far off the tourist track — and had hundreds of items picked up on the beach after the battle. Sentry posts. Jeeps. Trucks. Broken-down tanks. Rifles, grenades, shovels, helmets, gas masks, bayonets and knives, boots, shirts — all the debris of war. It forms the basis of our display.

Serious fund-raising began. It is the most difficult thing I've ever tried, exasperating, maddening, a thoroughgoing learning experience. Together with the board, Nick and I put together a list of who to see, usually CEOs of companies that the board members did some business with, always of companies who made a contribution to — and made money off of — the war effort. I persuaded Bill Colby, the former head of the CIA and an OSS agent during the war, to accompany me to ask for the money. I thought they could not possibly say no to Bill Colby. We called on AT&T, American Express, McDonnell-Douglas, the automakers, the arms manufacturers, the shipbuilders, the railroads, others. I thought we had the perfect approach: "What did you do during the war, Daddy?" Their advertising departments could take full-page magazine ads showing jeeps, rifles, airplanes, aircraft carriers. "That's What We Did!"

I learned that American corporations hate to give away money, and that it does you no good to see the number two or number three man in the corporation — you have got to get through to number one. The vice presidents would listen to our pitch, then say, "Great idea — you should go see so-and-so." I could have screamed at those words.

We wanted to open on June 6, 1994, the fiftieth anniversary of D-Day in Normandy, but we were not even close. The board members would shake their heads, mumble that we would never make it, and resign. I never gave up, but I came close. The money from the federal government was just about spent and no more was coming in. At this point Bob Howson, after a two-year stint, decided to resign. I persuaded General James Livingston, USMC, to take up the job of CEO. We decided to go to Baton Rouge to ask the Louisiana legislature for a $2 million appropriation.

What an experience — to walk onto the floor of the Louisiana legislature at the side of a Marine general who is a recipient of a Medal of Honor. The politicians went weak in the knees (I already was). Livingston managed to get what we needed to keep going.

Masey and Guggenheim continued at work, mainly on my promise that somehow, some way, someday they would be paid. Jack was designing an exhibit that could never be equaled; Charley was putting together a documentary that we all felt deserved an Academy Award nomination. They were doing their work on their own time with their own money. Jack's designs had yet to be built. Charles was wondering about alternative venues to premiere his documentary.

By this time, 1996, my D-Day book had been a best-seller and I was receiving royalties far above anything I ever experienced. I had no doubt what to do. I gave $2 million to the National D-Day Museum, with more to follow in subsequent years.

General Livingston and I were learning to go to individuals rather than corporations for contributions. We went to New York to see Tim Forbes, of *American Heritage*. He was as gracious as could be and together with his brother Steve came up with $1 million. We were able to get other, smaller sums from others, enough to keep us going. The biggest came from local businessman Frank Stewart, who plunked down $2 million.

In 2000, Livingston had completed his term and wanted to drop out as CEO, while staying on the board. Bosie Bollinger, a local shipbuilder of international renown, agreed to become CEO of the board, while Nick Mueller continued to serve as director, a post he had taken on two years earlier. With Bosie and Nick running things it became obvious that the National D-Day Museum would come into existence. Between them, they know everything about how to raise money, deal with the media, consult with the designers, arrange grand openings and various big functions, in short how to run this superb museum in the best possible way.

An active-duty Coast Guard officer, Lieutenant Jimmy Duckworth, got interested. Many of the LCVP drivers during the war came from the Coast Guard. He joined the board. We had a set of blueprints for the original Higgins Boat. He decided to build one (none of the Higgins Boats from the war was intact and running) and got me to contribute enough money to buy Philippine mahogany — which was what the original boats were made from. Higgins had, in 1940, bought up the entire Philippine mahogany crop for that year. Jimmy raised money elsewhere, got American Standard to loan him an unused warehouse, put a notice in the newspaper that he needed former workers for Mr. Higgins to build an LCVP. They came, ten, a dozen, two dozen, more. They worked Saturday mornings. The boat began to take shape.

During the building a man walked into the warehouse to say he used to work for Mr. Higgins and could he help? Jimmy said that at the moment they were stuck on how this or that connection was made, they couldn't tell from the blueprints. He said, "Hell, that's what I used to do. Let me show you."

When the boat was completed, we christened it, with the top brass of the Coast Guard present, then launched it on the Industrial Canal. I got to drive it. Moira got to drive it. We got our picture in the paper, write-ups, the whole bit. As to cost, the entire cash outlay couldn't have been much more than the few thousand dollars I put up to buy the mahogany. The craft, fully commissioned, is today in the Louisiana Pavilion at the museum.

Now we were rolling. Past $10 million. Past $20 million. Up to $35 million. Then $40 million. By 2002, $55 million. The State of Louisiana, thanks to Nick's and Boisie's initiative, put up $4 million to build the Louisiana Pavilion. Senators Ted Stevens and Daniel Inouye joined with Louisiana's Senators Mary Landrieu and John Breaux to get more federal money for our museum. Individuals began making contributions of some significance. Hank Greenberg, who had been a Ranger at Pt. du Hoc, gave $1 million. People were buying bricks, which would be placed on the walkway, with the name of a veteran from the family stamped on the brick. And we continued to sell memberships for $25.

Artifacts kept coming. Thanks to local oilman Pat Taylor, we got a vintage Spitfire, with its log showing it had flown reconnaissance on D-Day over Normandy. Pat had it refurbished and hung in the Pavilion. Commodore Tom Lupo, on the board, got us an Avenger, the plane he flew in the war. That was also the plane George Bush flew in the war when he got shot down.

In 1998 Steven Spielberg released his *Saving Private Ryan*. I was the historical consultant for the movie, which was based in large part on my book on D-Day. The movie got us tons of publicity and more contributions, best of all large sums from Spielberg, Tom Hanks, and Tom Brokaw.

The Grand Opening of the Normandy Wing, held on June 6, 2000, was a smashing success. We had some 10,000 veterans in the parade. More than two dozen Medal of Honor recipients. French ships, Norwegian ships, American ships, British ships. American World War II airplanes, as well as modern planes, flew over. Secretary of Defense William Cohen was a speaker, along with former President George Bush. Senators. Congressmen. Governors. The Mayor. More than a half-million people watched the parade. We were on all the national TV shows, plus C-SPAN worldwide.

There was more, but what I thought was best was the reaction of Spielberg and Hanks. When a Ranger group marched by, they jumped out of the viewing stands, handed over their camera, pulled out a pad and pencil, and asked if they could have an autograph and their picture taken. The stars became the spectators. The same thing happened with the various senators and other politicians, with the TV anchormen, with the men who had put up the money. George McGovern, who was there for the entire four days, told me it was the best time he had ever had in his life.

The Pavilion was jammed. I noticed an older man wearing his medals on his civilian suit, something the British often do. I introduced myself, asked him where he was from. London, he said. I asked how he had found out about this event.

"In the London *Times*," he answered. "I wouldn't have missed it for the world."

"What did you do during the war?" I asked.

He pointed to the Spitfire suspended from the Pavilion roof. "I flew that plane. Six times that day, on reconnaissance." We got out the log of the plane, and sure enough, there he was.

Since that opening, we have had another, for the Pacific Wing, on December 7, 2001, just as grand and sweeping. The documentary movie that goes with the Pacific exhibit was financed by Steven Spielberg and Shell Oil, directed by James Moll, and produced by me and Spielberg; entitled *Price for Peace*, it premiered on NBC-TV in prime time on Memorial Day, 2002. We are now adding a wing on the China-Burma-India

312

Theater; on medics, nurses, and doctors in the war; on North Africa, Sicily, and Italy; and more. It is our hope and plan that we will become the best World War II museum in America, if not the world.

When I'm at the museum for this or that function, reporters and others often say to me, "You must be very proud." My reply is that first of all I was not a participant in the action, that second I hardly built this museum by myself, that it would not be here if not for the construction workers, the designers, the men and women who gave us the artifacts, and most of all those who made financial contributions. So I'm not proud. But I surely am very pleased.

One of the things I like most about the museum is its ability to reach out to the young and inform them of who went before them, and what they owe to them. Museums that commemorate events of a half-century or less ago pull the generations together. The grandest sight for me in the National D-Day Museum comes when a busload of students comes in and the kids spot a group of veterans, often in town for a reunion. The students and the veterans are drawn together in the way a magnet attracts metal. The kids want to know what the veteran did in the war; the veterans are delighted to be asked and to have a receptive, indeed almost a worshipping, audience.

You can see dancing through the kids' heads the question, "Could I have done that?" And you can see the veterans' thoughts: "Kid, like me you are a child of democracy, and I can count on it that if the challenge comes, you too will fight for democracy."

That is what we in the military history museum business try to teach the children. We do what we can, which is quite a lot, to inspire them to be the successors of those who helped make this country into the freest and richest ever.

# Chapter Sixteen

# *American Racism*

When I was eleven years old, there was a photograph on the sports pages of the *Milwaukee Journal*. It was of Jackie Robinson, showing him opening the door of a baseball training facility in Florida. Above the door there was a sign saying, "Players Only."

Fifty-six years later that photo is still etched in my memory. My father was a Navy doctor and we lived in Pensacola, Florida, the second half of 1945. Back then I had become accustomed to seeing "Whites Only" signs or "Colored Only" on water fountains, rest rooms (designated additionally "Men" or "Women"), the front half of city buses, movie theaters, and almost everywhere else. They meant nothing to me, except to check to make sure I was drinking out of the right water fountain or pissing in the right rest room.

But the sign over Robinson's head said nothing about skin color, or race, or gender. The only criterion for entering was to be a baseball player. This was immediately after World War II, when America and her Allies had defeated the world's worst racists ever, Nazi Germany and Imperial Japan. It was my thought that in America we made no distinction between black and white men. You got ahead by doing well whatever it was you did. I thought his coming into the major leagues was a great thing, quite right and proper, and through that year and the next two or three, I followed his career avidly. It did not occur to this child to wonder why it had taken so long for black men to enter "Players Only."

Race relations in America are a complicated subject. Slavery fed American racism, something Thomas Jefferson knew but never acted on. It was not possible to hold slaves, and nearly impossible to live in the slaveocracy (as the abolitionists called the South), without regarding African Americans as inferior in every way — except hard physical labor — to whites.

When the slaves were freed during the Civil War, the liberated Negroes were emancipated but were not citizens. During Reconstruction some of them could vote and a few held elective office, but although President Grant tried to enforce the law, the Ku Klux Klan drove the blacks back into something close to bondage. The newly freed blacks found that the Fourteenth Amendment was ignored; private slavery had been replaced by public slavery. They were segregated, uneducated, subject to violence, any time, any place, for any offense. Even slaves had never been lynched in such numbers as the freed blacks. (Slaves, after all, were private property and worth money.) The system of apartheid that came to dominate the South, the border states, and much of the North (recall that *Brown v. Board of Education* applied to Topeka, Kansas — once an abolitionist town, by 1954 a segregated town), was dreadful.

Black soldiers were strictly segregated in World War I and World War II. Most were truck drivers, unloading at the wharves, or cooks or construction men. The 92nd Infantry Division (Colored) had black enlisted men and white officers. The Army, Navy, Coast Guard, Marines were as segregated as almost every other institution in America. This had always been the way, on the excuse that it was not the armed forces' task to bring about a social revolution. Only a few blacks got into combat, then only in their own outfits — the Tuskegee Airmen, flying P-51s, black antiaircraft batteries, black antitank units, the 92nd Infantry Division, and some other units. During the crisis of the Battle of the Bulge, when Eisenhower had run out of replacements, he offered black soldiers serving in the Service of Supply an opportunity to join units already in the line, on an integrated basis. They would have to give up their stripes to do so, but they would fight side by side with white soldiers. Thousands of blacks responded. They received much praise from their white regimental and division officers, and their fellow soldiers.

So the United States fought Germany and Japan, racist societies, with a segregated army. I only began to learn about it later, in college. Where I was in my thinking and feeling about race as a boy, was, in truth, nowhere. Except for sports, I knew nothing and apparently did not want to know.

One reason for this ignorance was that few people in America, at least none that I knew, talked about race. In 1945, when Dad got out of the Navy, we moved to Whitewater, Wisconsin. In Wisconsin, you didn't have to check a sign to see if you were at the right drinking fountain or eating in the right restaurant. Unlike in Florida, the grade schools (and high schools and colleges) in Wisconsin were not segregated by race. But of course outside Milwaukee, Madison, and Beloit there were few Negroes.

Until Robinson there had been no Negroes in the major leagues. It was the greatest sports story of my life. It was one of the greatest American stories of the century. Robinson lifted my heart. Then and ever since, I felt that whatever America's sins and shortcomings, we Americans could, would, change them.

In 1952, playing high school football, I can recall my heart swelling when the band played "The Star-Spangled Banner" before our game with Delavan because there was a Negro on the Delavan team. To my knowledge, he came from the first Negro family to live in Walworth

County, and the rumor around the league was that he had been "recruited," that his father had been given a job in Delavan to move there from Chicago because his son was an outstanding halfback. Maybe so, maybe not. How would I know? But he certainly was the first Negro I had played against, and I thought, as the National Anthem was being played, what a wonderful country we live in, a place where blacks can play against whites.

In 1953, I went off to college, where things didn't seem quite so simple, not even in sports. The Big Ten league was made up of Midwestern universities, all from abolitionist states that had fought for the Union, yet it was having a difficult time integrating its teams or even its undergraduate student bodies. Madison was well known for its liberalism, but the Wisconsin football team (on which I played as an offensive guard and a defensive middle-linebacker, good enough to have once been selected the Big Ten Player of the Week) had only five or six black players. In 1956 Wisconsin was the first Big Ten team — and as far as I know the first major college team — to have a black quarterback. His name was Sid Williams. To give some indication of the times, this simple fact brought forth many articles in the sports pages, and even in the editorial pages across the nation. Sid and I were friends, and as he was easily the best athlete on the team, all the players were glad to have him as our quarterback. We were concerned with winning.

I hung around with the black players after practice or on road trips, not for any political reasons but because they smoked cigarettes and so did I. We were almost the only ones on the team who did, so we would sneak off to do our puffing.

I was a history major, learning about slavery and the Civil War and the postwar South. The book that had the biggest impact on me, as it did or would have on millions of others, was C. Vann Woodward's 1955 classic, *The Strange Career of Jim Crow*. Half a century later it remains by far the single best book on the origins of segregation in the South because it puts the blame where it belongs, on politics. Racism dominated all Southern thinking about Negroes during the slavery days because it explained why it was that one race was master, the other slave. Racism was the justification for a system of segregation. If you don't believe this, read Woodward.

In 1957 I graduated from the University of Wisconsin and went to Louisiana State University to get my M.A. degree, studying under T. Harry Williams. In the summer of that year, my wife, Judy, and I got an apartment in Baton Rouge and I got a job on the west bank of the river as a teamster, working on the construction of a Dow Chemical plant in Plaquemines Parish. That meant a ferry ride each morning and evening, a good way to get to know that part of the Mississippi River. The plant was five miles away from the ferry landing, so I drove to it.

One afternoon, walking to the parking lot, I was talking sports with a co-worker, a guy about my age. I had learned that Southerners were nuts about sports and it was a safe subject to discuss, even argue about. As we were comparing the Southeastern Conference with the Big Ten, we walked past a car that had an American flag tied to the radio antenna.

"Nigger," he spat out.

"How could you possibly know that?" I asked in astonishment.

"Down here, we white guys fly the Confederate flag. Only the niggers put the Stars and Stripes on their cars."

"Wait a minute!" I blurted out. "That's our flag. All of us."

"Not down here," he said. He then gave me a short lecture on race and its position in the South, and ended up exclaiming, "I can kill a nigger anytime I want to."

I protested. Vehemently. He replied that there never had been a white person convicted of killing a nigger in Louisiana, and never would be.

I thought that was a terrible way to grow up, thinking you had a right to murder.

That fall I began my student career at LSU. My fellow graduate students were mainly from Louisiana, with a few from other parts of the South. We were all worshippers of T. Harry Williams and fascinated by the Civil War, and we bonded. Of course I argued for the Northern side.

That November, I was walking in downtown Baton Rouge after a heavy shower. I stepped into a mud hole. I picked up a stick and began scraping the mud off my shoe. An old black man came over to me, took the stick from my hand, explained that what I was doing was "nigger work," dropped to his knees, and began doing the scraping.

I was shocked and embarrassed down to my toes. I just stood there. When he finished with one shoe, still on his knees, he went to work on the other one. When he finished he stood. I gave him whatever change I had — a quarter probably, maybe a dime. My face was burning. I said thank you and fled.

The history graduate students shared office space so when I got there I related what had just happened to me. I expected the others would be as outraged as I was, or at least as embarrassed — imagine an old man doing something like that for a twenty-one-year-old kid. They wanted to know how big a tip I had given, then laughed me to scorn. They told me, patiently, that that was the way he made his living, that I should have given him more, that I was a typical Yankee abolitionist liberal, ready to extend sympathy but not money.

In the forty-plus years since I finished my graduate studies, what seemed improbable, then at least, has happened. There have been African-American doctors, scientists of all kinds, lawyers, professors, college presidents, mayors, Army and Air Force generals, Navy admirals, senators, representatives, Cabinet officials, big businessmen, governors, poets, novelists, historians. I think about what has happened in the South, and throughout America, in my lifetime. When I was a graduate student at LSU in the late 1950s, at a service station black men washed your windshield and filled your automobile with gas, swept the inside, and did whatever else needed doing. But they never, ever, handled your money. You paid the white employer, the only one to handle money.

Other than at work, black people stayed — overwhelmingly — with other blacks, for their housing, eating out, entertainment, church-going, schooling. There may have been interracial couples, but I never saw them. Professional sports teams were beginning to be integrated, and some colleges — even in the Deep South — but almost no local schools.

After World War II young officers in the Army began to question the wisdom of consigning some 12 percent of the Army's enlisted strength to labor battalions. They — and the black soldiers — were ready to integrate. So in 1948, President Harry Truman, running for election and threatened by A. Philip Randolph, a prominent black organizer and politician, with a "March on Washington," signed an executive order outlawing segregation in the armed forces.

Over the next four decades, the integration of the armed forces made most, if not all, of the difference. The Army led the way, with the Air Force following, then the Navy and the Marines. There were problems, difficulties, incidents, disgruntlement — but overall, by far, there was success. It is pretty hard to maintain a system of segregation in civilian life when there are black sergeants, lieutenants, colonels giving orders to white soldiers in uniform. It is pretty hard to maintain racial prejudices that know no limits when you live in a country that is defended by an Army that has only one color — green. The Army (and then the other services) became and has remained the most successfully integrated institution in America. More so than the universities. More so than politics or business life. More so than the churches.

In my first job, at LSU in New Orleans, I taught a course on the Civil War. One of my students was Raphael Cassimere. When I arranged a field trip to Vicksburg, Cassimere, who was my best student, told me no, he could not go to Mississippi in a caravan of cars with a white professor and white students. He was sure he would be arrested — all of us might be — and beaten and jailed or worse. I insisted that would not happen to us, riding in vans marked LSUNO, but he insisted. We went to Vicksburg without him. A month later, in June 1963, civil rights leader Medgar Evers was shot in the back and killed in an ambush outside his home in Jackson, Mississippi.

He was right. It was dangerous.

But I was right about him. He graduated, went to graduate school in history, became a member of the History Department at our school, by then called the University of New Orleans. He has been there ever since, a wonderful teacher, much admired by his colleagues and by students who now include Asian Americans, Mexican Americans, Latin Americans.

This is part of an awfully big change. I see it myself in my home state of Mississippi, where I have lived for a decade and a half, but which I once thought was at least as bad as South Africa used to be — and it was. An African American in the White House would cause no stir at all in Mississippi today, as it did in Theodore Roosevelt's day. It happens all the time, as we all know. For me, one of the great things in my life is riding my bike in my little town of Bay St. Louis and seeing black and white children playing together in the school yard. I see black businessmen, bankers, lawyers, doctors, teachers, and mixed couples walking on our beaches or sidewalks, holding hands. This is Martin Luther King, Jr.'s, dream, what he hoped for and what he got started.

# Chapter Seventeen

# Women's Rights and Immigration

When I was a boy in the 1940s, in high school and college in the 1950s, and at my first teaching job in the 1960s, women had a place in American society that I thought was privileged, enviable, unshakable, and much preferred by the women themselves. They knew their place, which was in the home, taking care of husband and children. Men opened the doors for them, held their chairs as they were seated at dinner, spoke carefully, without any curse words, when they were present. In college their majors were home economics, art, English, education, library science, music. A sex life for a middle- or upper-class woman before marriage was unthinkable (which doesn't mean it didn't happen, only that it was never flaunted and seldom known about). When they got married they took on the husband's family name.

This seemed to me to be entirely right and proper, if only because that is the way things were in my family and with my parents' friends.

My dad grew up on a farm in central Illinois, went on to medical school, and was a general practitioner in a small town in Wisconsin. My mother was the daughter of an Army Corps of Engineers colonel and a granddaughter of the leading family in town. She had lived with her parents in the Panama Canal Zone and other exotic places, while Dad got out of Illinois and Wisconsin only during the war. Yet there was no question about who ran the family — not in her mind, not in his, not in mine nor my brothers'. He made the decisions. She took care of us. For us children, all through grade and high school, walking in the front door for lunch or after school meant calling out, "Mom, I'm home!" We expected an answer, then a treat of some sort, cookies or the like, and questions about how our day was going.

They were both interested in our academic progress, Dad more so than Mom. They both went to our high school football and basketball games, at home or away, he because he was the team doctor, she because her sons were playing. Dad didn't much care about how well we did in sports. Our mother, who never missed a game, did. Dad insisted that we take the toughest academic programs — algebra, Latin, chemistry, physics. Funny thing: he never worried about our grades but only about how much we were learning, while she was obsessed with grades. She insisted that we learn to play a musical instrument in the band, learn to type.

Mother had more money than Dad did, although neither of them would have ever put it that way. She had inherited eighty acres and a cabin and a lake from her father, and a small ranch from her mother. He had his education. She read constantly, mainly historical romances that she took out of the library. He read medical journals and not much more. I spent much of my time in the local Carnegie Library, reading history books, especially about Napoleon, Washington, Jefferson, and Lincoln. Both had a casual interest in Wisconsin history and on occasion I'd get them to take me to historical sites.

Mother was far more talkative than he was, much more of a social creature. She wanted adventure. Dad wanted to take care of his patients, work in his garden, raise his kids. When my brothers and I reached high school age, and she could take care of our needs with the back of her hand, she told Dad she wanted a job. He absolutely refused. No wife of his was going to work — what would people say? Harry, Bill, and I agreed with Dad, wholeheartedly. What on earth would she do? Why would she do it? What made her want to do it? It would be degrading to have the wife of the town doctor working for a wage.

Finally, in self-defense, Dad gave her permission to become active in local politics. Otherwise she would not stop pestering him, and more importantly, she drank too much and smoked too much, played too much bridge and had too many friends. So he told her to try politics. She ended up as an elected member of the Walworth County Board and the Whitewater School Board. She certainly could have been a member of the Wisconsin state legislature and perhaps even a representative in Congress if he had given her permission to try, but that he would never do.

Eventually, when all her boys had gone off to college, Mother persuaded Dad to allow her to take a job at a travel agency. She had done a considerable amount of traveling and the agency was next door to his office, so they could drive to work and back home together. And she clearly would not be making much money.

In 1974, she went to work, at an age when most working women retire, and she loved it. She was very good at helping people plan a trip, keeping the costs to what they could afford, urging them to go see this or that. She had made a lot of the trips herself, even if sometimes only in her mind.

One day in the summer of 1975, she returned to her office from lunch (with Dad, of course), hung up her jacket, announced, "I'm back," and fell down, dead. The others in the office rushed next door to get Dad, who came and examined her but could do nothing about her stroke.

She was a great wife, mother, and grandmother. Her grandchildren adored her. She could have been a successful businesswoman, or a skilled and capable politician, or a leader in any part of the medical field (Dad had met her when he was an intern at St. Luke's Hospital in Chicago, where she was studying to be a dietitian). She would have made an outstanding reporter or a fine writer of novels or nonfiction. She never got to try these professions or any other. Before the travel agency the only job she ever held was during World War II, when she worked at the local pea cannery, alongside German POWs captured in North Africa. Somehow during that time she worked eight hours per day, six days a week, and managed to raise us children, all still in grade school.

The Second World War was a seminal experience for nearly all Americans. Sixteen million young men went into the armed services, a wholly new experience for most of them, and nearly all of them went overseas. They learned to do things they had always counted on women to do for them — cook the food, wash the dishes, make their beds, clean and press their clothes, and they learned to take orders without protest, to do as told, to forget their individual preferences and act together, as a team. Most of all, to prepare for and engage in combat.

Women's lives were also altered in radical ways. They could vote, since 1920, and hold elective office — Nellie Tayloe Ross in 1925 became the Governor of Wyoming, the first woman Governor in America. They began doing unthinkable things. In 1932 Amelia Earhart flew alone across the Atlantic. When America entered the war in 1941, a popular saying among women was "We are in this war too." They flocked to join up and pressured the Congress in May 1942 to provide for the Women's Army Auxiliary Corps (WAAC, later WAC), the Women Accepted for Volunteer Emergency Service (WAVES, Navy), Women's Auxiliary Ferrying Squadron (WAFS, Air Force), and Women's Reserve of the U.S. Marine Corps (WM). They got to wear uniforms but not carry arms. They were discriminated against in rank and pay. Everywhere they were welcome, not because of their sex or looks but because of the job they did.

The women officers in the WAFS flew hundreds of B-17s, B-24s, and B-25s over the Atlantic to their bases in England, Italy, and North Africa. They never lost a plane. When Colonel Paul Tibbets was training the 509th Composite Group to fly B-29 Superfortress bombers, some of his men said they were not going up in that thing, it was too dangerous. Tibbets got three WAFS to take off and land the plane, had the reluctant male fliers watch, and got rid of that problem.

It would not be possible to praise the nurses too highly. They did a magnificent job, in forward hospitals, in permanent hospitals, in aircraft used as flying ambulances, in ships set up as hospitals, generally in conditions never encountered in civilian life. By 1944, the armed forces needed more nurses, and President Roosevelt introduced a bill that would have drafted nurses (which would have been the first draft of women in American history), but it lost by one vote in Congress.

The women in service did their part and took on a whole new role in American life. But where the vast majority of American women served was on the home front, in the factories and assembly plants, making guns, ammunition, ships, landing craft, helmets, boots, and clothes, preparing canned food, packaging medical supplies, and so much more. They worked eight to ten hours per day, often six days a week. They learned new skills, made new friends. They were paid, not as well as men on the same job but more than they ever had before the war. Collectively they were called Rosie the Riveter. They were proud of the contribution they made and pleased at the new-found freedom they gained by having a well-paying job.

Men were fearful about what would happen when the war was over. Wartime jobs would disappear as the men would be coming home. They wanted their old jobs back. But the women wanted them too. And the women had learned how to do a job, how to fix a car, how to entertain themselves, how to open doors and pull up their own chairs at a table. The men wanted to come home to an America unchanged since December 6, 1941, and that clearly would not be possible.

The great worry never materialized. Young men and young women, freed from their war-time responsibilities, courted and got married. Women who had been financially independent during the war were glad to put some of the burden on their husbands. Life went on.

But not as it had. Rosie the Riveter had a new outlook.

Despite my mother having been a Rosie the Riveter, all this more or less passed me by. Whatever strides the women's movement was making in the two decades after the war took place without my noticing. I agreed with Dad, and most male Americans, as to the role of women. I married Judy Dorlester in 1957, the day I graduated from Wisconsin. She had just completed her junior year on a scholarship given by the Ford Foundation. Her test scores pegged her as a genius. We drove south to Baton Rouge for my graduate work. With no discussion about alternatives, I informed her (which is different from "we agreed") that she would have a job in the administration at LSU so I could afford to go to graduate school. For that year, she worked forty hours a week at a calculating machine. We returned to Wisconsin for my Ph.D. and again she went to work to pay the bills. After two years, and the birth of our first child, Stephenie, we went down to New Orleans and my first job. Now she didn't have to work anymore — I was pulling in a real salary — so she stayed home to take care of Stephenie and our new son, Barry.

Maybe three times a month, we would splurge on a baby-sitter and go to a party given by one of my colleagues. Never, in my memory, out to dinner at a restaurant. Sometimes we would go to a movie, or I would go out to play penny-ante poker. When we moved to Baltimore in 1964, I was making enough money finally to allow her to go back to school for her degree. I thought what we were doing was perfectly normal. It was what was right and proper.

In 1966, after Judy committed suicide — she was a depressive — I married Moira Buckley. She had a job at the Johns Hopkins hospital working on the bulletin there, but she could not stay with it and raise five kids at the same time. Then she met Stephanie Pascoff, wife of one of my students, Bob Pascoff. Stephanie invited her to a consciousness-raising meeting. She came home and began talking, and I realized — either right then or very soon thereafter — that my whole life had been changed. She brought with her, after that first meeting, a point of view that was brand-new to her and to me. Look at the history books, she said. Look at literature, entertainment, politics, and see which sex takes precedence. For my part, I thought, What on earth is she talking about? For her part, she was developing a new way of looking at what she was learning and doing.

Betty Friedan had published *The Feminine Mystique* in 1963. Moira read it, carefully, and more than once. Friedan contended that the "mystique of feminine fulfillment," the image to which many women attempted to conform, relegated them to the roles of wife, mother, homemaker, and consumer. The mystique was perpetuated by the advertising business, the mainstream media, TV comedies, education. It caused uneasiness, frustration, and despair among its victims.

Friedan became one of the most influential writers of the century. Her message spread across the country. In 1966 a civil rights group calling itself the National Organization for Women (NOW) came together to work for a "fully equal partnership of the sexes." It promoted a proposed Equal Rights Amendment, equal employment opportunities, an end to abortion laws, free day-care centers, an end to discriminatory educational quotas, and more.

Moira was always reading, talking, learning. More intellectually than in the practice of daily life. There was no bra burning. Still, our home life changed. She wanted me to do more in helping to raise five kids, all under ten years of age. More cleaning. Some cooking. Getting the little ones dressed for an outing. I continued to go out one night a week to play poker with the boys, and she started going out one night per week with Stephanie Pascoff and her group. They talked about consciousness raising. They vented long pent-up rage. And they went to work on their husbands, to educate them.

It wasn't just the older conservative men who resisted. So did those in their early thirties, like me, even those who regarded themselves as radicals, revolutionaries, or at least reformers. Bob Pascoff was heavily involved in civil rights and the antiwar crusade. He thought of himself and his mates as part of the Movement. Occasionally the members of the Movement would invite their wives and girlfriends to a meeting, usually to plan a demonstration. At such meetings, the men expected the women to make the coffee, bring the cookies, and serve them. When the women complained, demanding a role in forming the plans for the demonstration, they were put down.

While I was at Johns Hopkins, Milton Eisenhower put me on the Board of Governors of the Hopkins Club, presumably to bring some fresh, young ideas to a rather stodgy group. The club, in a splendid and refurbished colonial house on the campus, was divided at lunchtime into the men's side and the women's side. The kitchen was in between. Men could eat in the women's side, but not vice versa except in the evening, when the sexes could mingle on the men's side. Women professors complained that the "men only" lunch kept them out of the mainstream of what always goes on at a faculty club — gossip, discussions about what is happening on campus and in one's particular field, job openings.

The question came to a vote of the board. There were three votes to change policy, three to resist. It came down to me. I voted against the women, and "men only" it remained for the next year or so. Why I did what I did I can't explain today, but that is what I did. I compounded the mistake by mentioning it to Moira when I got home from the board meeting. She was appalled. Three decades later it is not something we laugh about.

By 1969, Moira had taught some of what she had learned to our kids, especially our two girls. I had learned not much but something. In the academic year 1969–70, we moved to Newport, Rhode Island, where I taught at the Naval War College. Everyone we knew was in the Navy and most of the wives and all of the husbands wanted no part of women's liberation. Moira read the publications of the National Organization of Women, but mainly she was on her own. She was passionately opposed to the Vietnam War. So was I, in my own way. But Newport was not a place conducive to speaking out on the subject.

Our only political commitment seemed safe enough. Moira organized the kids and got me to go along to a supermarket to support César Chávez's campaign for the grape pickers in California. The idea was to boycott the non-union-picked grapes. We marched around the entrance, carrying signs and chanting, "We won't go in until the grapes come out." That wasn't much but at least it gave our family the sense of having done something for the oppressed of America.

In 1970 we moved to Manhattan, Kansas,

where we had many adventures. The best, most important, with the longest-lasting consequences, was meeting and joining with the antiwar, pro–civil rights activists at Kansas State University. It was a cow college and we never expected what we found — organized groups trying to change America. My own life was tied to my teaching duties at KSU, and my research at the Eisenhower Library in nearby Abilene, Kansas, but Moira could finally start setting off on her own. It helped that the kids were older and required less care. It helped that in Manhattan there was a sympathetic group to support her and encourage her.

She got involved in building a geodesic dome. She took classes at the "Free University" run by the students and some members of the administration at KSU. She got into yoga. She spent time with her reading group, getting new points of view, adding her own. In these and other meetings, she gained the strength to look at women in newspaper, magazine, and TV advertisements, or to hear the jokes about women current at the time, and laugh rather than cry. She learned to trust other women, to see them as her sisters. Insofar as women's liberation was seen by its male (and some female) detractors as bra burning, growing long hair, wearing sacklike dresses, scorning lipstick — that was not for her nor her friends. What they were seeking and finding was consciousness. They were teaching themselves to be aware of their circumstances.

They were trying to avoid behaving like second-class citizens. They were searching to find explanations for the huge difference between men and women in American society.

For the Ambrose family, not just Moira, there was a lot to learn, and one way or another we did. When we moved to New Orleans in 1971, she taught for a couple of years, then went to graduate school in English at UNO. She completed her course work but could not find a sponsor to guide her through a dissertation on the marriage dialogues of Robert Frost. She switched to Special Education to get her certification in that field, which she did. I helped, or at least like to think I did.

I told Moira that since Judy had made it possible for me to go through graduate school, I wanted to do at least that much for her. So for two years I did all the cooking — not quite all, of course, especially not on weekends — the shopping, the clothes washing, and some of the cleaning around the house. Every Monday afternoon I'd go to the supermarket, fill a cart with groceries — lots of hot dogs, beans, and buns, lots of hamburger, a canned ham, much cereal and milk, quarts of juice — and try to get by through the week. On Tuesday afternoons I cleaned the house, on Friday afternoons I washed the clothes. The rest of my time I'd teach and try to write a book.

For the young men and women — younger than us but older than our kids — the biggest difference in those early years in New Orleans was the Vietnam War. The boys had to carry a draft card and were always subject to being called into the armed services and sent to war. The girls did not. That was a major reason why the boys' views on the war carried far more weight than what the girls thought and said. It was the war that broke down some parts of the world of the 1950s and early 1960s; in an ironic way, that breakdown in social mores and political outlook caused terrible anguish among the staunch supporters of the war, the hawks who were generally older and more conservative. One of the biggest changes of all, the success of the civil rights movement, would have happened without the Vietnam War, but at a different pace and in a different way.

So also women's liberation. The demands that grew out of the Rosie the Riveter experience were already there and would have grown. Women would have started going to law schools in increasing numbers, and to medical schools, and attending business colleges without the war in Vietnam. Other things were aiding women's liberation. New washing machines, dishwashing machines, improved vacuum cleaners, wash-and-wear clothes, automobiles that were not laid up in the shop half the time, frozen foods. And the Vietnam War contributed too, as it got the younger generation of women to question authority and the established way of doing things. But it is also impossible to imagine drug use, hippie lifestyles, a march on the Pentagon, the riots at the 1968 Democratic National Convention, popular music, and more of the things the old folks loved to hate without the Vietnam War.

America led the way in pop culture, which attracted lots of attention and condemnation, especially from the British, French, and Germans, but it also led the way in the women's movement and civil rights, in attracting immigrants, in accepting immigrants, in creating a society that was open and embracing, that welcomes all that was good in whatever was new.

There have been many profound changes in my life and in that of most others over the past sixty-five years. In America, which has led the way, these include racial and ethnic attitudes, an ever broadening and deeper commitment to democracy in all nations and every phase of life, a wholly new attitude toward the environment, a determination to save rather than profit from the wonders of nature. But the place that America has shown the way to the biggest and most satisfactory change, the one that above all others that has led us, if not to, but at least toward, the promised land, is women's rights. Women's liberation is not completed, but it is the direction in which we are all heading. It is to the great benefit of all of us.

Because women's liberation covers 50 percent

341

of the population, of course, it always must come first in any list of significant changes, but not too far behind come changes in racial attitudes and in our immigration policy.

One hundred years ago, people from Eastern and Central and Southern Europe were "white," "Christian" (generally Catholic), usually literate, a part of what was then called "the melting pot." They were referred to, disparagingly, as Wops or Eye-ties, Poles, Polacks, Huns, Russkis, Jews or Shinnies or Kikes, Mackerel Snappers or Paddies, and on and on in a long list of cruel or derogatory nicknames. Mainly they lived in urban slums, working long hours for small wages, living in tiny rooms, exploited in every way possible. Almost no immigrants from Asia, the Middle East, or Africa were allowed into the country, and few from Mexico. No Asians or Spanish-speaking Americans could participate in amateur or professional sports against white Americans. The prejudice against these ethnic groups and against their countries or continents of origin was almost total. The full extent of that feeling at the beginning of the twentieth century cannot be overstated.

By the end of the century immigration laws limiting the numbers of East Europeans and all but forbidding Asians, Africans, and Middle Eastern people from coming into the country were gone. Chinese, Japanese, Vietnamese, Indians, Filipinos, and many others have come to the United States and become an integral part of the nation. So too Mexicans, Puerto Ricans, and other Spanish-speaking peoples. All these groups not only participate in the economic and cultural life of the country, but in sports as well. Their literature sparkles. So do their movies and music. Their contribution to popular dress is immense. We have all learned to enjoy their food. Presidential candidates strive to speak to them directly in their own language; their representatives and local politicians do so as a matter of course. We are a far more diverse culture than ever before, far ahead of the rest of the world, and all of us are the beneficiaries as a consequence. Like much else that has happened in the last century — flying in machines, for example — none of this would have seemed even remotely possible to the people of 1901.

A partial list of immigrants in the twentieth century would include our most famous rocket scientists, moviemakers, musicians, automobile manufacturers, airplane designers, educators, medical personnel, and so many more that one has to wonder where we might be today had it not been for them.

From the beginning we have been a nation of immigrants. We would never have developed without them. We quite possibly would not have survived without them, from the Revolutionary War to Andrew Jackson's army at New Orleans, to the immigrants who fought in the Civil War, to the Chinese and Irish and others who built the transcontinental railroad, or those who worked in the factories, mines, and mills to turn us into the industrial power that went on to win World War II.

Immigrants do more than help us win our wars, or set up cleaning shops or ethnic restaurants. Here is a story from the Cajun country of southern Louisiana. Beginning in the mid-1970s, people fleeing Indochina flocked to Louisiana. They liked the weather and the opportunity to fish for a living. They borrowed money and bought some old, falling-apart Cajun shrimp boats. The Cajuns laughed and laughed at the fast one they had pulled on the Vietnamese. By the mid-1980s, the Vietnamese were buying specially crafted shrimp boats, for big sums of money. What had happened?

This is the story a resident of Larose, Louisiana, heard from a game warden. One day the warden came into the dock, half laughing and half crying. "What is going on?" asked my friend.

"Well, you see that shrimp boat out there?" It was Vietnamese, he said, and quite unlike anything the Cajuns used. When the Cajuns went out to trawl for shrimp, they brought along the TV so they could watch the football game. They had two or three ice chests filled with steaks and beer. They had a Coleman stove to cook the steaks. And they took only young men. They went through their catch when they hauled in the net, took out and threw away the trash fish, put ice over the shrimp, and after a few hours came back to port.

The Vietnamese, the warden said, went out with the whole family, old and young. They carried some water but nothing to eat. When they hauled in the net, they separated the trash fish from the shrimp, put ice on the shrimp, and gutted the trash fish, to bring them home to sell at a penny or two a pound to a nearby cat food factory. Running around on the deck were naked seagulls.

"What the hell?" asked the warden. The Vietnamese explained that the gulls flew down to pick up the guts of the fish. The Vietnamese caught them by the foot, yanked out their feathers, and let them run loose until it was time for dinner. Then they recaptured the seagulls, killed and gutted them, and cooked them over a small grill.

The warden protested that although the seagull was not protected by any law, it was illegal to commit cruelty to wild animals, and this pulling of feathers was cruelty. Besides, why didn't they just cut off the heads and throw the gulls on the ice until they were ready to eat them?

"What," the Vietnamese replied. "And waste all that ice?"

# Chapter Eighteen

# *The United States and Nation Building*

It became a commonplace because of Vietnam to say that no matter what, America should not engage in nation building. It was thought to be an expression of hubris. No matter our intentions, nation building is costly and, worse, unworkable. Americans believed we could not change Vietnam into a democratic, modern, progressive country by war. We cannot transform African states.

America made only a halfhearted, ill-thought-out attempt to introduce democracy and a free economy to Vietnam. President Thieu was elected, but no opposition candidate was allowed. Generals ran the show in Saigon. Instead of democracy and free enterprise, the American presence in the persons of hundreds of thousands of GIs brought widespread drug use, rampant prostitution, thousands of babies who were abandoned when their American fathers took off when their tours of duty were over. Criminal activities of all kinds abounded and the destruction of its villages, towns, cities, and the environment was the result of years of war. It got so bad that many Americans came to believe that the communists in North Vietnam were fighting on the right side, while our South Vietnamese allies were on the wrong side. Thousands said, God help any country that gets into a war on the American side.

In fact, we have done more than any other country in bringing democracy, a free economy, and progress to Japan, Germany, and South Korea. Rather than taking a negative historical lesson from Vietnam, we should take the positive lessons of World War II's aftermath. So, what happened in Japan, our most hated enemy?

In September 1945, American occupation troops began to move into and take control of Japan. The country had been a feudal monarchy for more than 1,000 years. The Emperor was worshipped. Young men flew kamikaze, sacrificing their lives for him. The country was ruled by the few families that owned the major businesses, held the largest farms, ran the military. Women had no rights. No Japanese worker or serf had ever voted in a meaningful election.

In 1945, the Americans determined to change the system. General Douglas MacArthur wrote Japan's new constitution, basing it on the Americans'. Under his efficient and autocratic direction, the occupation, which lasted until 1951, officially eliminated militarist, ultranationalist, and feudal vestiges. Japan's political system, its economy, labor relations, society, public health and welfare programs, and educational structure were reformed. Its Emperor was no longer divine. The new constitution included land reform and women's rights to education and the vote and provided for Japan's demilitarization. Amicable relations between Japan and the United States were established.

In less time than the Second World War lasted, MacArthur transformed Japan from a feudal totalitarian state into a modern, progressive, democratic country. His biographer, D. Clayton James, writes that, "His leadership in occupied Japan may be viewed by future authorities as the most important phase of his career. His administration in Japan was one of the most enlightened of any occupation in history." This was nation building such as had never before been seen, anywhere. It brought immense good for Japan, for Asia, for the world. From his headquarters in Tokyo, MacArthur ran a large bureaucratic structure, composed of U.S. armed forces, State Department and Commerce Department personnel, and other civilian Americans, effectively. There was freedom of political association to the point that, in early 1950, the Japanese Communist Party staged a series of violent demonstrations against American military personnel in Tokyo.

MacArthur did not do all this alone, obviously. What made the American occupation of Japan a success for the Japanese and the Americans was all the more remarkable for the hatred between the two countries between December 7, 1941, and September 1945, and before.

Here is one story, among scores. A young GI in the American occupation force came ashore in early September 1945. He was stationed in a small village in the countryside. His unit's job was to protect the police station and city hall. The next morning, he saw not one Japanese. This went on for two weeks and he was getting bored, as his unit was never allowed out of its headquarters in the police station. He had a baseball glove and a ball with him, and he began throwing the ball against a wall in the courtyard, then catching it on the rebound. One day he saw, on the other side of the wall, a Japanese teenager watching him. The Japanese youth had an old, badly battered softball and a stick for a bat. The GI invited the boy by sign language to play catch. The boy did. The next day, the GI found a glove for him, and the next week a bat and more gloves and some balls. Soon the courtyard was filled with Japanese boys and GIs playing catch. After a few days they all moved into the street. A few days later they had laid out a baseball field and were playing the game.

I know that nothing like that ever happened when German troops occupied Russian villages, or when Red Army men took over German villages, or when Japanese troops invaded China, the Philippines, and elsewhere. MacArthur did not order this done. It just happened because that is the way Americans acted.

Korea had been for most of the first half of the twentieth century a Japanese colony, with most Koreans serving their Japanese masters as slaves. In 1945, American troops occupied the area south of the thirty-eighth parallel and the Soviet Union the area to the north. In 1947, the United States submitted the Korean question of unification to the United Nations General Assembly for disposition. The Soviet Union refused to cooperate in this effort to unify the country. Elections held in South Korea in May 1948, under U.N. supervision, led to Syngman Rhee becoming President of the Republic of Korea. The Soviet Union set up a communist puppet government in North Korea under Kim Il Sung — whose son, Kim Jong Il, more than half a century later, still rules.

In June 1950, with Soviet prodding and weapons, the North Koreans invaded South Korea. President Truman immediately went to South Korea's aid, with MacArthur in command. A long, costly war ensued, not finished until the summer of 1953. More than a half-century later, American troops are still in South Korea, helping to defend it. Further, thanks to the efforts of the South Koreans and extensive American reconstruction aid, South Korea became one of the most progressive, productive democratic nations in Asia. North Korea, still under communist rule, remains just about the poorest nation in the world. There is a difference between having the United States and the Soviet Union as a military occupier.

America sent her troops overseas, around the world, in the Second World War. She kept them there through the second half of the twentieth century. American troops ended up spreading democracy wherever they were.

It has not stopped. At Thanksgiving 2001, Moira and I went to Bosnia under the sponsorship of the USO to speak to the American troops stationed there. In a way, I was playing Bob Hope. Not that I can tell jokes like Hope did, but I do know how to tell stories about men at war. The American troops were members of the 29th Division (the "Blue and Gray"), the division that led the way ashore on Omaha Beach on D-Day, 1944, and with us were a dozen or so veterans of that landing, mainly sergeants but junior officers and two men who went on to make general officer. The current 29th Division troops were, of course, in awe of the veterans. Obviously I don't have that kind of status, but I could tell the hospital personnel about the division's medics on D-Day and the riflemen about how their predecessors got ashore on June 6, and what they did, or the communications men about scouts and runners back in 1944.

We were in Bosnia for more than a week. It

was our best trip ever, both because of what it represented and because of the promise it held for the future. To begin with, we saw things we never could have imagined possible. There are thirty national contingents, all United Nations, under American command. The commander was General Steve Blum, head of the 29th Division. All the troops were part of the Stabilization Force (SFOR). A large curved sign over the gate at the command post, Eagle Base, proclaimed "Home of the Peacekeepers." We saw a Greek and a Turk soldier, patrolling, in uniform, armed, working together. We saw Germans and Frenchmen, Poles and Estonians, Latvian and Swedish troops, Lithuanians and British, Irish and Austrian.

We arrived at one observation post, Connor, in two Black Hawk helicopters, with General Blum, Moira and me sitting in the middle, armed men behind us, and two men at machine guns at the forward windows, all loaded and ready. We talked with the troops, made a presentation, and prepared to leave. General Blum said wait a minute. Two incoming helicopters came over the low mountain heading for our landing strip. They were Russian, part of the air-landing brigade that serves as part of Blum's command. They landed about fifty meters from the Black Hawks, Russian armed men, landing combat-ready, in the presence of American armed men, also ready for combat. They greeted each other. The last time that happened was at Torgau on the banks of the Elbe River in 1945. With this difference: an American general now commanded a Russian unit, the first time ever.

All this was happening in the middle of Europe, in a country that is one-third Croat, one-third Muslim, one-third Serb, where people have been killing one another for 1,000 years. And it was the Americans, the men and women from the New World, who were setting the example and leading the way.

These American troops were superb, and a big surprise, men and women, all armed, carrying their loaded weapons, including women with BARs. We drove to Forward Observation Base Comanche, a small outpost of 120 soldiers, sixty-five of whom were from the Mississippi National Guard. They had replaced the Georgia National Guard when it had completed its six-month deployment, and they had three months to go. They were very young. They came from a Southern state known everywhere for its defense of the past, but they were now preparing for the future. They wore an American flag shoulder patch. They were black, brown, yellow, red, white. This is not the way things used to be in the Mississippi National Guard. The troops wear baseball caps when off duty. The caps proclaim at the front, "Hard Rock Café: SFOR Bosnia," and on the back, "Love All, Serve All." That is not the way things used to be in the Mississippi National Guard.

Blum's UN command, the Multi National

Division North (4,700 troops), was anchored by the 2,672 Americans (down from 20,000 in 1995), part of the 29th Division. It included regulars, and reserve units, and National Guard contingents. Eagle Base was the largest employer in the city of Tuzla, providing construction jobs, service jobs, and many others at fair wages — for women as well as men. Muslims worked beside Serbs along with Croats. The people of Bosnia saw black and white, yellow and brown, male and female Americans working together.

It has been the pattern, over the past decade, for troops sent into a region — Serbs into Bosnia, for example, or Indonesians into East Timor, or African soldiers into other parts of Africa — to engage in wanton slaughter of civilians, especially women and children. That did not happen when American troops went into a country, not even after September 11, 2001, into a country of Muslims. Individual atrocities occur, that is true, but nowhere has it been American policy to kill civilians. Indeed, it is the other way around — American troops went into Bosnia signaling "Love All, Serve All." General Blum remarked, "The American flag on the troops' shoulders is what the people of Bosnia respect — and they don't mess with them."

Americans are there to lend their resources and personnel to rebuilding. One example: clearing minefields. The mines are everywhere, laid down by all three sides during the Bosnian war. One civilian a day is killed or maimed by a mine. American soldiers go out to remove them, using dog teams to sniff them out. By the end of 2001, 267,000 square miles had been swept by men and women, black and white.

What the Mississippi National Guard is doing in Bosnia is setting precedent for what lies ahead for American foreign and military policy. Like it or not, we are the world's only superpower and we have taken on the job of rebuilding, restoring, educating. This is what much of modern American soldiering is going to look like.

General Blum has a singular task. At fifty-five, he has made 1,500 air drops. He has had open heart surgery. He talks so well and thinks so swiftly and knows so much that he reminds me of Eisenhower in 1945, when Ike was fifty-five years old. We flew in helicopters together, we attended ceremonies, briefings, meals with the troops. He was always fully concentrated. He is outstanding in his job as military commander and diplomat, as good as Ike was in Germany after World War II, although on a much smaller scale.

Quotes from General Blum during a helicopter ride: "No other army in the world could do this. Our soldiers have to be social workers one minute, combat soldiers the next." The difficulty of his task is clear: "Our aim is one country, one army." Bosnia currently has three armies: Muslim, Croat, and Serb. In Bosnia, he reminds us, "There are more weapons per person than anywhere else in the world. So many that to celebrate a wedding they throw grenades and shoot their AK-47s."

We flew by helicopter to Sarajevo. It is a bowl surrounded by splendid mountains. The city was host to the 1982 Winter Olympics. In 1914, the terrorist act of a crazed Serb killing the Austrian Archduke led directly to the First World War. In 1998, the mountains belonged to the Serbs. From there they shelled the largely Muslim city. There are parts of Sarajevo today that look like Berlin in 1945.

We also flew to Srebrenica, another Muslim city under U.N. protection during the war, which the Serbs overran. The U.N. peacekeepers failed to stop them. The Serbs executed many men — rounded them up and shot them. The Serb assault on Srebrenica killed more than 7,000 people (out of about 24,000). It was the significant event that impelled the Western powers to take action against the Serbs.

Blum warns that it will take twenty years for Srebrenica to come back. At least there is some peace; the streetcars are running. Armed Dutch troops do the sweep of the airfield. At the headquarters, Camp Bitmer, there is a Norwegian PX, a French PX, an American PX, and a British PX.

Blum showed us the site of the Vicoko airfield raid, Operation Dragnet. On September 27, 2001, elements from the U.S. 10th Mountain Division, urban warfare specialists, carried out a search and seize mission. Along with illegal arms discovered, they arrested six Algerian nationals who were associated with Osama bin Laden. On October 28, in Operation Omaha, Blum's troops made a ground-air assault on two sites, where they found illegal weapons, including six surface-to-air missiles hidden underground.

Blum showed us a site where he had found a mass grave. "Same thing as 1945 — just new names." More than 200,000 were killed in Bosnia, no one knows how many injured. More than a million refugees. To escape cities being shelled, the women, children, and old men fled, following the power lines across the roughest mountains. This was the worst war in Europe in fifty years.

Flying to Srebrenica we had passed over farm-land that looked like America in the 1930s. No tractors. Horses pulled the plows. The roads were a ruin. The Saudis sent in money, but Blum said it was used to pay Muslim men to grow beards or to fund children's camps, which are for males only and in fact were military camps.

Every house was destroyed, but rebuilding is beginning. The new police station, Blum said, was built with American funds. When it was completed, he ordered that it not be opened until there were both Muslim and Serb police. It sat empty for some months, but finally his condition was met and he opened the station.

An international force commanded by an

American, working for the United Nations to keep peace. That was a dream General Eisenhower had a half-century ago. In 1947 he advocated a United Nations peacekeeping force, with one uniform and one commander. He expected the United States to send a sizable contingent to it, larger than any of the others, and he assigned command to one of his best officers, General Matthew Ridgway. He believed that sooner or later, the U.N. force would have control of atomic weapons, an outcome he favored. In the meantime, he opted for a British-American Combined Chiefs of Staff, but only until a genuine U.N. peacekeeping force was established. At that point the CCS would have to be abolished.

Eisenhower's proposal for a United Nations force languished, but his optimism remained. In his Farewell Address as President, on January 17, 1961, he declared: "We pray that peoples of all faiths, all races, all nations, may have their great human needs satisfied; that those now denied opportunity shall come to enjoy it to the full; that all who yearn for freedom may experience its spiritual blessings; that those who have freedom will understand, also, its heavy responsibilities; that all who are insensitive to the needs of others will learn charity; that the scourges of poverty, disease, and ignorance will be made to disappear from the earth, and that, in the goodness of time, all peoples will come to live together in a peace guaranteed by the binding

358

force of mutual respect and love."

From almost anyone else, that would be pie-in-the-sky optimism, but from the Supreme Commander, Allied Expeditionary Force, World War II, it was the American Spirit, clearly enunciated. Someday it will happen. My faith is based on what happened in Japan, Germany, and South Korea after World War II, and what is happening today in Bosnia. The American Spirit. By no means are we as a people all that special, or all-embracing, but we are part of a country that outshines those that have gone before us and most of those in existence today. I realize that sounds like some politician talking. I'm no politician. I am an historian who has learned through a lifetime of studying that nothing in the world beats universal education, women's rights, freedom of religion, democracy, an openness to all ethnic groups, the will to admit that terrible mistakes have been made — slavery, imperialism, segregation — and a determination to correct those mistakes.

Except for a tiny number of the twentieth century's leading religious figures — Gandhi, Pope John XXIII — no one outside America has ever produced a leader who could speak as General and President Eisenhower did in his Farewell Address.

# Chapter Nineteen

# *Nothing Like It in the World*

In 1959 Robert L. Heilbroner published *The Future as History: The Historic Currents of Our Time and the Direction in Which They Are Taking America*. I read the book then and again in June 2002. I am struck by how much he got right, as well as what he missed.

Heilbroner's major theme is optimism. He calls it "a philosophy that is an historic attitude toward the future. . . . Over most of human history it has been untenable. . . . Indeed as an enduring trait of national character it could almost be called exclusively American." The coming of the Industrial Revolution brought many changes, including this: "Nature, which had hitherto been the master of man, now became his great slave." That was true through the period Heilbroner is discussing, culminating with the atomic bomb. That optimism was summed up by Saint-Just, Robespierre's young colleague. Happiness, he said, was a new idea in Europe. It was, and it grew, through the remainder of the eighteenth century and the nineteenth century and into the twentieth century.

But then in 1914–18 Europe experienced a compression of horror without parallel in history. "The carnage of the First World War, the exhaustion of the Depression, the agonizing descent of Germany into its fascist nightmare, the suicide of Spain, the humiliation of Italy, the French decay, the English decline — and finally the culminating fury of World War II. Before the cumulative tragedy of these years all optimistic views failed. . . . We could only note with incredulous dismay the supine acquiescence with which the masses of Germany and Italy had received — not to say welcomed — Caesarism."

Despite Heilbroner's pessimistic judgment, America nevertheless held to its optimism, partly because it had no enemies on its borders, but also because "unlike its mother-nations, America has never experienced the dragging weight of a changeless past; has never had to cope with the peasant tradition or with its resistance to change." The American attitude has been (and is): Whatever doesn't work, we will fix and change. Thus, "as few peoples on earth, we were permitted the belief that we were the sole masters of our destiny, and as few peoples on earth have been, we were," Heilbroner wrote.

World War II, the atomic bomb, the Cold War, made it hard for Americans to continue in their optimism. The idea of progress, so central to the Western World in the nineteenth century, gave way to a sense of despair. At first we feared and then came to believe that we were no longer in control. But in the half-century since Heilbroner wrote, the Cold War has ended. With America victorious and today the only superpower in the world, our optimism has been restored. As to whether this is justifiable we must leave to our children's grandchildren, and their progeny.

American optimism from 1776 to 1940 had many sources: an abundance of free or almost free land; no feudal past to encumber that land; great mineral deposits; magnificent lakes and rivers; a diverse and self-chosen population. Except for the War of 1812, it had been an American decision whether or not to get into foreign wars — the Mexican War, the war with Spain, World War I — until 1941. Also feeding the optimism was the feeling that we were exceptional, unique among nations, which we certainly were in terms of the fertility of our soil, the mineral deposits, our size. Most important of all, we were unique because of our Constitution.

The American Constitution is the greatest governing document, and at some 7,000 words just about the shortest. Since 1788, it has been our guidepost. It took a while, but with the Thirteenth, Fourteenth, Fifteenth, and Nineteenth Amendments, it came to embrace everyone born in the United States, or naturalized. Its principles are known throughout the world: One person, one vote. Three branches of government. Nationwide elections at stated periods. Trial by jury. Live wherever you can make a living. And so much more — how could a government based on such principles fail?

The pillars on which that government stands embrace goals and aims that are felt worldwide. Everyone, everywhere, knows these principles and struggles for them. Those who live in colonies want independence. Those in dictatorships long for freedom. The pillars that the Founding Fathers, and their successors, rejected were kingship (despotism), an heredity noble class, and a state religion.

A chief characteristic of the nineteenth century was putting the best minds to work discovering and describing nature — men like Lewis and Clark, Charles Darwin, Alexander von Humboldt, and so many others, who opened up the world for all of us. Nation states that went to war in the nineteenth century and early twentieth century fought with such ferocity as to almost wipe each other out. That does not compare to war in the later twentieth century, when nation states were able to use the conquest of nature to build weapons that could kill masses of people quickly and easily. The nineteenth century had ended with high hopes and a commitment to progress — with the steamboat and the railroad leading the way and the automobile and airplane just around the corner in the year 1900. But the technological improvements that inspired optimism throughout the Western world and made the nineteenth century one of great hope soon became killing machines. As a consequence, the great wars of the twentieth century made it into the worst century ever.

But things that Heilbroner did not see coming brought with them a renewed sense of optimism. The United States won the Cold War. It is democracy, not totalitarianism, that is on the march. The scientific and technological advances of the twentieth century, so heavily based on weapons, have also produced advances in scientific agriculture, including pesticides and irrigation, new sources of fuel and power, new medicines of all types.

If the nineteenth century was the age of the discovery and description of nature, and the twentieth century was the great age of the conquest of nature, the twenty-first century must be the great age of nature's restoration. One place to begin is with dams.

Dams across rivers go far back in time. Those of the twentieth century surpassed anything previously seen, as did the "lakes" they created upstream. American governments, mostly in President Franklin Roosevelt's administration, built dams on most major and many smaller rivers. The idea was to put people to work. Roosevelt could have built an interstate highway system, but he feared political opposition to great expanses of concrete stretching from one coast to another. Dams, on the other hand, would have many supporters and hardly any opponents. An announcement of a new dam here or there was almost everywhere greeted with great enthusiasm.

The promise was that dams would control floods, create more irrigated farmland, and provide a constant source of power for electricity. But dams and the higher levees the government also built do not control floods. They just pass them on downstream. Taken altogether, the dam-building projects of the twentieth century were misguided, especially those on the Missouri, the Columbia, and the Salmon rivers. When the rains come the water spreads out. It tops the dams and crests the levees, spreads across the floodplains and inundates the cornfields and the houses built on them. This is an act of nature, rather like a forest fire. We have to learn to live with it, not fight it, because if we fight it we will always lose.

In the past century the U.S. Army Corps of Engineers spent billions of dollars on the Mississippi, Missouri, Columbia, and other rivers in an attempt to make them floodproof, but it is the river that wins.

Dams have also harmed wildlife and made rivers less useful for recreation. Dammed rivers, hemmed in by levees, flow faster and are much narrower than those without dams and levees — the Missouri River today flows three to five times as fast as it did when Lewis and Clark first went up it in 1804. This tampering with nature has diminished fish and bird and deer life and makes canoeing, camping, and swimming difficult to impossible. We were promised as the dams went in that they would have stepping-blocks for the salmon to make their way upstream, past the dams, to their spawning ground. But today the salmon runs on the Columbia River — once the most prolific river in the world for salmon — are reduced to less than 5 percent of what they were.

We need to get rid of those dams and let the rivers flow the way God intended them to run. The generation that will be taking power in America, and those following it, will determine to restore nature. When I was a college student, I was taught in Econ. 101 that the two chief ingredients to life come for free — water and air. Since then I have learned that that is the opposite of the truth. Clean air and water cost money. We will have to clean up the rivers and lakes and air, and make automobiles that are powered by hydrogen rather than fossil fuels. And much more.

There are many other problems brought on by human progress. As things are now, the more sophisticated we get, the more advanced our vehicles and buildings become, the more vulnerable we are.

It is safe to predict that war will be our greatest threat in the twenty-first century, but we cannot say what kind of war, fought where, to what end. For the United States, now, the danger comes from the Islamic world, which has what seems a nearly unstoppable weapon, in some ways the ultimate weapon. It is the man, woman, boy, or girl willing to give up his or her life. In World War II, the U.S. Navy took its most severe losses at Iwo Jima and Okinawa — some 20 percent of all naval losses in the war. The kamikazes got them. There was no machine then, and is no computer now, that can respond as fast or as accurately as the human eye and brain. Suicide bombers are relatively easy to train, difficult to stop, and all they have to do is walk — or fly — to their target.

We are now engaged in a war which will not end with the killing of this or that Islamic leader, or the destruction of Arab headquarters on the West Bank, or any other temporary triumph. This war must end the way the wars with Germany and Japan ended, when Islamic nations begin educating their women, allowing everyone to vote, encouraging freedom of religion. These are things being done in some Muslim states. Some say it is impossible to nation-build in the Islamic world. That is by no means true. Some 1.2 billion people are Muslims, which means that 600 million are women. The vast majority of them are not allowed to learn to read or write. But think of what a constituency that is. It is a war between modernity and medievalism. As things are now, whenever an Islamic militant sees a Muslim woman without a veil, or a Muslim woman watching TV or driving a car, they blame the United States. The fanatics among them want to be in absolute control of their women, their children, their economy, their religion, their society, their politics. There is nothing the United States can do that will satisfy these authoritarian extremists, short of transporting our country to another planet.

Consider what the United States has accomplished since 1776. We began with some severe problems — slavery, the condition of women in the body politic, the terrible way we treated the Native Americans, using our national resources as if they were inexhaustible, then colonialism in Panama and the Philippines, a virtual ban on immigration from outside Western Europe, and so much more. Nor have we solved them all — racism is still with us, as is sexism. We face new foreign threats — terrorism, weapons of mass destruction in the hands of fanatics.

But we've accomplished so much in these areas and others, both at home and abroad, that we are right to remain the most optimistic of people. We've made the world a better place and we will continue to do so. Our American Spirit comes from the Founding Fathers, was developed by Jackson, Grant, and both Roosevelts, taken abroad. That Spirit got us through September 11, 2001, and it will see us through the future.

# Acknowledgments

My wife, Moira, and my son Hugh listened to each chapter of this book as it emerged from the computer, made helpful suggestions on word choices and placement, and kept me going. Friends and other family members who came to Bay St. Louis to see me while I was writing had to listen also, and also made useful changes and suggestions. These include Stephenie Ambrose Tubbs, Barry Ambrose, Andrew Ambrose, Grace Ambrose and her fiancé, Benjamin Zake; Edie Ambrose and Yakir Katz; Bill and Pris Ambrose; Ron and Judy Drez; Harry Ambrose; Jim and Sue Burt; Mary Alice Wimmer; Dick Lamm; John Holcomb; Nick Mueller; Raphael Cassimere; Tammie Cimalore; Homer and Dougie Hitt and others at the Bay St. Louis "Da Beach House," including Colleen and Todd Read.

The dedication is to the three medical people who convinced me I could most successfully fight cancer by continuing my regular regime, which meant sleeping and eating, riding a bike, swimming, working out at the gym, reading — and writing. They not only convinced me, they made it possible.

Like Moira, Alice Mayhew always gets first

mention in my acknowledgments, but in this case I need to single out Roger Labrie and Anja Schmidt, her assistants at Simon & Schuster and two of the finest editors I've ever worked with, full of suggestions, corrections, additions, deletions, ideas. After writing more than a dozen books with Alice as my editor, I should have thought I had little to learn — but I did, and Roger and Anja taught me.

# About the Author

Stephen E. Ambrose is the author of numerous books of history, including the *New York Times* best-sellers *The Wild Blue, Nothing Like It in the World, Band of Brothers, Citizen Soldiers, Undaunted Courage, and D-Day*, as well as multi-volume biographies of Dwight D. Eisenhower and Richard Nixon. He lives in Bay St. Louis, Mississippi, and Helena, Montana.

The employees of Thorndike Press hope you have enjoyed this Large Print book. All our Thorndike and Wheeler Large Print titles are designed for easy reading, and all our books are made to last. Other Thorndike Press Large Print books are available at your library, through selected bookstores, or directly from us.

For information about titles, please call:

(800) 223-1244

or visit our Web site at:

www.gale.com/thorndike
www.gale.com/wheeler

To share your comments, please write:

Publisher
Thorndike Press
295 Kennedy Memorial Drive
Waterville, ME   04901

6|17

6|12  5|14

5|12  5|15

6|15      5|17